I0018759

Yocto Project Reference Manual

A catalogue record for this book is available from the Hong Kong Public Libraries.

Published in Hong Kong by Samurai Media Limited.

Email: info@samuraimedia.org

ISBN 978-988-8381-98-2

Copyright © 2010-2015 Linux Foundation
Permission is granted to copy, distribute and/or modify this document under the terms of the Creative Commons Attribution-Share Alike 2.0 UK: England & Wales http://creativecommons.org/licenses/by-sa/2.0/uk/ as published by Creative Commons.

Minor modifications for publication Copyright 2015 Samurai Media Limited.

Background Cover Image by https://www.flickr.com/people/webtreatsetc/

Table of Contents

Chapter 1. Introduction

1.1. Introduction

This manual provides reference information for the current release of the Yocto Project. The Yocto Project is an open-source collaboration project focused on embedded Linux developers. Amongst other things, the Yocto Project uses the OpenEmbedded build system, which is based on the Poky project, to construct complete Linux images. You can find complete introductory and getting started information on the Yocto Project by reading the Yocto Project Quick Start [http://www.yoctoproject.org/docs/1.7.2/yocto-project-qs/yocto-project-qs.html]. For task-based information using the Yocto Project, see the Yocto Project Development Manual [http://www.yoctoproject.org/docs/1.7.2/dev-manual/dev-manual.html] and the Yocto Project Linux Kernel Development Manual [http://www.yoctoproject.org/docs/1.7.2/kernel-dev/kernel-dev.html]. For Board Support Package (BSP) structure information, see the Yocto Project Board Support Package (BSP) Developer's Guide [http://www.yoctoproject.org/docs/1.7.2/bsp-guide/bsp-guide.html]. You can find information on tracing and profiling in the Yocto Project Profiling and Tracing Manual [http://www.yoctoproject.org/docs/1.7.2/profile-manual/profile-manual.html#profile-manual]. For information on BitBake, which is the task execution tool the OpenEmbedded build system is based on, see the BitBake User Manual [http://www.yoctoproject.org/docs/1.7.2/bitbake-user-manual/bitbake-user-manual.html#bitbake-user-manual]. Finally, you can also find lots of Yocto Project information on the Yocto Project website [http://www.yoctoproject.org].

1.2. Documentation Overview

This reference manual consists of the following:

- Using the Yocto Project: Provides an overview of the components that make up the Yocto Project followed by information about debugging images created in the Yocto Project.

- A Closer Look at the Yocto Project Development Environment: Provides a more detailed look at the Yocto Project development environment within the context of development.

- Technical Details: Describes fundamental Yocto Project components as well as an explanation behind how the Yocto Project uses shared state (sstate) cache to speed build time.

- Migrating to a Newer Yocto Project Release: Describes release-specific information that helps you move from one Yocto Project Release to another.

- Directory Structure: Describes the Source Directory [http://www.yoctoproject.org/docs/1.7.2/dev-manual/dev-manual.html#source-directory] created either by unpacking a released Yocto Project tarball on your host development system, or by cloning the upstream Poky [http://www.yoctoproject.org/docs/1.7.2/dev-manual/dev-manual.html#poky] Git repository.

- Classes: Describes the classes used in the Yocto Project.

- Tasks: Describes the tasks defined by the OpenEmbedded build system.

- QA Error and Warning Messages: Lists and describes QA warning and error messages.

- Images: Describes the standard images that the Yocto Project supports.

- Features: Describes mechanisms for creating distribution, machine, and image features during the build process using the OpenEmbedded build system.

- Variables Glossary: Presents most variables used by the OpenEmbedded build system, which uses BitBake. Entries describe the function of the variable and how to apply them.

- Variable Context: Provides variable locality or context.

- FAQ: Provides answers for commonly asked questions in the Yocto Project development environment.

- Contributing to the Yocto Project: Provides guidance on how you can contribute back to the Yocto Project.

1.3. System Requirements

For general Yocto Project system requirements, see the "What You Need and How You Get It [http://www.yoctoproject.org/docs/1.7.2/yocto-project-qs/yocto-project-qs.html#yp-resources]" section in the Yocto Project Quick Start. The remainder of this section provides details on system requirements not covered in the Yocto Project Quick Start.

1.3.1. Supported Linux Distributions

Currently, the Yocto Project is supported on the following distributions:

Note

Yocto Project releases are tested against the stable Linux distributions in the following list. The Yocto Project should work on other distributions but validation is not performed against them.

In particular, the Yocto Project does not support and currently has no plans to support rolling-releases or development distributions due to their constantly changing nature. We welcome patches and bug reports, but keep in mind that our priority is on the supported platforms listed below.

If you encounter problems, please go to Yocto Project Bugzilla [http://bugzilla.yoctoproject.org] and submit a bug. We are interested in hearing about your experience.

- Ubuntu 12.04 (LTS)

- Ubuntu 13.10

- Ubuntu 14.04 (LTS)

- Fedora release 19 (Schrödinger's Cat)

- Fedora release 20 (Heisenbug)

- CentOS release 6.4

- CentOS release 6.5

- Debian GNU/Linux 7.0 (Wheezy)

- Debian GNU/Linux 7.1 (Wheezy)

- Debian GNU/Linux 7.2 (Wheezy)

- Debian GNU/Linux 7.3 (Wheezy)

- Debian GNU/Linux 7.4 (Wheezy)

- Debian GNU/Linux 7.5 (Wheezy)

- Debian GNU/Linux 7.6 (Wheezy)

- openSUSE 12.2

- openSUSE 12.3

- openSUSE 13.1

Note
While the Yocto Project Team attempts to ensure all Yocto Project releases are one hundred percent compatible with each officially supported Linux distribution, instances might exist where you encounter a problem while using the Yocto Project on a specific distribution. For example, the CentOS 6.4 distribution does not include the Gtk+ 2.20.0 and PyGtk 2.21.0 (or higher) packages, which are required to run Hob [http://www.yoctoproject.org/tools-resources/projects/hob].

1.3.2. Required Packages for the Host Development System

The list of packages you need on the host development system can be large when covering all build scenarios using the Yocto Project. This section provides required packages according to Linux distribution and function.

1.3.2.1. Ubuntu and Debian

The following list shows the required packages by function given a supported Ubuntu or Debian Linux distribution:

- Essentials: Packages needed to build an image on a headless system:

```
$ sudo apt-get install gawk wget git-core diffstat unzip texinfo gcc-multilib \
build-essential chrpath socat
```

- Graphical and Eclipse Plug-In Extras: Packages recommended if the host system has graphics support or if you are going to use the Eclipse IDE:

```
$ sudo apt-get install libsdl1.2-dev xterm
```

- Documentation: Packages needed if you are going to build out the Yocto Project documentation manuals:

```
$ sudo apt-get install make xsltproc docbook-utils fop dblatex xmlto
```

- ADT Installer Extras: Packages needed if you are going to be using the Application Development Toolkit (ADT) Installer [http://www.yoctoproject.org/docs/1.7.2/adt-manual/adt-manual.html#using-the-adt-installer]:

```
$ sudo apt-get install autoconf automake libtool libglib2.0-dev
```

1.3.2.2. Fedora Packages

The following list shows the required packages by function given a supported Fedora Linux distribution:

- Essentials: Packages needed to build an image for a headless system:

```
$ sudo yum install gawk make wget tar bzip2 gzip python unzip perl patch \
diffutils diffstat git cpp gcc gcc-c++ glibc-devel texinfo chrpath \
ccache perl-Data-Dumper perl-Text-ParseWords perl-Thread-Queue socat
```

- Graphical and Eclipse Plug-In Extras: Packages recommended if the host system has graphics support or if you are going to use the Eclipse IDE:

```
$ sudo yum install SDL-devel xterm perl-Thread-Queue
```

- Documentation: Packages needed if you are going to build out the Yocto Project documentation manuals:

```
$ sudo yum install make docbook-style-dsssl docbook-style-xsl \
```

```
docbook-dtds docbook-utils fop libxslt dblatex xmlto
```

- ADT Installer Extras: Packages needed if you are going to be using the Application Development Toolkit (ADT) Installer [http://www.yoctoproject.org/docs/1.7.2/adt-manual/adt-manual.html#using-the-adt-installer]:

```
$ sudo yum install autoconf automake libtool glib2-devel
```

1.3.2.3. openSUSE Packages

The following list shows the required packages by function given a supported openSUSE Linux distribution:

- Essentials: Packages needed to build an image for a headless system:

```
$ sudo zypper install python gcc gcc-c++ git chrpath make wget python-xml \
diffstat texinfo python-curses patch socat
```

- Graphical and Eclipse Plug-In Extras: Packages recommended if the host system has graphics support or if you are going to use the Eclipse IDE:

```
$ sudo zypper install libSDL-devel xterm
```

- Documentation: Packages needed if you are going to build out the Yocto Project documentation manuals:

```
$ sudo zypper install make fop xsltproc dblatex xmlto
```

- ADT Installer Extras: Packages needed if you are going to be using the Application Development Toolkit (ADT) Installer [http://www.yoctoproject.org/docs/1.7.2/adt-manual/adt-manual.html#using-the-adt-installer]:

```
$ sudo zypper install autoconf automake libtool glib2-devel
```

1.3.2.4. CentOS Packages

The following list shows the required packages by function given a supported CentOS Linux distribution:

Note

For CentOS 6.x, some of the versions of the components provided by the distribution are too old (e.g. Git, Python, and tar). It is recommended that you install the buildtools in order to provide versions that will work with the OpenEmbedded build system. For information on how to install the buildtools tarball, see the "Required Git, Tar, and Python Versions" section.

- Essentials: Packages needed to build an image for a headless system:

```
$ sudo yum install gawk make wget tar bzip2 gzip python unzip perl patch \
diffutils diffstat git cpp gcc gcc-c++ glibc-devel texinfo chrpath socat
```

- Graphical and Eclipse Plug-In Extras: Packages recommended if the host system has graphics support or if you are going to use the Eclipse IDE:

```
$ sudo yum install SDL-devel xterm
```

- Documentation: Packages needed if you are going to build out the Yocto Project documentation manuals:

```
$ sudo yum install make docbook-style-dsssl docbook-style-xsl \
docbook-dtds docbook-utils fop libxslt dblatex xmlto
```

- ADT Installer Extras: Packages needed if you are going to be using the Application Development Toolkit (ADT) Installer [http://www.yoctoproject.org/docs/1.7.2/adt-manual/adt-manual.html#using-the-adt-installer]:

```
$ sudo yum install autoconf automake libtool glib2-devel
```

1.3.3. Required Git, tar, and Python Versions

In order to use the build system, your host development system must meet the following version requirements for Git, tar, and Python:

- Git 1.7.8 or greater

- tar 1.24 or greater

- Python 2.7.3 or greater not including Python 3.x, which is not supported.

If your host development system does not meet all these requirements, you can resolve this by installing a buildtools tarball that contains these tools. You can get the tarball one of two ways: download a pre-built tarball or use BitBake to build the tarball.

1.3.3.1. Downloading a Pre-Built**buildtools** Tarball

Downloading and running a pre-built buildtools installer is the easiest of the two methods by which you can get these tools:

1. Locate and download the *.sh at http://downloads.yoctoproject.org/releases/yocto/yocto-1.7.2/buildtools/.

2. Execute the installation script. Here is an example:

```
$ sh poky-glibc-x86_64-buildtools-tarball-x86_64-buildtools-nativesdk-standalone-1.7.2.s
```

During execution, a prompt appears that allows you to choose the installation directory. For example, you could choose the following:

```
/home/your-username/buildtools
```

3. Source the tools environment setup script by using a command like the following:

```
$ source /home/your-username/buildtools/environment-setup-i586-poky-linux
```

Of course, you need to supply your installation directory and be sure to use the right file (i.e. i585 or x86-64).

After you have sourced the setup script, the tools are added to PATH and any other environment variables required to run the tools are initialized. The results are working versions versions of Git, tar, Python and chrpath.

1.3.3.2. Building Your Own**buildtools** Tarball

Building and running your own buildtools installer applies only when you have a build host that can already run BitBake. In this case, you use that machine to build the .sh file and then take steps to transfer and run it on a machine that does not meet the minimal Git, tar, and Python requirements.

Here are the steps to take to build and run your own buildtools installer:

1. On the machine that is able to run BitBake, be sure you have set up your build environment with the setup script (oe-init-build-env or oe-init-build-env-memres).

2. Run the BitBake command to build the tarball:

```
$ bitbake buildtools-tarball
```

> **Note**
> The SDKMACHINE variable in your local.conf file determines whether you build tools for a 32-bit or 64-bit system.

   Once the build completes, you can find the .sh file that installs the tools in the tmp/deploy/ sdk subdirectory of the Build Directory [http://www.yoctoproject.org/docs/1.7.2/dev-manual/dev-manual.html#build-directory]. The installer file has the string "buildtools" in the name.

3. Transfer the .sh file from the build host to the machine that does not meet the Git, tar, or Python requirements.

4. On the machine that does not meet the requirements, run the .sh file to install the tools. Here is an example:

```
$ sh poky-glibc-x86_64-buildtools-tarball-x86_64-buildtools-nativesdk-standalone-1.7.2.sh
```

   During execution, a prompt appears that allows you to choose the installation directory. For example, you could choose the following:

```
/home/your-username/buildtools
```

5. Source the tools environment setup script by using a command like the following:

```
$ source /home/your-username/buildtools/environment-setup-i586-poky-linux
```

   Of course, you need to supply your installation directory and be sure to use the right file (i.e. i585 or x86-64).

   After you have sourced the setup script, the tools are added to PATH and any other environment variables required to run the tools are initialized. The results are working versions versions of Git, tar, Python and chrpath.

1.4. Obtaining the Yocto Project

The Yocto Project development team makes the Yocto Project available through a number of methods:

- Source Repositories: Working from a copy of the upstream poky repository is the preferred method for obtaining and using a Yocto Project release. You can view the Yocto Project Source Repositories at http://git.yoctoproject.org/cgit.cgi. In particular, you can find the poky repository at http://git.yoctoproject.org/cgit/cgit.cgi/poky/.

- Releases: Stable, tested releases are available as tarballs through http://downloads.yoctoproject.org/releases/yocto/.

- Nightly Builds: These tarball releases are available at http://autobuilder.yoctoproject.org/nightly. These builds include Yocto Project releases, meta-toolchain tarball installation scripts, and experimental builds.

- Yocto Project Website: You can find tarball releases of the Yocto Project and supported BSPs at the Yocto Project website [http://www.yoctoproject.org]. Along with these downloads, you can find lots of other information at this site.

1.5. Development Checkouts

Development using the Yocto Project requires a local Source Directory [http://www.yoctoproject.org/docs/1.7.2/dev-manual/dev-manual.html#source-directory]. You can set up the Source Directory by cloning a copy of the upstream poky [http://www.yoctoproject.org/docs/1.7.2/dev-manual/dev-manual.html#poky] Git repository. For information on how to do this, see the "Getting Set Up [http://www.yoctoproject.org/docs/1.7.2/dev-manual/dev-manual.html#getting-setup]" section in the Yocto Project Development Manual.

Chapter 2. Using the Yocto Project

This chapter describes common usage for the Yocto Project. The information is introductory in nature as other manuals in the Yocto Project documentation set provide more details on how to use the Yocto Project.

2.1. Running a Build

This section provides a summary of the build process and provides information for less obvious aspects of the build process. For general information on how to build an image using the OpenEmbedded build system, see the "Building an Image [http://www.yoctoproject.org/docs/1.7.2/yocto-project-qs/yocto-project-qs.html#building-image]" section of the Yocto Project Quick Start.

2.1.1. Build Overview

The first thing you need to do is set up the OpenEmbedded build environment by sourcing an environment setup script (i.e. oe-init-build-env or oe-init-build-env-memres). Here is an example:

```
$ source oe-init-build-env [build_dir]
```

The build_dir argument is optional and specifies the directory the OpenEmbedded build system uses for the build - the Build Directory [http://www.yoctoproject.org/docs/1.7.2/dev-manual/dev-manual.html#build-directory]. If you do not specify a Build Directory, it defaults to a directory named build in your current working directory. A common practice is to use a different Build Directory for different targets. For example, ~/build/x86 for a qemux86 target, and ~/build/arm for a qemuarm target.

Once the build environment is set up, you can build a target using:

```
$ bitbake target
```

The target is the name of the recipe you want to build. Common targets are the images in meta/recipes-core/images, meta/recipes-sato/images, etc. all found in the Source Directory [http://www.yoctoproject.org/docs/1.7.2/dev-manual/dev-manual.html#source-directory]. Or, the target can be the name of a recipe for a specific piece of software such as BusyBox. For more details about the images the OpenEmbedded build system supports, see the "Images" chapter.

Note
Building an image without GNU General Public License Version 3 (GPLv3), or similarly licensed, components is supported for only minimal and base images. See the "Images" chapter for more information.

2.1.2. Building an Image Using GPL Components

When building an image using GPL components, you need to maintain your original settings and not switch back and forth applying different versions of the GNU General Public License. If you rebuild using different versions of GPL, dependency errors might occur due to some components not being rebuilt.

2.2. Installing and Using the Result

Once an image has been built, it often needs to be installed. The images and kernels built by the OpenEmbedded build system are placed in the Build Directory [http://www.yoctoproject.org/docs/1.7.2/dev-manual/dev-manual.html#build-directory] in tmp/deploy/images. For information on how to run pre-built images such as qemux86 and qemuarm, see the "Using Pre-Built Binaries and QEMU [http://www.yoctoproject.org/docs/1.7.2/yocto-project-qs/yocto-project-qs.html#using-pre-built]" section in the Yocto Project Quick Start. For information about how to install these images, see the documentation for your particular board or machine.

2.3. Debugging Build Failures

The exact method for debugging build failures depends on the nature of the problem and on the system's area from which the bug originates. Standard debugging practices such as comparison against the last known working version with examination of the changes and the re-application of steps to identify the one causing the problem are valid for the Yocto Project just as they are for any other system. Even though it is impossible to detail every possible potential failure, this section provides some general tips to aid in debugging.

A useful feature for debugging is the error reporting tool. Configuring the Yocto Project to use this tool causes the OpenEmbedded build system to produce error reporting commands as part of the console output. You can enter the commands after the build completes to log error information into a common database, that can help you figure out what might be going wrong. For information on how to enable and use this feature, see the "Using the Error Reporting Tool [http://www.yoctoproject.org/docs/1.7.2/dev-manual/dev-manual.html#using-the-error-reporting-tool]" section in the Yocto Project Development Manual.

For discussions on debugging, see the "Debugging With the GNU Project Debugger (GDB) Remotely [http://www.yoctoproject.org/docs/1.7.2/dev-manual/dev-manual.html#platdev-gdb-remotedebug]" and "Working within Eclipse [http://www.yoctoproject.org/docs/1.7.2/dev-manual/dev-manual.html#adt-eclipse]" sections in the Yocto Project Development Manual.

Note

The remainder of this section presents many examples of the bitbake command. You can learn about BitBake by reading the BitBake User Manual [http://www.yoctoproject.org/docs/1.7.2/bitbake-user-manual/bitbake-user-manual.html#bitbake-user-manual].

2.3.1. Task Failures

The log file for shell tasks is available in ${WORKDIR}/temp/log.do_taskname.pid. For example, the do_compile task for the QEMU minimal image for the x86 machine (qemux86) might be tmp/work/qemux86-poky-linux/core-image-minimal/1.0-r0/temp/log.do_compile.20830. To see what BitBake [http://www.yoctoproject.org/docs/1.7.2/dev-manual/dev-manual.html#bitbake-term] runs to generate that log, look at the corresponding run.do_taskname.pid file located in the same directory.

Presently, the output from Python tasks is sent directly to the console.

2.3.2. Running Specific Tasks

Any given package consists of a set of tasks. The standard BitBake behavior in most cases is: do_fetch, do_unpack, do_patch, do_configure, do_compile, do_install, do_package, do_package_write_*, and do_build. The default task is do_build and any tasks on which it depends build first. Some tasks, such as do_devshell, are not part of the default build chain. If you wish to run a task that is not part of the default build chain, you can use the -c option in BitBake. Here is an example:

```
$ bitbake matchbox-desktop -c devshell
```

If you wish to rerun a task, use the -f force option. For example, the following sequence forces recompilation after changing files in the work directory.

```
$ bitbake matchbox-desktop
       .
       .
   make some changes to the source code in the work directory
       .
       .
```

```
$ bitbake matchbox-desktop -c compile -f
$ bitbake matchbox-desktop
```

This sequence first builds and then recompiles matchbox-desktop. The last command reruns all tasks (basically the packaging tasks) after the compile. BitBake recognizes that the do_compile task was rerun and therefore understands that the other tasks also need to be run again.

You can view a list of tasks in a given package by running the do_listtasks task as follows:

```
$ bitbake matchbox-desktop -c listtasks
```

The results appear as output to the console and are also in the file ${WORKDIR}/temp/log.do_listtasks.

2.3.3. Dependency Graphs

Sometimes it can be hard to see why BitBake wants to build other packages before building a given package you have specified. The bitbake -g targetname command creates the pn-buildlist, pn-depends.dot, package-depends.dot, and task-depends.dot files in the current directory. These files show what will be built and the package and task dependencies, which are useful for debugging problems. You can use the bitbake -g -u depexp targetname command to display the results in a more human-readable form.

2.3.4. General BitBake Problems

You can see debug output from BitBake by using the -D option. The debug output gives more information about what BitBake is doing and the reason behind it. Each -D option you use increases the logging level. The most common usage is -DDD.

The output from bitbake -DDD -v targetname can reveal why BitBake chose a certain version of a package or why BitBake picked a certain provider. This command could also help you in a situation where you think BitBake did something unexpected.

2.3.5. Development Host System Issues

Sometimes issues on the host development system can cause your build to fail. Following are known, host-specific problems. Be sure to always consult the Release Notes [http://www.yoctoproject.org/downloads/core/dizzy172] for a look at all release-related issues.

- glibc-initial fails to build: If your development host system has the unpatched GNU Make 3.82, the do_install task fails for glibc-initial during the build.

  Typically, every distribution that ships GNU Make 3.82 as the default already has the patched version. However, some distributions, such as Debian, have GNU Make 3.82 as an option, which is unpatched. You will see this error on these types of distributions. Switch to GNU Make 3.81 or patch your make to solve the problem.

2.3.6. Building with No Dependencies

To build a specific recipe (.bb file), you can use the following command form:

```
$ bitbake -b somepath/somerecipe.bb
```

This command form does not check for dependencies. Consequently, you should use it only when you know existing dependencies have been met.

Note
You can also specify fragments of the filename. In this case, BitBake checks for a unique match.

2.3.7. Variables

You can use the -e BitBake option to display the parsing environment for a configuration. The following displays the general parsing environment:

```
$ bitbake -e
```

This next example shows the parsing environment for a specific recipe:

```
$ bitbake -e recipename
```

2.3.8. Recipe Logging Mechanisms

Best practices exist while writing recipes that both log build progress and act on build conditions such as warnings and errors. Both Python and Bash language bindings exist for the logging mechanism:

- Python: For Python functions, BitBake supports several loglevels: bb.fatal, bb.error, bb.warn, bb.note, bb.plain, and bb.debug.

- Bash: For Bash functions, the same set of loglevels exist and are accessed with a similar syntax: bbfatal, bberror, bbwarn, bbnote, bbplain, and bbdebug.

For guidance on how logging is handled in both Python and Bash recipes, see the logging.bbclass file in the meta/classes folder of the Source Directory [http://www.yoctoproject.org/docs/1.7.2/dev-manual/dev-manual.html#source-directory].

2.3.8.1. Logging With Python

When creating recipes using Python and inserting code that handles build logs, keep in mind the goal is to have informative logs while keeping the console as "silent" as possible. Also, if you want status messages in the log, use the "debug" loglevel.

Following is an example written in Python. The code handles logging for a function that determines the number of tasks needed to be run. See the "do_listtasks" section for additional information:

```python
python do_listtasks() {
    bb.debug(2, "Starting to figure out the task list")
    if noteworthy_condition:
        bb.note("There are 47 tasks to run")
    bb.debug(2, "Got to point xyz")
    if warning_trigger:
        bb.warn("Detected warning_trigger, this might be a problem later.")
    if recoverable_error:
        bb.error("Hit recoverable_error, you really need to fix this!")
    if fatal_error:
        bb.fatal("fatal_error detected, unable to print the task list")
    bb.plain("The tasks present are abc")
    bb.debug(2, "Finished figuring out the tasklist")
}
```

2.3.8.2. Logging With Bash

When creating recipes using Bash and inserting code that handles build logs, you have the same goals - informative with minimal console output. The syntax you use for recipes written in Bash is similar to that of recipes written in Python described in the previous section.

Following is an example written in Bash. The code logs the progress of the do_my_function function.

```bash
do_my_function() {
```

```
    bbdebug 2 "Running do_my_function"
    if [ exceptional_condition ]; then
        bbnote "Hit exceptional_condition"
    fi
    bbdebug 2  "Got to point xyz"
    if [ warning_trigger ]; then
        bbwarn "Detected warning_trigger, this might cause a problem later."
    fi
    if [ recoverable_error ]; then
        bberror "Hit recoverable_error, correcting"
    fi
    if [ fatal_error ]; then
        bbfatal "fatal_error detected"
    fi
    bbdebug 2 "Completed do_my_function"
}
```

2.3.9. Other Tips

Here are some other tips that you might find useful:

- When adding new packages, it is worth watching for undesirable items making their way into compiler command lines. For example, you do not want references to local system files like /usr/lib/ or /usr/include/.

- If you want to remove the psplash boot splashscreen, add psplash=false to the kernel command line. Doing so prevents psplash from loading and thus allows you to see the console. It is also possible to switch out of the splashscreen by switching the virtual console (e.g. Fn+Left or Fn+Right on a Zaurus).

2.4. Maintaining Build Output Quality

Many factors can influence the quality of a build. For example, if you upgrade a recipe to use a new version of an upstream software package or you experiment with some new configuration options, subtle changes can occur that you might not detect until later. Consider the case where your recipe is using a newer version of an upstream package. In this case, a new version of a piece of software might introduce an optional dependency on another library, which is auto-detected. If that library has already been built when the software is building, the software will link to the built library and that library will be pulled into your image along with the new software even if you did not want the library.

The buildhistory class exists to help you maintain the quality of your build output. You can use the class to highlight unexpected and possibly unwanted changes in the build output. When you enable build history, it records information about the contents of each package and image and then commits that information to a local Git repository where you can examine the information.

The remainder of this section describes the following:

- How you can enable and disable build history

- How to understand what the build history contains

- How to limit the information used for build history

- How to examine the build history from both a command-line and web interface

2.4.1. Enabling and Disabling Build History

Build history is disabled by default. To enable it, add the following INHERIT statement and set the BUILDHISTORY_COMMIT variable to "1" at the end of your conf/local.conf file found in the Build Directory [http://www.yoctoproject.org/docs/1.7.2/dev-manual/dev-manual.html#build-directory]:

```
    INHERIT += "buildhistory"
    BUILDHISTORY_COMMIT = "1"
```

Enabling build history as previously described causes the build process to collect build output information and commit it to a local Git [http://www.yoctoproject.org/docs/1.7.2/dev-manual/dev-manual.html#git] repository.

Note
Enabling build history increases your build times slightly, particularly for images, and increases the amount of disk space used during the build.

You can disable build history by removing the previous statements from your conf/local.conf file.

2.4.2. Understanding What the Build History Contains

Build history information is kept in ${TOPDIR}/buildhistory in the Build Directory as defined by the BUILDHISTORY_DIR variable. The following is an example abbreviated listing:

At the top level, there is a metadata-revs file that lists the revisions of the repositories for the layers enabled when the build was produced. The rest of the data splits into separate packages, images and sdk directories, the contents of which are described below.

2.4.2.1. Build History Package Information

The history for each package contains a text file that has name-value pairs with information about the package. For example, buildhistory/packages/i586-poky-linux/busybox/busybox/latest contains the following:

```
PV = 1.22.1
PR = r32
RPROVIDES =
RDEPENDS = glibc (>= 2.20) update-alternatives-opkg
RRECOMMENDS = busybox-syslog busybox-udhcpc update-rc.d
PKGSIZE = 540168
FILES = /usr/bin/* /usr/sbin/* /usr/lib/busybox/* /usr/lib/lib*.so.* \
    /etc /com /var /bin/* /sbin/* /lib/*.so.* /lib/udev/rules.d \
    /usr/lib/udev/rules.d /usr/share/busybox /usr/lib/busybox/* \
    /usr/share/pixmaps /usr/share/applications /usr/share/idl \
```

```
                     /usr/share/omf /usr/share/sounds /usr/lib/bonobo/servers
    FILELIST = /bin/busybox /bin/busybox.nosuid /bin/busybox.suid /bin/sh \
        /etc/busybox.links.nosuid /etc/busybox.links.suid
```

Most of these name-value pairs correspond to variables used to produce the package. The exceptions are FILELIST, which is the actual list of files in the package, and PKGSIZE, which is the total size of files in the package in bytes.

There is also a file corresponding to the recipe from which the package came (e.g. buildhistory/packages/i586-poky-linux/busybox/latest):

```
    PV = 1.22.1
    PR = r32
    DEPENDS = initscripts kern-tools-native update-rc.d-native \
        virtual/i586-poky-linux-compilerlibs virtual/i586-poky-linux-gcc \
        virtual/libc virtual/update-alternatives
    PACKAGES = busybox-ptest busybox-httpd busybox-udhcpd busybox-udhcpc \
        busybox-syslog busybox-mdev busybox-hwclock busybox-dbg \
        busybox-staticdev busybox-dev busybox-doc busybox-locale busybox
```

Finally, for those recipes fetched from a version control system (e.g., Git), a file exists that lists source revisions that are specified in the recipe and lists the actual revisions used during the build. Listed and actual revisions might differ when SRCREV is set to ${AUTOREV}. Here is an example assuming buildhistory/packages/qemux86-poky-linux/linux-yocto/latest_srcrev):

```
    # SRCREV_machine = "38cd560d5022ed2dbd1ab0dca9642e47c98a0aa1"
    SRCREV_machine = "38cd560d5022ed2dbd1ab0dca9642e47c98a0aa1"
    # SRCREV_meta = "a227f20eff056e511d504b2e490f3774ab260d6f"
    SRCREV_meta = "a227f20eff056e511d504b2e490f3774ab260d6f"
```

You can use the buildhistory-collect-srcrevs command with the -a option to collect the stored SRCREV values from build history and report them in a format suitable for use in global configuration (e.g., local.conf or a distro include file) to override floating AUTOREV values to a fixed set of revisions. Here is some example output from this command:

```
    $ buildhistory-collect-srcrevs -a
    # i586-poky-linux
    SRCREV_pn-glibc = "b8079dd0d360648e4e8de48656c5c38972621072"
    SRCREV_pn-glibc-initial = "b8079dd0d360648e4e8de48656c5c38972621072"
    SRCREV_pn-opkg-utils = "53274f087565fd45d8452c5367997ba6a682a37a"
    SRCREV_pn-kmod = "fd56638aed3fe147015bfa10ed4a5f7491303cb4"
    # x86_64-linux
    SRCREV_pn-gtk-doc-stub-native = "1dea266593edb766d6d898c79451ef193eb17cfa"
    SRCREV_pn-dtc-native = "65cc4d2748a2c2e6f27f1cf39e07a5dbabd80ebf"
    SRCREV_pn-update-rc.d-native = "eca680ddf28d024954895f59a241a622dd575c11"
    SRCREV_glibc_pn-cross-localedef-native = "b8079dd0d360648e4e8de48656c5c38972621072"
    SRCREV_localedef_pn-cross-localedef-native = "c833367348d39dad7ba018990bfdaffaec8e9ed3"
    SRCREV_pn-prelink-native = "faa069deec99bf61418d0bab831c83d7c1b797ca"
    SRCREV_pn-opkg-utils-native = "53274f087565fd45d8452c5367997ba6a682a37a"
    SRCREV_pn-kern-tools-native = "23345b8846fe4bd167efdf1bd8a1224b2ba9a5ff"
    SRCREV_pn-kmod-native = "fd56638aed3fe147015bfa10ed4a5f7491303cb4"
    # qemux86-poky-linux
    SRCREV_machine_pn-linux-yocto = "38cd560d5022ed2dbd1ab0dca9642e47c98a0aa1"
    SRCREV_meta_pn-linux-yocto = "a227f20eff056e511d504b2e490f3774ab260d6f"
    # all-poky-linux
    SRCREV_pn-update-rc.d = "eca680ddf28d024954895f59a241a622dd575c11"
```

Note
Here are some notes on using the buildhistory-collect-srcrevs command:

- By default, only values where the SRCREV was not hardcoded (usually when AUTOREV was used) are reported. Use the -a option to see all SRCREV values.

- The output statements might not have any effect if overrides are applied elsewhere in the build system configuration. Use the -f option to add the forcevariable override to each output line if you need to work around this restriction.

- The script does apply special handling when building for multiple machines. However, the script does place a comment before each set of values that specifies which triplet to which they belong as shown above (e.g., i586-poky-linux).

2.4.2.2. Build History Image Information

The files produced for each image are as follows:

- image-files: A directory containing selected files from the root filesystem. The files are defined by BUILDHISTORY_IMAGE_FILES.

- build-id.txt: Human-readable information about the build configuration and metadata source revisions. This file contains the full build header as printed by BitBake.

- *.dot: Dependency graphs for the image that are compatible with graphviz.

- files-in-image.txt: A list of files in the image with permissions, owner, group, size, and symlink information.

- image-info.txt: A text file containing name-value pairs with information about the image. See the following listing example for more information.

- installed-package-names.txt: A list of installed packages by name only.

- installed-package-sizes.txt: A list of installed packages ordered by size.

- installed-packages.txt: A list of installed packages with full package filenames.

Note
Installed package information is able to be gathered and produced even if package management is disabled for the final image.

Here is an example of image-info.txt:

```
DISTRO = poky
DISTRO_VERSION = 1.7
USER_CLASSES = buildstats image-mklibs image-prelink
IMAGE_CLASSES = image_types
IMAGE_FEATURES = debug-tweaks
IMAGE_LINGUAS =
IMAGE_INSTALL = packagegroup-core-boot run-postinsts
BAD_RECOMMENDATIONS =
NO_RECOMMENDATIONS =
PACKAGE_EXCLUDE =
ROOTFS_POSTPROCESS_COMMAND = write_package_manifest; license_create_manifest; \
    write_image_manifest ; buildhistory_list_installed_image ; \
    buildhistory_get_image_installed ; ssh_allow_empty_password;  \
    postinst_enable_logging; rootfs_update_timestamp ; ssh_disable_dns_lookup ;
IMAGE_POSTPROCESS_COMMAND =   buildhistory_get_imageinfo ;
IMAGESIZE = 6900
```

Other than IMAGESIZE, which is the total size of the files in the image in Kbytes, the name-value pairs are variables that may have influenced the content of the image. This information is often useful when you are trying to determine why a change in the package or file listings has occurred.

2.4.2.3. Using Build History to Gather Image Information Only

As you can see, build history produces image information, including dependency graphs, so you can see why something was pulled into the image. If you are just interested in this information and not interested in collecting specific package or SDK information, you can enable writing only image information without any history by adding the following to your conf/local.conf file found in the Build Directory [http://www.yoctoproject.org/docs/1.7.2/dev-manual/dev-manual.html#build-directory]:

```
INHERIT += "buildhistory"
BUILDHISTORY_COMMIT = "0"
BUILDHISTORY_FEATURES = "image"
```

Here, you set the BUILDHISTORY_FEATURES variable to use the image feature only.

2.4.2.4. Build History SDK Information

Build history collects similar information on the contents of SDKs (e.g. meta-toolchain or bitbake -c populate_sdk imagename) as compared to information it collects for images. The following list shows the files produced for each SDK:

- files-in-sdk.txt: A list of files in the SDK with permissions, owner, group, size, and symlink information. This list includes both the host and target parts of the SDK.

- sdk-info.txt: A text file containing name-value pairs with information about the SDK. See the following listing example for more information.

- The following information appears under each of the host and target directories for the portions of the SDK that run on the host and on the target, respectively:

  - depends.dot: Dependency graph for the SDK that is compatible with graphviz.

  - installed-package-names.txt: A list of installed packages by name only.

  - installed-package-sizes.txt: A list of installed packages ordered by size.

  - installed-packages.txt: A list of installed packages with full package filenames.

Here is an example of sdk-info.txt:

```
DISTRO = poky
DISTRO_VERSION = 1.3+snapshot-20130327
SDK_NAME = poky-glibc-i686-arm
SDK_VERSION = 1.3+snapshot
SDKMACHINE =
SDKIMAGE_FEATURES = dev-pkgs dbg-pkgs
BAD_RECOMMENDATIONS =
SDKSIZE = 352712
```

Other than SDKSIZE, which is the total size of the files in the SDK in Kbytes, the name-value pairs are variables that might have influenced the content of the SDK. This information is often useful when you are trying to determine why a change in the package or file listings has occurred.

2.4.2.5. Examining Build History Information

You can examine build history output from the command line or from a web interface.

To see any changes that have occurred (assuming you have BUILDHISTORY_COMMIT = "1"), you can simply use any Git command that allows you to view the history of a repository. Here is one method:

```
$ git log -p
```

You need to realize, however, that this method does show changes that are not significant (e.g. a package's size changing by a few bytes).

A command-line tool called buildhistory-diff does exist, though, that queries the Git repository and prints just the differences that might be significant in human-readable form. Here is an example:

```
$ ~/poky/poky/scripts/buildhistory-diff . HEAD^
Changes to images/qemux86_64/glibc/core-image-minimal (files-in-image.txt):
   /etc/anotherpkg.conf was added
   /sbin/anotherpkg was added
   * (installed-package-names.txt):
   *    anotherpkg was added
Changes to images/qemux86_64/glibc/core-image-minimal (installed-package-names.txt):
   anotherpkg was added
packages/qemux86_64-poky-linux/v86d: PACKAGES: added "v86d-extras"
   * PR changed from "r0" to "r1"
   * PV changed from "0.1.10" to "0.1.12"
packages/qemux86_64-poky-linux/v86d/v86d: PKGSIZE changed from 110579 to 144381 (+30%)
   * PR changed from "r0" to "r1"
   * PV changed from "0.1.10" to "0.1.12"
```

To see changes to the build history using a web interface, follow the instruction in the README file here. http://git.yoctoproject.org/cgit/cgit.cgi/buildhistory-web/.

Here   is   a   sample   screenshot   of   the   interface:

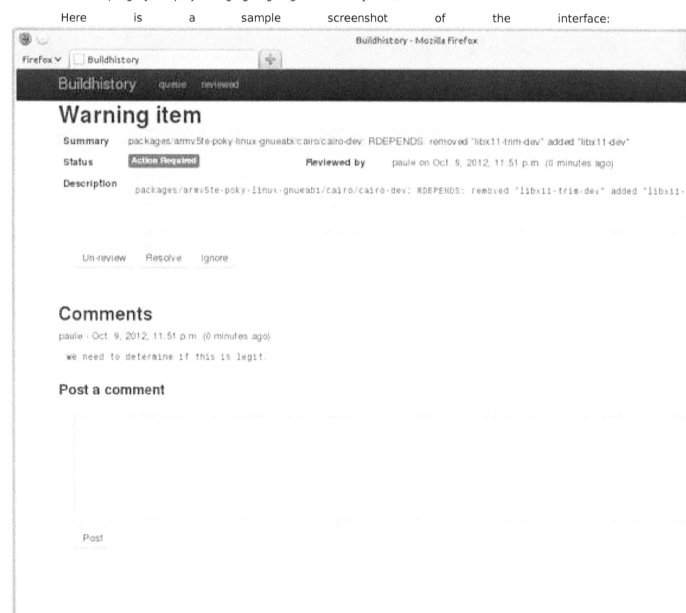

Chapter 3. A Closer Look at the Yocto Project Development Environment

This chapter takes a more detailed look at the Yocto Project development environment. The following diagram represents the development environment at a high level. The remainder of this chapter expands on the fundamental input, output, process, and Metadata [http://www.yoctoproject.org/docs/1.7.2/dev-manual/dev-manual.html#metadata]) blocks in the Yocto Project development environment.

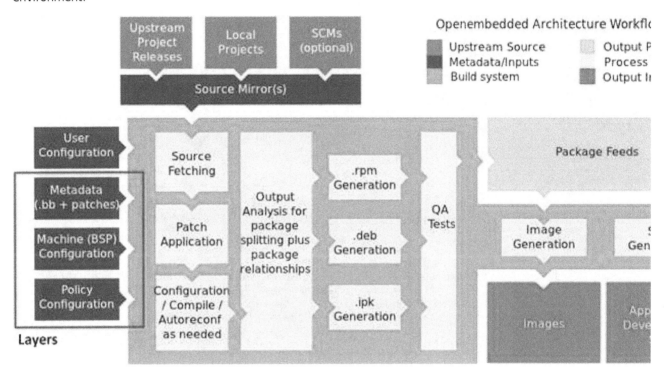

The generalized Yocto Project Development Environment consists of several functional areas:

• User Configuration: Metadata you can use to control the build process.

• Metadata Layers: Various layers that provide software, machine, and distro Metadata.

• Source Files: Upstream releases, local projects, and SCMs.

• Build System: Processes under the control of BitBake [http://www.yoctoproject.org/docs/1.7.2/dev-manual/dev-manual.html#bitbake-term]. This block expands on how BitBake fetches source, applies patches, completes compilation, analyzes output for package generation, creates and tests packages, generates images, and generates cross-development tools.

• Package Feeds: Directories containing output packages (RPM, DEB or IPK), which are subsequently used in the construction of an image or SDK, produced by the build system. These feeds can also be copied and shared using a web server or other means to facilitate extending or updating existing images on devices at runtime if runtime package management is enabled.

• Images: Images produced by the development process.

• Application Development SDK: Cross-development tools that are produced along with an image or separately with BitBake.

3.1. User Configuration

User configuration helps define the build. Through user configuration, you can tell BitBake the target architecture for which you are building the image, where to store downloaded source, and other build properties.

The following figure shows an expanded representation of the "User Configuration" box of the general Yocto Project Development Environment figure [18]:

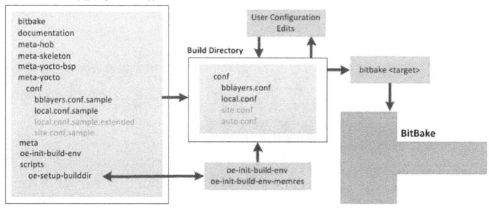

BitBake needs some basic configuration files in order to complete a build. These files are *.conf files. The minimally necessary ones reside as example files in the Source Directory [http://www.yoctoproject.org/docs/1.7.2/dev-manual/dev-manual.html#source-directory]. For simplicity, this section refers to the Source Directory as the "Poky Directory."

When you clone the poky Git repository or you download and unpack a Yocto Project release, you can set up the Source Directory to be named anything you want. For this discussion, the cloned repository uses the default name poky.

Note
The Poky repository is primarily an aggregation of existing repositories. It is not a canonical upstream source.

The meta-yocto layer inside Poky contains a conf directory that has example configuration files. These example files are used as a basis for creating actual configuration files when you source the build environment script (i.e. oe-init-build-env or oe-init-build-env-memres).

Sourcing the build environment script creates a Build Directory [http://www.yoctoproject.org/docs/1.7.2/dev-manual/dev-manual.html#build-directory] if one does not already exist. BitBake uses the Build Directory for all its work during builds. The Build Directory has a conf directory that contains default versions of your local.conf and bblayers.conf configuration files. These default configuration files are created only if versions do not already exist in the Build Directory at the time you source the build environment setup script.

Because the Poky repository is fundamentally an aggregation of existing repositories, some users might be familiar with running the oe-init-build-env or oe-init-build-env-memres script in the context of separate OpenEmbedded-Core and BitBake repositories rather than a single Poky repository. This discussion assumes the script is executed from within a cloned or unpacked version of Poky.

Depending on where the script is sourced, different sub-scripts are called to set up the Build Directory (Yocto or OpenEmbedded). Specifically, the script scripts/oe-setup-builddir inside the poky directory sets up the Build Directory and seeds the directory (if necessary) with configuration files appropriate for the Yocto Project development environment.

Note

The `scripts/oe-setup-builddir` script uses the `$TEMPLATECONF` variable to determine which sample configuration files to locate.

The `local.conf` file provides many basic variables that define a build environment. Here is a list of a few. To see the default configurations in a `local.conf` file created by the build environment script, see the `local.conf.sample` in the `meta-yocto` layer:

• Parallelism Options: Controlled by the BB_NUMBER_THREADS and PARALLEL_MAKE variables.

• Target Machine Selection: Controlled by the MACHINE variable.

• Download Directory: Controlled by the DL_DIR variable.

• Shared State Directory: Controlled by the SSTATE_DIR variable.

• Build Output: Controlled by the TMPDIR variable.

Note

Configurations set in the `conf/local.conf` file can also be set in the `conf/site.conf` and `conf/auto.conf` configuration files.

The `bblayers.conf` file tells BitBake what layers you want considered during the build. By default, the layers listed in this file include layers minimally needed by the build system. However, you must manually add any custom layers you have created. You can find more information on working with the `bblayers.conf` file in the "Enabling Your Layer [http://www.yoctoproject.org/docs/1.7.2/dev-manual/dev-manual.html#enabling-your-layer]" section in the Yocto Project Development Manual.

The files `site.conf` and `auto.conf` are not created by the environment initialization script. If you want these configuration files, you must create them yourself:

• `site.conf`: You can use the `conf/site.conf` configuration file to configure multiple build directories. For example, suppose you had several build environments and they shared some common features. You can set these default build properties here. A good example is perhaps the level of parallelism you want to use through the BB_NUMBER_THREADS and PARALLEL_MAKE variables.

One useful scenario for using the `conf/site.conf` file is to extend your BBPATH variable to include the path to a `conf/site.conf`. Then, when BitBake looks for Metadata using BBPATH, it finds the `conf/site.conf` file and applies your common configurations found in the file. To override configurations in a particular build directory, alter the similar configurations within that build directory's `conf/local.conf` file.

• `auto.conf`: This file is not hand-created. Rather, the file is usually created and written to by an autobuilder. The settings put into the file are typically the same as you would find in the `conf/local.conf` or the `conf/site.conf` files.

You can edit all configuration files to further define any particular build environment. This process is represented by the "User Configuration Edits" box in the figure.

When you launch your build with the `bitbake target` command, BitBake sorts out the configurations to ultimately define your build environment.

3.2. Metadata, Machine Configuration, and Policy Configuration

The previous section described the user configurations that define BitBake's global behavior. This section takes a closer look at the layers the build system uses to further control the build. These layers provide Metadata for the software, machine, and policy.

In general, three types of layer input exist:

• Policy Configuration: Distribution Layers provide top-level or general policies for the image or SDK being built. For example, this layer would dictate whether BitBake produces RPM or IPK packages.

• Machine Configuration: Board Support Package (BSP) layers provide machine configurations. This type of information is specific to a particular target architecture.

• Metadata: Software layers contain user-supplied recipe files, patches, and append files.

The following figure shows an expanded representation of the Metadata, Machine Configuration, and Policy Configuration input (layers) boxes of the general Yocto Project Development Environment figure [18]:

Layers

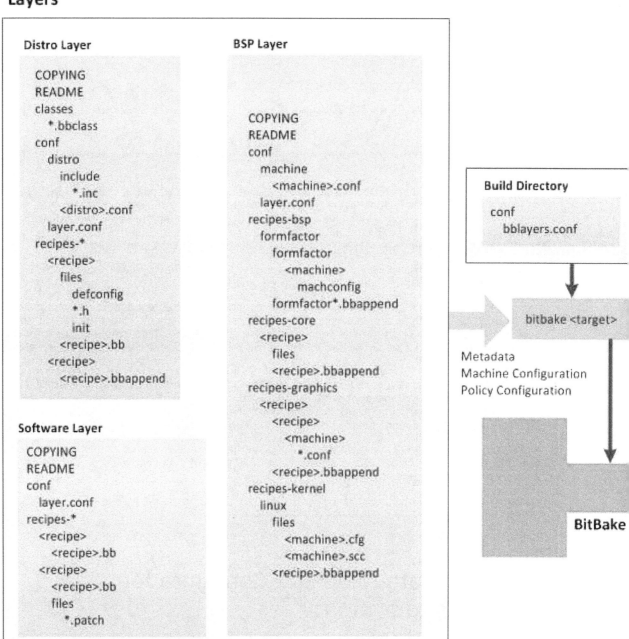

In general, all layers have a similar structure. They all contain a licensing file (e.g. COPYING) if the layer is to be distributed, a README file as good practice and especially if the layer is to be distributed, a configuration directory, and recipe directories.

The Yocto Project has many layers that can be used. You can see a web-interface listing of them on the Source Repositories [http://git.yoctoproject.org/] page. The layers are shown at the bottom categorized under "Yocto Metadata Layers." These layers are fundamentally a subset of the OpenEmbedded Metadata Index [http://layers.openembedded.org/layerindex/layers/], which lists all layers provided by the OpenEmbedded community.

Note

Layers exist in the Yocto Project Source Repositories that cannot be found in the OpenEmbedded Metadata Index. These layers are either deprecated or experimental in nature.

BitBake uses the `conf/bblayers.conf` file, which is part of the user configuration, to find what layers it should be using as part of the build.

For more information on layers, see the "Understanding and Creating Layers [http://www.yoctoproject.org/docs/1.7.2/dev-manual/dev-manual.html#understanding-and-creating-layers]" section in the Yocto Project Development Manual.

3.2.1. Distro Layer

The distribution layer provides policy configurations for your distribution. Best practices dictate that you isolate these types of configurations into their own layer. Settings you provide in `conf/distro/distro.conf` override similar settings that BitBake finds in your `conf/local.conf` file in the Build Directory.

The following list provides some explanation and references for what you typically find in the distribution layer:

- classes: Class files (`.bbclass`) hold common functionality that can be shared among recipes in the distribution. When your recipes inherit a class, they take on the settings and functions for that class. You can read more about class files in the "Classes" section.

- conf: This area holds configuration files for the layer (`conf/layer.conf`), the distribution (`conf/distro/distro.conf`), and any distribution-wide include files.

- recipes-*: Recipes and append files that affect common functionality across the distribution. This area could include recipes and append files to add distribution-specific configuration, initialization scripts, custom image recipes, and so forth.

3.2.2. BSP Layer

The BSP Layer provides machine configurations. Everything in this layer is specific to the machine for which you are building the image or the SDK. A common structure or form is defined for BSP layers. You can learn more about this structure in the Yocto Project Board Support Package (BSP) Developer's Guide [http://www.yoctoproject.org/docs/1.7.2/bsp-guide/bsp-guide.html].

Note

In order for a BSP layer to be considered compliant with the Yocto Project, it must meet some structural requirements.

The BSP Layer's configuration directory contains configuration files for the machine (`conf/machine/machine.conf`) and, of course, the layer (`conf/layer.conf`).

The remainder of the layer is dedicated to specific recipes by function: `recipes-bsp`, `recipes-core`, `recipes-graphics`, and `recipes-kernel`. Metadata can exist for multiple formfactors, graphics support systems, and so forth.

Note

While the figure shows several `recipes-*` directories, not all these directories appear in all BSP layers.

3.2.3. Software Layer

The software layer provides the Metadata for additional software packages used during the build. This layer does not include Metadata that is specific to the distribution or the machine, which are found in their respective layers.

This layer contains any new recipes that your project needs in the form of recipe files.

3.3. Sources

In order for the OpenEmbedded build system to create an image or any target, it must be able to access source files. The general Yocto Project Development Environment figure [18] represents source files using the "Upstream Project Releases", "Local Projects", and "SCMs (optional)" boxes. The figure represents mirrors, which also play a role in locating source files, with the "Source Mirror(s)" box.

The method by which source files are ultimately organized is a function of the project. For example, for released software, projects tend to use tarballs or other archived files that can capture the state of a release guaranteeing that it is statically represented. On the other hand, for a project that is more dynamic or experimental in nature, a project might keep source files in a repository controlled by a Source Control Manager (SCM) such as Git. Pulling source from a repository allows you to control the point in the repository (the revision) from which you want to build software. Finally, a combination of the two might exist, which would give the consumer a choice when deciding where to get source files.

BitBake uses the SRC_URI variable to point to source files regardless of their location. Each recipe must have a SRC_URI variable that points to the source.

Another area that plays a significant role in where source files come from is pointed to by the DL_DIR variable. This area is a cache that can hold previously downloaded source. You can also instruct the OpenEmbedded build system to create tarballs from Git repositories, which is not the default behavior, and store them in the DL_DIR by using the BB_GENERATE_MIRROR_TARBALLS variable.

Judicious use of a DL_DIR directory can save the build system a trip across the Internet when looking for files. A good method for using a download directory is to have DL_DIR point to an area outside of your Build Directory. Doing so allows you to safely delete the Build Directory if needed without fear of removing any downloaded source file.

The remainder of this section provides a deeper look into the source files and the mirrors. Here is a more detailed look at the source file area of the base figure:

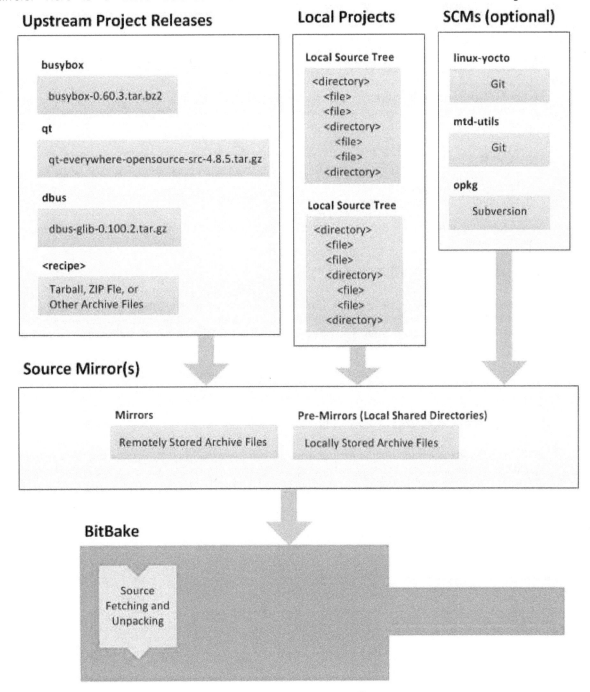

3.3.1. Upstream Project Releases

Upstream project releases exist anywhere in the form of an archived file (e.g. tarball or zip file). These files correspond to individual recipes. For example, the figure uses specific releases each for BusyBox, Qt, and Dbus. An archive file can be for any released product that can be built using a recipe.

3.3.2. Local Projects

Local projects are custom bits of software the user provides. These bits reside somewhere local to a project - perhaps a directory into which the user checks in items (e.g. a local directory containing a development source tree used by the group).

The canonical method through which to include a local project is to use the externalsrc class to include that local project. You use either the local.conf or a recipe's append file to override or set the recipe to point to the local directory on your disk to pull in the whole source tree.

For information on how to use the externalsrc class, see the "externalsrc.bbclass" section.

3.3.3. Source Control Managers (Optional)

Another place the build system can get source files from is through an SCM such as Git or Subversion. In this case, a repository is cloned or checked out. The do_fetch task inside BitBake uses the SRC_URI variable and the argument's prefix to determine the correct fetcher module.

Note

For information on how to have the OpenEmbedded build system generate tarballs for Git repositories and place them in the DL_DIR directory, see the BB_GENERATE_MIRROR_TARBALLS variable.

When fetching a repository, BitBake uses the SRCREV variable to determine the specific revision from which to build.

3.3.4. Source Mirror(s)

Two kinds of mirrors exist: pre-mirrors and regular mirrors. The PREMIRRORS and MIRRORS variables point to these, respectively. BitBake checks pre-mirrors before looking upstream for any source files. Pre-mirrors are appropriate when you have a shared directory that is not a directory defined by the DL_DIR variable. A Pre-mirror typically points to a shared directory that is local to your organization.

Regular mirrors can be any site across the Internet that is used as an alternative location for source code should the primary site not be functioning for some reason or another.

3.4. Package Feeds

When the OpenEmbedded build system generates an image or an SDK, it gets the packages from a package feed area located in the Build Directory [http://www.yoctoproject.org/docs/1.7.2/dev-manual/dev-manual.html#build-directory]. The general Yocto Project Development Environment figure [18] shows this package feeds area in the upper-right corner.

This section looks a little closer into the package feeds area used by the build system. Here is a more detailed look at the area:

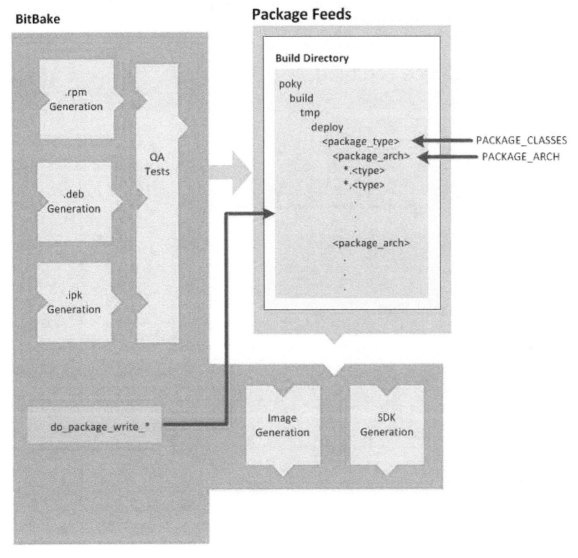

Package feeds are an intermediary step in the build process. BitBake generates packages whose types are defined by the PACKAGE_CLASSES variable. Before placing the packages into package feeds, the build process validates them with generated output quality assurance checks through the insane class.

The package feed area resides in tmp/deploy of the Build Directory. Folders are created that correspond to the package type (IPK, DEB, or RPM) created. Further organization is derived through the value of the PACKAGE_ARCH variable for each package. For example, packages can exist for the i586 or qemux86 architectures. The package files themselves reside within the appropriate architecture folder.

BitBake uses the do_package_write_* tasks to place generated packages into the package holding area (e.g. do_package_write_ipk for IPK packages). See the "do_package_write_deb", "do_package_write_ipk", "do_package_write_rpm", and "do_package_write_tar" sections for additional information.

3.5. BitBake

The OpenEmbedded build system uses BitBake [http://www.yoctoproject.org/docs/1.7.2/dev-manual/dev-manual.html#bitbake-term] to produce images. You can see from the general Yocto Project

Development Environment figure [18], the BitBake area consists of several functional areas. This section takes a closer look at each of those areas.

Separate documentation exists for the BitBake tool. See the BitBake User Manual [http://www.yoctoproject.org/docs/1.7.2/bitbake-user-manual/bitbake-user-manual.html#bitbake-user-manual] for reference material on BitBake.

3.5.1. Source Fetching

The first stages of building a recipe are to fetch and unpack the source code:

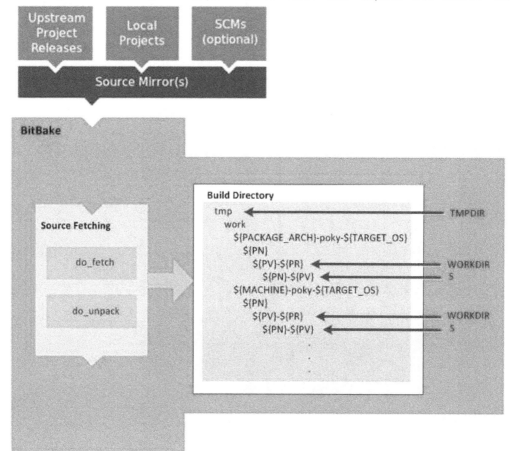

The do_fetch and do_unpack tasks fetch the source files and unpack them into the work directory.

Note

For every local file (e.g. file://) that is part of a recipe's SRC_URI statement, the OpenEmbedded build system takes a checksum of the file for the recipe and inserts the checksum into the signature for the do_fetch. If any local file has been modified, the do_fetch task and all tasks that depend on it are re-executed.

By default, everything is accomplished in the Build Directory [http://www.yoctoproject.org/docs/1.7.2/dev-manual/dev-manual.html#build-directory], which has a defined structure. For additional general information on the Build Directory, see the "build/" section.

Unpacked source files are pointed to by the S variable. Each recipe has an area in the Build Directory where the unpacked source code resides. The name of that directory for any given recipe is defined from several different variables. You can see the variables that define these directories by looking at the figure:

• TMPDIR - The base directory where the OpenEmbedded build system performs all its work during the build.

• PACKAGE_ARCH - The architecture of the built package or packages.

- TARGET_OS - The operating system of the target device.

- PN - The name of the built package.

- PV - The version of the recipe used to build the package.

- PR - The revision of the recipe used to build the package.

- WORKDIR - The location within TMPDIR where a specific package is built.

- S - Contains the unpacked source files for a given recipe.

3.5.2. Patching

Once source code is fetched and unpacked, BitBake locates patch files and applies them to the source files:

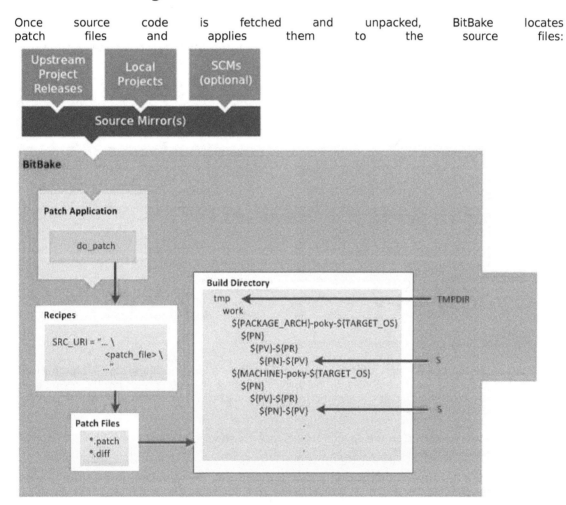

The do_patch task processes recipes by using the SRC_URI variable to locate applicable patch files, which by default are *.patch or *.diff files, or any file if "apply=yes" is specified for the file in SRC_URI.

BitBake finds and applies multiple patches for a single recipe in the order in which it finds the patches. Patches are applied to the recipe's source files located in the S directory.

For more information on how the source directories are created, see the "Source Fetching" section.

3.5.3. Configuration and Compilation

After source code is patched, BitBake executes tasks that configure and compile the source code:

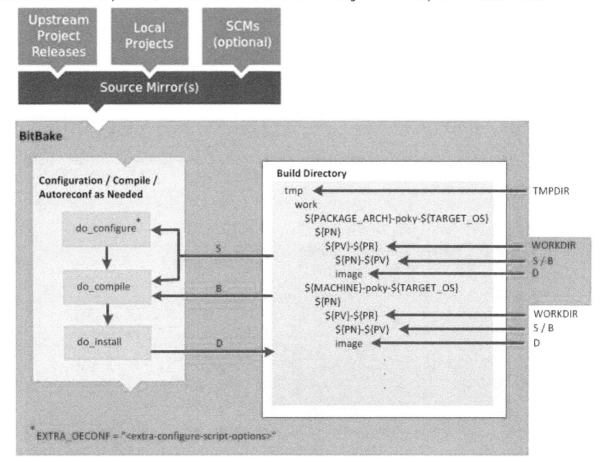

This step in the build process consists of three tasks:

- do_configure: This task configures the source by enabling and disabling any build-time and configuration options for the software being built. Configurations can come from the recipe itself as well as from an inherited class. Additionally, the software itself might configure itself depending on the target for which it is being built.

  The configurations handled by the do_configure task are specific to source code configuration for the source code being built by the recipe.

  If you are using the autotools class, you can add additional configuration options by using the EXTRA_OECONF variable. For information on how this variable works within that class, see the meta/classes/autotools.bbclass file.

- do_compile: Once a configuration task has been satisfied, BitBake compiles the source using the do_compile task. Compilation occurs in the directory pointed to by the B variable. Realize that the B directory is, by default, the same as the S directory.

- do_install: Once compilation is done, BitBake executes the do_install task. This task copies files from the B directory and places them in a holding area pointed to by the D variable.

3.5.4. Package Splitting

After source code is configured and compiled, the OpenEmbedded build system analyzes the results and splits the output into packages:

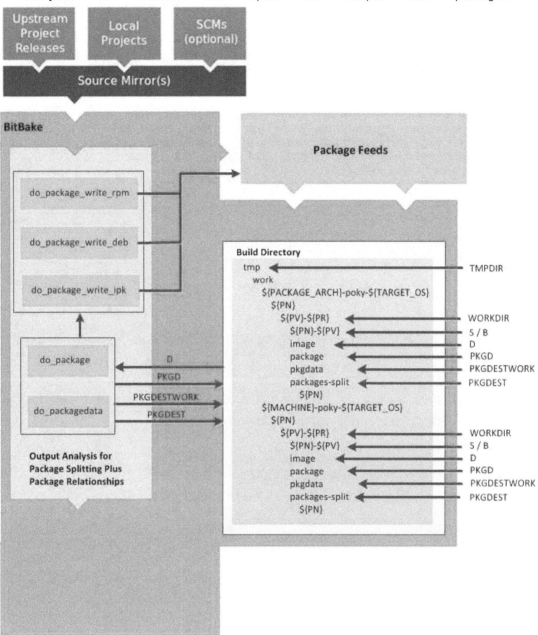

The do_package and do_packagedata tasks combine to analyze the files found in the D directory and split them into subsets based on available packages and files. The analyzing process involves the following as well as other items: splitting out debugging symbols, looking at shared library dependencies between packages, and looking at package relationships. The do_packagedata task creates package metadata based on the analysis such that the OpenEmbedded build system can generate the final packages. Working, staged, and intermediate results of the analysis and package splitting process use these areas:

- PKGD - The destination directory for packages before they are split.

- PKGDATA_DIR - A shared, global-state directory that holds data generated during the packaging process.

- PKGDESTWORK - A temporary work area used by the do_package task.

- PKGDEST - The parent directory for packages after they have been split.

The FILES variable defines the files that go into each package in PACKAGES. If you want details on how this is accomplished, you can look at the package class.

Depending on the type of packages being created (RPM, DEB, or IPK), the do_package_write_* task creates the actual packages and places them in the Package Feed area, which is ${TMPDIR}/deploy. You can see the "Package Feeds" section for more detail on that part of the build process.

Note

Support for creating feeds directly from the deploy/* directories does not exist. Creating such feeds usually requires some kind of feed maintenance mechanism that would upload the new packages into an official package feed (e.g. the Ångström distribution). This functionality is highly distribution-specific and thus is not provided out of the box.

3.5.5. Image Generation

Once packages are split and stored in the Package Feeds area, the OpenEmbedded build system uses BitBake to generate the root filesystem image:

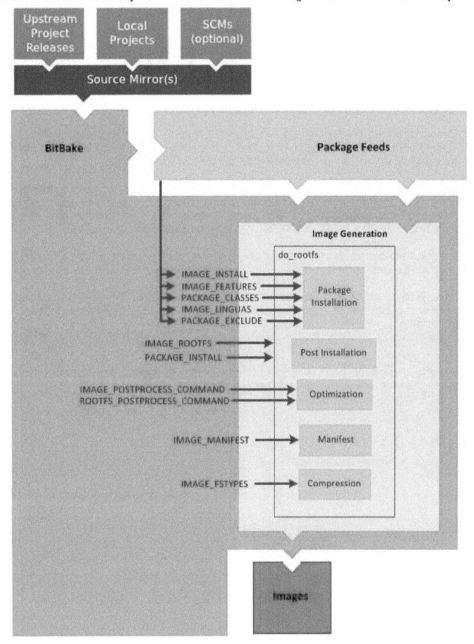

The image generation process consists of several stages and depends on many variables. The do_rootfs task uses these key variables to help create the list of packages to actually install:

- IMAGE_INSTALL: Lists out the base set of packages to install from the Package Feeds area.

- PACKAGE_EXCLUDE: Specifies packages that should not be installed.

- IMAGE_FEATURES: Specifies features to include in the image. Most of these features map to additional packages for installation.

- PACKAGE_CLASSES: Specifies the package backend to use and consequently helps determine where to locate packages within the Package Feeds area.

- IMAGE_LINGUAS: Determines the language(s) for which additional language support packages are installed.

Package installation is under control of the package manager (e.g. smart/rpm, opkg, or apt/dpkg) regardless of whether or not package management is enabled for the target. At the end of the process, if package management is not enabled for the target, the package manager's data files are deleted from the root filesystem.

During image generation, the build system attempts to run all post-installation scripts. Any that fail to run on the build host are run on the target when the target system is first booted. If you are using a read-only root filesystem [http://www.yoctoproject.org/docs/1.7.2/dev-manual/dev-manual.html#creating-a-read-only-root-filesystem], all the post installation scripts must succeed during the package installation phase since the root filesystem is read-only.

During Optimization, optimizing processes are run across the image. These processes include mklibs and prelink. The mklibs process optimizes the size of the libraries. A prelink process optimizes the dynamic linking of shared libraries to reduce start up time of executables.

Along with writing out the root filesystem image, the do_rootfs task creates a manifest file (.manifest) in the same directory as the root filesystem image that lists out, line-by-line, the installed packages. This manifest file is useful for the testimage class, for example, to determine whether or not to run specific tests. See the IMAGE_MANIFEST variable for additional information.

Part of the image generation process includes compressing the root filesystem image. Compression is accomplished through several optimization routines designed to reduce the overall size of the image.

After the root filesystem has been constructed, the image generation process turns everything into an image file or a set of image files. The formats used for the root filesystem depend on the IMAGE_FSTYPES variable.

Note

The entire image generation process is run under Pseudo. Running under Pseudo ensures that the files in the root filesystem have correct ownership.

3.5.6. SDK Generation

The OpenEmbedded build system uses BitBake to generate the Software Development Kit (SDK) installer script:

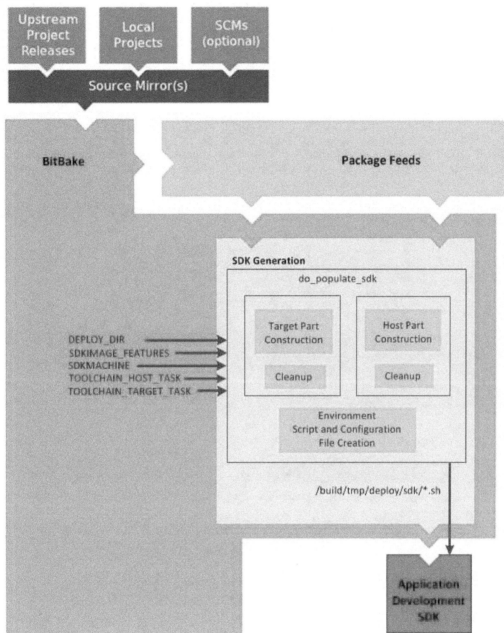

Note

For more information on the cross-development toolchain generation, see the "Cross-Development Toolchain Generation" section. For information on advantages gained when building a cross-development toolchain using the do_populate_sdk task, see the "Optionally Building a Toolchain Installer [http://www.yoctoproject.org/docs/1.7.2/adt-manual/adt-manual.html#optionally-building-a-toolchain-installer]" section in the Yocto Project Application Developer's Guide.

Like image generation, the SDK script process consists of several stages and depends on many variables. The do_populate_sdk task uses these key variables to help create the list of packages to actually install. For information on the variables listed in the figure, see the "Application Development SDK" section.

The do_populate_sdk task handles two parts: a target part and a host part. The target part is the part built for the target hardware and includes libraries and headers. The host part is the part of the SDK that runs on the SDKMACHINE.

Once both parts are constructed, the do_populate_sdk task performs some cleanup on both parts. After the cleanup, the task creates a cross-development environment setup script and any configuration files that might be needed.

The final output of the task is the Cross-development toolchain installation script (.sh file), which includes the environment setup script.

3.6. Images

The images produced by the OpenEmbedded build system are compressed forms of the root filesystem that are ready to boot on a target device. You can see from the general Yocto Project Development Environment figure [18] that BitBake output, in part, consists of images. This section is going to look more closely at this output:

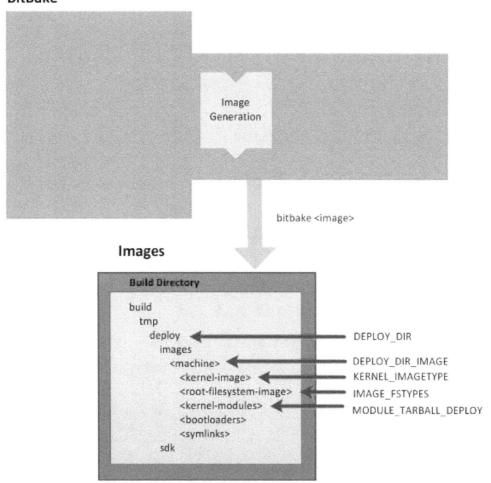

For a list of example images that the Yocto Project provides, see the "Images" chapter.

Images are written out to the Build Directory [http://www.yoctoproject.org/docs/1.7.2/dev-manual/dev-manual.html#build-directory] inside the tmp/deploy/images/machine/ folder as shown in the figure. This folder contains any files expected to be loaded on the target device. The DEPLOY_DIR variable points to the deploy directory, while the DEPLOY_DIR_IMAGE variable points to the appropriate directory containing images for the current configuration.

- kernel-image: A kernel binary file. The KERNEL_IMAGETYPE variable setting determines the naming scheme for the kernel image file. Depending on that variable, the file could begin with a variety of naming strings. The deploy/images/machine directory can contain multiple image files for the machine.

- root-filesystem-image: Root filesystems for the target device (e.g. *.ext3 or *.bz2 files). The IMAGE_FSTYPES variable setting determines the root filesystem image type. The deploy/ images/machine directory can contain multiple root filesystems for the machine.

- kernel-modules: Tarballs that contain all the modules built for the kernel. Kernel module tarballs exist for legacy purposes and can be suppressed by setting the MODULE_TARBALL_DEPLOY variable to "0". The deploy/images/machine directory can contain multiple kernel module tarballs for the machine.

- bootloaders: Bootloaders supporting the image, if applicable to the target machine. The deploy/ images/machine directory can contain multiple bootloaders for the machine.

- symlinks: The deploy/images/machine folder contains a symbolic link that points to the most recently built file for each machine. These links might be useful for external scripts that need to obtain the latest version of each file.

3.7. Application Development SDK

In the general Yocto Project Development Environment figure [18], the output labeled "Application Development SDK" represents an SDK. This section is going to take a closer look at this output:

The specific form of this output is a self-extracting SDK installer (*.sh) that, when run, installs the SDK, which consists of a cross-development toolchain, a set of libraries and headers, and an SDK environment setup script. Running this installer essentially sets up your cross-development environment. You can think of the cross-toolchain as the "host" part because it runs on the SDK machine. You can think of the libraries and headers as the "target" part because they are built for the target hardware. The setup script is added so that you can initialize the environment before using the tools.

Note

The Yocto Project supports several methods by which you can set up this cross-development environment. These methods include downloading pre-built SDK installers, building and installing your own SDK installer, or running an Application Development Toolkit (ADT) installer to install not just cross-development toolchains but also additional tools to help in this type of development.

For background information on cross-development toolchains in the Yocto Project development environment, see the "Cross-Development Toolchain Generation" section. For information on setting up a cross-development environment, see the "Installing the ADT and Toolchains [http://www.yoctoproject.org/docs/1.7.2/adt-manual/adt-manual.html#installing-the-adt]" section in the Yocto Project Application Developer's Guide.

Once built, the SDK installers are written out to the deploy/sdk folder inside the Build Directory [http://www.yoctoproject.org/docs/1.7.2/dev-manual/dev-manual.html#build-directory] as shown in the figure at the beginning of this section. Several variables exist that help configure these files:

• DEPLOY_DIR: Points to the deploy directory.

• SDKMACHINE: Specifies the architecture of the machine on which the cross-development tools are run to create packages for the target hardware.

• SDKIMAGE_FEATURES: Lists the features to include in the "target" part of the SDK.

• TOOLCHAIN_HOST_TASK: Lists packages that make up the host part of the SDK (i.e. the part that runs on the SDKMACHINE). When you use bitbake -c populate_sdk imagename to create the SDK, a set of default packages apply. This variable allows you to add more packages.

• TOOLCHAIN_TARGET_TASK: Lists packages that make up the target part of the SDK (i.e. the part built for the target hardware).

• SDKPATH: Defines the default SDK installation path offered by the installation script.

Chapter 4. Technical Details

This chapter provides technical details for various parts of the Yocto Project. Currently, topics include Yocto Project components, cross-toolchain generation, shared state (sstate) cache, x32, Wayland support, and Licenses.

4.1. Yocto Project Components

The BitBake [http://www.yoctoproject.org/docs/1.7.2/dev-manual/dev-manual.html#bitbake-term] task executor together with various types of configuration files form the OpenEmbedded Core. This section overviews these components by describing their use and how they interact.

BitBake handles the parsing and execution of the data files. The data itself is of various types:

- Recipes: Provides details about particular pieces of software.

- Class Data: Abstracts common build information (e.g. how to build a Linux kernel).

- Configuration Data: Defines machine-specific settings, policy decisions, and so forth. Configuration data acts as the glue to bind everything together.

BitBake knows how to combine multiple data sources together and refers to each data source as a layer. For information on layers, see the "Understanding and Creating Layers [http://www.yoctoproject.org/docs/1.7.2/dev-manual/dev-manual.html#understanding-and-creating-layers]" section of the Yocto Project Development Manual.

Following are some brief details on these core components. For additional information on how these components interact during a build, see the "A Closer Look at the Yocto Project Development Environment" Chapter.

4.1.1. BitBake

BitBake is the tool at the heart of the OpenEmbedded build system and is responsible for parsing the Metadata [http://www.yoctoproject.org/docs/1.7.2/dev-manual/dev-manual.html#metadata], generating a list of tasks from it, and then executing those tasks.

This section briefly introduces BitBake. If you want more information on BitBake, see the BitBake User Manual [http://www.yoctoproject.org/docs/1.7.2/bitbake-user-manual/bitbake-user-manual.html#bitbake-user-manual].

To see a list of the options BitBake supports, use either of the following commands:

```
$ bitbake -h
$ bitbake --help
```

The most common usage for BitBake is `bitbake packagename`, where packagename is the name of the package you want to build (referred to as the "target" in this manual). The target often equates to the first part of a recipe's filename (e.g. "foo" for a recipe named `foo_1.3.0-r0.bb`). So, to process the `matchbox-desktop_1.2.3.bb` recipe file, you might type the following:

```
$ bitbake matchbox-desktop
```

Several different versions of `matchbox-desktop` might exist. BitBake chooses the one selected by the distribution configuration. You can get more details about how BitBake chooses between different target versions and providers in the "Preferences [http://www.yoctoproject.org/docs/1.7.2/bitbake-user-manual/bitbake-user-manual.html#bb-bitbake-preferences]" section of the BitBake User Manual.

BitBake also tries to execute any dependent tasks first. So for example, before building `matchbox-desktop`, BitBake would build a cross compiler and `glibc` if they had not already been built.

A useful BitBake option to consider is the -k or --continue option. This option instructs BitBake to try and continue processing the job as long as possible even after encountering an error. When an error occurs, the target that failed and those that depend on it cannot be remade. However, when you use this option other dependencies can still be processed.

4.1.2. Metadata (Recipes)

Files that have the .bb suffix are "recipes" files. In general, a recipe contains information about a single piece of software. This information includes the location from which to download the unaltered source, any source patches to be applied to that source (if needed), which special configuration options to apply, how to compile the source files, and how to package the compiled output.

The term "package" is sometimes used to refer to recipes. However, since the word "package" is used for the packaged output from the OpenEmbedded build system (i.e. .ipk or .deb files), this document avoids using the term "package" when referring to recipes.

4.1.3. Classes

Class files (.bbclass) contain information that is useful to share between Metadata [http://www.yoctoproject.org/docs/1.7.2/dev-manual/dev-manual.html#metadata] files. An example is the autotools class, which contains common settings for any application that Autotools uses. The "Classes" chapter provides details about classes and how to use them.

4.1.4. Configuration

The configuration files (.conf) define various configuration variables that govern the OpenEmbedded build process. These files fall into several areas that define machine configuration options, distribution configuration options, compiler tuning options, general common configuration options, and user configuration options in local.conf, which is found in the Build Directory [http://www.yoctoproject.org/docs/1.7.2/dev-manual/dev-manual.html#build-directory].

4.2. Cross-Development Toolchain Generation

The Yocto Project does most of the work for you when it comes to creating cross-development toolchains [http://www.yoctoproject.org/docs/1.7.2/dev-manual/dev-manual.html#cross-development-toolchain]. This section provides some technical background on how cross-development toolchains are created and used. For more information on toolchains, you can also see the Yocto Project Application Developer's Guide [http://www.yoctoproject.org/docs/1.7.2/adt-manual/adt-manual.html].

In the Yocto Project development environment, cross-development toolchains are used to build the image and applications that run on the target hardware. With just a few commands, the OpenEmbedded build system creates these necessary toolchains for you.

The following figure shows a high-level build environment regarding toolchain construction and use.

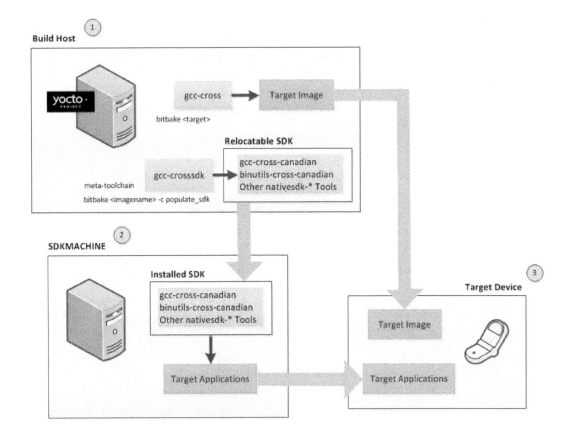

The Build Host produces three toolchains: 1) gcc-cross, which builds the target image. 2) gcc-crosssdk, which is a transitory toolchain and produces relocatable code that executes on the SDKMACHINE. 3) gcc-cross-canadian, which executes on the SDKMACHINE and produces target applications.

The SDKMACHINE, which may or may not be the same as the Build Host, runs gcc-cross-canadian to create target applications.

The Target Device run the Target Image and Target Applications.

Most of the work occurs on the Build Host. This is the machine used to build images and generally work within the the Yocto Project environment. When you run BitBake to create an image, the OpenEmbedded build system uses the host gcc compiler to bootstrap a cross-compiler named gcc-cross. The gcc-cross compiler is what BitBake uses to compile source files when creating the target image. You can think of gcc-cross simply as an automatically generated cross-compiler that is used internally within BitBake only.

The chain of events that occurs when gcc-cross is bootstrapped is as follows:

```
gcc -> binutils-cross -> gcc-cross-initial -> linux-libc-headers -> glibc-initial -> glibc
```

- gcc: The build host's GNU Compiler Collection (GCC).

- binutils-cross: The bare minimum binary utilities needed in order to run the gcc-cross-initial phase of the bootstrap operation.

- gcc-cross-initial: An early stage of the bootstrap process for creating the cross-compiler. This stage builds enough of the gcc-cross, the C library, and other pieces needed to finish building the final cross-compiler in later stages. This tool is a "native" package (i.e. it is designed to run on the build host).

- linux-libc-headers: Headers needed for the cross-compiler.

- glibc-initial: An initial version of the Embedded GLIBC needed to bootstrap glibc.

- gcc-cross: The final stage of the bootstrap process for the cross-compiler. This stage results in the actual cross-compiler that BitBake uses when it builds an image for a targeted device.

  ## Note
  If you are replacing this cross compiler toolchain with a custom version, you must replace gcc-cross.
  This tool is also a "native" package (i.e. it is designed to run on the build host).

- gcc-runtime: Runtime libraries resulting from the toolchain bootstrapping process. This tool produces a binary that consists of the runtime libraries need for the targeted device.

You can use the OpenEmbedded build system to build an installer for the relocatable SDK used to develop applications. When you run the installer, it installs the toolchain, which contains the development tools (e.g., the gcc-cross-canadian), binutils-cross-canadian, and other nativesdk-* tools you need to cross-compile and test your software. The figure shows the commands you use to easily build out this toolchain. This cross-development toolchain is built to execute on the SDKMACHINE, which might or might not be the same machine as the Build Host.

Note
If your target architecture is supported by the Yocto Project, you can take advantage of pre-built images that ship with the Yocto Project and already contain cross-development toolchain installers.

Here is the bootstrap process for the relocatable toolchain:

```
gcc -> binutils-crosssdk -> gcc-crosssdk-initial -> linux-libc-headers ->
    glibc-initial -> nativesdk-glibc -> gcc-crosssdk -> gcc-cross-canadian
```

- gcc: The build host's GNU Compiler Collection (GCC).

- binutils-crosssdk: The bare minimum binary utilities needed in order to run the gcc-crosssdk-initial phase of the bootstrap operation.

- gcc-crosssdk-initial: An early stage of the bootstrap process for creating the cross-compiler. This stage builds enough of the gcc-crosssdk and supporting pieces so that the final stage of the bootstrap process can produce the finished cross-compiler. This tool is a "native" binary that runs on the build host.

- linux-libc-headers: Headers needed for the cross-compiler.

- glibc-initial: An initial version of the Embedded GLIBC needed to bootstrap nativesdk-glibc.

- nativesdk-glibc: The Embedded GLIBC needed to bootstrap the gcc-crosssdk.

- gcc-crosssdk: The final stage of the bootstrap process for the relocatable cross-compiler. The gcc-crosssdk is a transitory compiler and never leaves the build host. Its purpose is to help in the bootstrap process to create the eventual relocatable gcc-cross-canadian compiler, which is relocatable. This tool is also a "native" package (i.e. it is designed to run on the build host).

- gcc-cross-canadian: The final relocatable cross-compiler. When run on the SDKMACHINE, this tool produces executable code that runs on the target device. Only one cross-canadian compiler is produced per architecture since they can be targeted at different processor optimizations using configurations passed to the compiler through the compile commands. This circumvents the need for multiple compilers and thus reduces the size of the toolchains.

Note
For information on advantages gained when building a cross-development toolchain installer, see the "Optionally Building a Toolchain Installer [http://www.yoctoproject.org/docs/1.7.2/adt-manual/adt-manual.html#optionally-building-a-toolchain-installer]" section in the Yocto Project Application Developer's Guide.

4.3. Shared State Cache

By design, the OpenEmbedded build system builds everything from scratch unless BitBake can determine that parts do not need to be rebuilt. Fundamentally, building from scratch is attractive as it means all parts are built fresh and there is no possibility of stale data causing problems. When developers hit problems, they typically default back to building from scratch so they know the state of things from the start.

Building an image from scratch is both an advantage and a disadvantage to the process. As mentioned in the previous paragraph, building from scratch ensures that everything is current and starts from a known state. However, building from scratch also takes much longer as it generally means rebuilding things that do not necessarily need to be rebuilt.

The Yocto Project implements shared state code that supports incremental builds. The implementation of the shared state code answers the following questions that were fundamental roadblocks within the OpenEmbedded incremental build support system:

• What pieces of the system have changed and what pieces have not changed?

• How are changed pieces of software removed and replaced?

• How are pre-built components that do not need to be rebuilt from scratch used when they are available?

For the first question, the build system detects changes in the "inputs" to a given task by creating a checksum (or signature) of the task's inputs. If the checksum changes, the system assumes the inputs have changed and the task needs to be rerun. For the second question, the shared state (sstate) code tracks which tasks add which output to the build process. This means the output from a given task can be removed, upgraded or otherwise manipulated. The third question is partly addressed by the solution for the second question assuming the build system can fetch the sstate objects from remote locations and install them if they are deemed to be valid.

Note
The OpenEmbedded build system does not maintain PR information as part of the shared state packages. Consequently, considerations exist that affect maintaining shared state feeds. For information on how the OpenEmbedded build system works with packages and can track incrementing PR information, see the "Incrementing a Package Revision Number [http://www.yoctoproject.org/docs/1.7.2/dev-manual/dev-manual.html#incrementing-a-package-revision-number]" section.

The rest of this section goes into detail about the overall incremental build architecture, the checksums (signatures), shared state, and some tips and tricks.

4.3.1. Overall Architecture

When determining what parts of the system need to be built, BitBake works on a per-task basis rather than a per-recipe basis. You might wonder why using a per-task basis is preferred over a per-recipe basis. To help explain, consider having the IPK packaging backend enabled and then switching to DEB. In this case, the do_install and do_package task outputs are still valid. However, with a per-recipe approach, the build would not include the .deb files. Consequently, you would have to invalidate the whole build and rerun it. Rerunning everything is not the best solution. Also, in this case, the core must be "taught" much about specific tasks. This methodology does not scale well and does not allow users to easily add new tasks in layers or as external recipes without touching the packaged-staging core.

4.3.2. Checksums (Signatures)

The shared state code uses a checksum, which is a unique signature of a task's inputs, to determine if a task needs to be run again. Because it is a change in a task's inputs that triggers a rerun, the process needs to detect all the inputs to a given task. For shell tasks, this turns out to be fairly easy because the build process generates a "run" shell script for each task and it is possible to create a checksum that gives you a good idea of when the task's data changes.

To complicate the problem, there are things that should not be included in the checksum. First, there is the actual specific build path of a given task - the WORKDIR. It does not matter if the work directory changes because it should not affect the output for target packages. Also, the build process has the objective of making native or cross packages relocatable. The checksum therefore needs to exclude WORKDIR. The simplistic approach for excluding the work directory is to set WORKDIR to some fixed value and create the checksum for the "run" script.

Another problem results from the "run" scripts containing functions that might or might not get called. The incremental build solution contains code that figures out dependencies between shell functions. This code is used to prune the "run" scripts down to the minimum set, thereby alleviating this problem and making the "run" scripts much more readable as a bonus.

So far we have solutions for shell scripts. What about Python tasks? The same approach applies even though these tasks are more difficult. The process needs to figure out what variables a Python function accesses and what functions it calls. Again, the incremental build solution contains code that first figures out the variable and function dependencies, and then creates a checksum for the data used as the input to the task.

Like the WORKDIR case, situations exist where dependencies should be ignored. For these cases, you can instruct the build process to ignore a dependency by using a line like the following:

```
PACKAGE_ARCHS[vardepsexclude] = "MACHINE"
```

This example ensures that the PACKAGE_ARCHS variable does not depend on the value of MACHINE, even if it does reference it.

Equally, there are cases where we need to add dependencies BitBake is not able to find. You can accomplish this by using a line like the following:

```
PACKAGE_ARCHS[vardeps] = "MACHINE"
```

This example explicitly adds the MACHINE variable as a dependency for PACKAGE_ARCHS.

Consider a case with in-line Python, for example, where BitBake is not able to figure out dependencies. When running in debug mode (i.e. using -DDD), BitBake produces output when it discovers something for which it cannot figure out dependencies. The Yocto Project team has currently not managed to cover those dependencies in detail and is aware of the need to fix this situation.

Thus far, this section has limited discussion to the direct inputs into a task. Information based on direct inputs is referred to as the "basehash" in the code. However, there is still the question of a task's indirect inputs - the things that were already built and present in the Build Directory [http://www.yoctoproject.org/docs/1.7.2/dev-manual/dev-manual.html#build-directory]. The checksum (or signature) for a particular task needs to add the hashes of all the tasks on which the particular task depends. Choosing which dependencies to add is a policy decision. However, the effect is to generate a master checksum that combines the basehash and the hashes of the task's dependencies.

At the code level, there are a variety of ways both the basehash and the dependent task hashes can be influenced. Within the BitBake configuration file, we can give BitBake some extra information to help it construct the basehash. The following statement effectively results in a list of global variable dependency excludes - variables never included in any checksum:

```
BB_HASHBASE_WHITELIST ?= "TMPDIR FILE PATH PWD BB_TASKHASH BBPATH DL_DIR \
    SSTATE_DIR THISDIR FILESEXTRAPATHS FILE_DIRNAME HOME LOGNAME SHELL TERM \
    USER FILESPATH STAGING_DIR_HOST STAGING_DIR_TARGET COREBASE PRSERV_HOST \
    PRSERV_DUMPDIR PRSERV_DUMPFILE PRSERV_LOCKDOWN PARALLEL_MAKE \
    CCACHE_DIR EXTERNAL_TOOLCHAIN CCACHE CCACHE_DISABLE LICENSE_PATH SDKPKGSUFFIX"
```

The previous example excludes WORKDIR since that variable is actually constructed as a path within TMPDIR, which is on the whitelist.

The rules for deciding which hashes of dependent tasks to include through dependency chains are more complex and are generally accomplished with a Python function. The code in meta/lib/oe/sstatesig.py shows two examples of this and also illustrates how you can insert your own policy into the system if so desired. This file defines the two basic signature generators OE-Core uses: "OEBasic" and "OEBasicHash". By default, there is a dummy "noop" signature handler enabled in BitBake. This means that behavior is unchanged from previous versions. OE-Core uses the "OEBasicHash" signature handler by default through this setting in the bitbake.conf file:

```
BB_SIGNATURE_HANDLER ?= "OEBasicHash"
```

The "OEBasicHash" BB_SIGNATURE_HANDLER is the same as the "OEBasic" version but adds the task hash to the stamp files. This results in any Metadata [http://www.yoctoproject.org/docs/1.7.2/dev-manual/dev-manual.html#metadata] change that changes the task hash, automatically causing the task to be run again. This removes the need to bump PR values, and changes to Metadata automatically ripple across the build.

It is also worth noting that the end result of these signature generators is to make some dependency and hash information available to the build. This information includes:

• BB_BASEHASH_task-taskname: The base hashes for each task in the recipe.

• BB_BASEHASH_filename:taskname: The base hashes for each dependent task.

• BBHASHDEPS_filename:taskname: The task dependencies for each task.

• BB_TASKHASH: The hash of the currently running task.

4.3.3. Shared State

Checksums and dependencies, as discussed in the previous section, solve half the problem of supporting a shared state. The other part of the problem is being able to use checksum information during the build and being able to reuse or rebuild specific components.

The sstate class is a relatively generic implementation of how to "capture" a snapshot of a given task. The idea is that the build process does not care about the source of a task's output. Output could be freshly built or it could be downloaded and unpacked from somewhere - the build process does not need to worry about its origin.

There are two types of output, one is just about creating a directory in WORKDIR. A good example is the output of either do_install or do_package. The other type of output occurs when a set of data is merged into a shared directory tree such as the sysroot.

The Yocto Project team has tried to keep the details of the implementation hidden in sstate class. From a user's perspective, adding shared state wrapping to a task is as simple as this do_deploy example taken from the deploy class:

```
DEPLOYDIR = "${WORKDIR}/deploy-${PN}"
SSTATETASKS += "do_deploy"
do_deploy[sstate-name] = "deploy"
do_deploy[sstate-inputdirs] = "${DEPLOYDIR}"
do_deploy[sstate-outputdirs] = "${DEPLOY_DIR_IMAGE}"

python do_deploy_setscene () {
    sstate_setscene(d)
}
addtask do_deploy_setscene
do_deploy[dirs] = "${DEPLOYDIR} ${B}"
```

In this example, we add some extra flags to the task, a name field ("deploy"), an input directory where the task sends data, and the output directory where the data from the task should eventually be copied. We also add a _setscene variant of the task and add the task name to the SSTATETASKS list.

If you have a directory whose contents you need to preserve, you can do this with a line like the following:

```
do_package[sstate-plaindirs] = "${PKGD} ${PKGDEST}"
```

This method, as well as the following example, also works for multiple directories.

```
do_package[sstate-inputdirs] = "${PKGDESTWORK} ${SHLIBSWORKDIR}"
do_package[sstate-outputdirs] = "${PKGDATA_DIR} ${SHLIBSDIR}"
do_package[sstate-lockfile] = "${PACKAGELOCK}"
```

These methods also include the ability to take a lockfile when manipulating shared state directory structures since some cases are sensitive to file additions or removals.

Behind the scenes, the shared state code works by looking in SSTATE_DIR and SSTATE_MIRRORS for shared state files. Here is an example:

```
SSTATE_MIRRORS ?= "\
file://.* http://someserver.tld/share/sstate/PATH \n \
file://.* file:///some/local/dir/sstate/PATH"
```

Note

The shared state directory (SSTATE_DIR) is organized into two-character subdirectories, where the subdirectory names are based on the first two characters of the hash. If the shared state directory structure for a mirror has the same structure as SSTATE_DIR, you must specify "PATH" as part of the URI to enable the build system to map to the appropriate subdirectory.

The shared state package validity can be detected just by looking at the filename since the filename contains the task checksum (or signature) as described earlier in this section. If a valid shared state package is found, the build process downloads it and uses it to accelerate the task.

The build processes use the *_setscene tasks for the task acceleration phase. BitBake goes through this phase before the main execution code and tries to accelerate any tasks for which it can find shared state packages. If a shared state package for a task is available, the shared state package is used. This means the task and any tasks on which it is dependent are not executed.

As a real world example, the aim is when building an IPK-based image, only the do_package_write_ipk tasks would have their shared state packages fetched and extracted. Since the sysroot is not used, it would never get extracted. This is another reason why a task-based approach is preferred over a recipe-based approach, which would have to install the output from every task.

4.3.4. Tips and Tricks

The code in the build system that supports incremental builds is not simple code. This section presents some tips and tricks that help you work around issues related to shared state code.

4.3.4.1. Debugging

When things go wrong, debugging needs to be straightforward. Because of this, the Yocto Project includes strong debugging tools:

- Whenever a shared state package is written out, so is a corresponding .siginfo file. This practice results in a pickled Python database of all the metadata that went into creating the hash for a given shared state package.

- If you run BitBake with the --dump-signatures (or -S) option, BitBake dumps out .siginfo files in the stamp directory for every task it would have executed instead of building the specified target package.

- There is a bitbake-diffsigs command that can process .siginfo files. If you specify one of these files, BitBake dumps out the dependency information in the file. If you specify two files, BitBake compares the two files and dumps out the differences between the two. This more easily helps answer the question of "What changed between X and Y?"

4.3.4.2. Invalidating Shared State

The OpenEmbedded build system uses checksums and shared state cache to avoid unnecessarily rebuilding tasks. Collectively, this scheme is known as "shared state code."

As with all schemes, this one has some drawbacks. It is possible that you could make implicit changes to your code that the checksum calculations do not take into account. These implicit changes affect a task's output but do not trigger the shared state code into rebuilding a recipe. Consider an example during which a tool changes its output. Assume that the output of rpmdeps changes. The result of the change should be that all the package and package_write_rpm shared state cache items become invalid. However, because the change to the output is external to the code and therefore implicit, the associated shared state cache items do not become invalidated. In this case, the build process uses the cached items rather than running the task again. Obviously, these types of implicit changes can cause problems.

To avoid these problems during the build, you need to understand the effects of any changes you make. Realize that changes you make directly to a function are automatically factored into the checksum calculation. Thus, these explicit changes invalidate the associated area of shared state cache. However, you need to be aware of any implicit changes that are not obvious changes to the code and could affect the output of a given task.

When you identify an implicit change, you can easily take steps to invalidate the cache and force the tasks to run. The steps you can take are as simple as changing a function's comments in the source code. For example, to invalidate package shared state files, change the comment statements of do_package or the comments of one of the functions it calls. Even though the change is purely cosmetic, it causes the checksum to be recalculated and forces the OpenEmbedded build system to run the task again.

Note
For an example of a commit that makes a cosmetic change to invalidate shared state, see this commit [http://git.yoctoproject.org/cgit.cgi/poky/commit/meta/classes/package.bbclass?id=737f8bbb4f27b4837047cb9b4fbfe01dfde36d54].

4.4. x32

x32 is a processor-specific Application Binary Interface (psABI) for x86_64. An ABI defines the calling conventions between functions in a processing environment. The interface determines what registers are used and what the sizes are for various C data types.

Some processing environments prefer using 32-bit applications even when running on Intel 64-bit platforms. Consider the i386 psABI, which is a very old 32-bit ABI for Intel 64-bit platforms. The i386 psABI does not provide efficient use and access of the Intel 64-bit processor resources, leaving the system underutilized. Now consider the x86_64 psABI. This ABI is newer and uses 64-bits for data sizes and program pointers. The extra bits increase the footprint size of the programs, libraries, and also increases the memory and file system size requirements. Executing under the x32 psABI enables user programs to utilize CPU and system resources more efficiently while keeping the memory footprint of the applications low. Extra bits are used for registers but not for addressing mechanisms.

4.4.1. Support

This Yocto Project release supports the final specifications of x32 psABI. Support for x32 psABI exists as follows:

• You can create packages and images in x32 psABI format on x86_64 architecture targets.

• You can successfully build many recipes with the x32 toolchain.

• You can create and boot core-image-minimal and core-image-sato images.

4.4.2. Completing x32

Future Plans for the x32 psABI in the Yocto Project include the following:

• Enhance and fix the few remaining recipes so they work with and support x32 toolchains.

- Enhance RPM Package Manager (RPM) support for x32 binaries.

- Support larger images.

4.4.3. Using x32 Right Now

Follow these steps to use the x32 spABI:

- Enable the x32 psABI tuning file for x86_64 machines by editing the conf/local.conf like this:

```
MACHINE = "qemux86-64"
DEFAULTTUNE = "x86-64-x32"
baselib = "${@d.getVar('BASE_LIB_tune-' + (d.getVar('DEFAULTTUNE', True) \
    or 'INVALID'), True) or 'lib'}"
#MACHINE = "genericx86"
#DEFAULTTUNE = "core2-64-x32"
```

- As usual, use BitBake to build an image that supports the x32 psABI. Here is an example:

```
$ bitbake core-image-sato
```

- As usual, run your image using QEMU:

```
$ runqemu qemux86-64 core-image-sato
```

4.5. Wayland

Wayland [http://en.wikipedia.org/wiki/Wayland_(display_server_protocol)] is a computer display server protocol that provides a method for compositing window managers to communicate directly with applications and video hardware and expects them to communicate with input hardware using other libraries. Using Wayland with supporting targets can result in better control over graphics frame rendering than an application might otherwise achieve.

The Yocto Project provides the Wayland protocol libraries and the reference Weston [http://en.wikipedia.org/wiki/Wayland_(display_server_protocol)#Weston] compositor as part of its release. This section describes what you need to do to implement Wayland and use the compositor when building an image for a supporting target.

4.5.1. Support

The Wayland protocol libraries and the reference Weston compositor ship as integrated packages in the meta layer of the Source Directory [http://www.yoctoproject.org/docs/1.7.2/dev-manual/dev-manual.html#source-directory]. Specifically, you can find the recipes that build both Wayland and Weston at meta/recipes-graphics/wayland.

You can build both the Wayland and Weston packages for use only with targets that accept the Mesa 3D and Direct Rendering Infrastructure [http://dri.freedesktop.org/wiki/], which is also known as Mesa DRI. This implies that you cannot build and use the packages if your target uses, for example, the Intel® Embedded Media and Graphics Driver (Intel® EMGD) that overrides Mesa DRI.

Note
Due to lack of EGL support, Weston 1.0.3 will not run directly on the emulated QEMU hardware. However, this version of Weston will run under X emulation without issues.

4.5.2. Enabling Wayland in an Image

To enable Wayland, you need to enable it to be built and enable it to be included in the image.

4.5.2.1. Building

To cause Mesa to build the wayland-egl platform and Weston to build Wayland with Kernel Mode Setting (KMS [https://wiki.archlinux.org/index.php/Kernel_Mode_Setting]) support, include the "wayland" flag in the DISTRO_FEATURES statement in your local.conf file:

```
DISTRO_FEATURES_append = " wayland"
```

Note
If X11 has been enabled elsewhere, Weston will build Wayland with X11 support

4.5.2.2. Installing

To install the Wayland feature into an image, you must include the following CORE_IMAGE_EXTRA_INSTALL statement in your local.conf file:

```
CORE_IMAGE_EXTRA_INSTALL += "wayland weston"
```

4.5.3. Running Weston

To run Weston inside X11, enabling it as described earlier and building a Sato image is sufficient. If you are running your image under Sato, a Weston Launcher appears in the "Utility" category.

Alternatively, you can run Weston through the command-line interpretor (CLI), which is better suited for development work. To run Weston under the CLI, you need to do the following after your image is built:

1. Run these commands to export XDG_RUNTIME_DIR:

```
mkdir -p /tmp/$USER-weston
chmod 0700 /tmp/$USER-weston
export XDG_RUNTIME_DIR=/tmp/$USER-weston
```

2. Launch Weston in the shell:

```
weston
```

4.6. Licenses

This section describes the mechanism by which the OpenEmbedded build system tracks changes to licensing text. The section also describes how to enable commercially licensed recipes, which by default are disabled.

For information that can help you maintain compliance with various open source licensing during the lifecycle of the product, see the "Maintaining Open Source License Compliance During Your Project's Lifecycle [http://www.yoctoproject.org/docs/1.7.2/dev-manual/dev-manual.html#maintaining-open-source-license-compliance-during-your-products-lifecycle]" section in the Yocto Project Development Manual.

4.6.1. Tracking License Changes

The license of an upstream project might change in the future. In order to prevent these changes going unnoticed, the LIC_FILES_CHKSUM variable tracks changes to the license text. The checksums are validated at the end of the configure step, and if the checksums do not match, the build will fail.

4.6.1.1. Specifying the**LIC_FILES_CHKSUM** Variable

The LIC_FILES_CHKSUM variable contains checksums of the license text in the source code for the recipe. Following is an example of how to specify LIC_FILES_CHKSUM:

```
LIC_FILES_CHKSUM = "file://COPYING;md5=xxxx \
                    file://licfile1.txt;beginline=5;endline=29;md5=yyyy \
                    file://licfile2.txt;endline=50;md5=zzzz \
                    ..."
```

The build system uses the S variable as the default directory when searching files listed in LIC_FILES_CHKSUM. The previous example employs the default directory.

Consider this next example:

```
LIC_FILES_CHKSUM = "file://src/ls.c;beginline=5;endline=16;\
                        md5=bb14ed3c4cda583abc85401304b5cd4e"
LIC_FILES_CHKSUM = "file://${WORKDIR}/license.html;md5=5c94767cedb5d6987c902ac850ded2c6"
```

The first line locates a file in ${S}/src/ls.c. The second line refers to a file in WORKDIR.

Note that LIC_FILES_CHKSUM variable is mandatory for all recipes, unless the LICENSE variable is set to "CLOSED".

4.6.1.2. Explanation of Syntax

As mentioned in the previous section, the LIC_FILES_CHKSUM variable lists all the important files that contain the license text for the source code. It is possible to specify a checksum for an entire file, or a specific section of a file (specified by beginning and ending line numbers with the "beginline" and "endline" parameters, respectively). The latter is useful for source files with a license notice header, README documents, and so forth. If you do not use the "beginline" parameter, then it is assumed that the text begins on the first line of the file. Similarly, if you do not use the "endline" parameter, it is assumed that the license text ends with the last line of the file.

The "md5" parameter stores the md5 checksum of the license text. If the license text changes in any way as compared to this parameter then a mismatch occurs. This mismatch triggers a build failure and notifies the developer. Notification allows the developer to review and address the license text changes. Also note that if a mismatch occurs during the build, the correct md5 checksum is placed in the build log and can be easily copied to the recipe.

There is no limit to how many files you can specify using the LIC_FILES_CHKSUM variable. Generally, however, every project requires a few specifications for license tracking. Many projects have a "COPYING" file that stores the license information for all the source code files. This practice allows you to just track the "COPYING" file as long as it is kept up to date.

Tip
If you specify an empty or invalid "md5" parameter, BitBake returns an md5 mis-match error and displays the correct "md5" parameter value during the build. The correct parameter is also captured in the build log.

Tip
If the whole file contains only license text, you do not need to use the "beginline" and "endline" parameters.

4.6.2. Enabling Commercially Licensed Recipes

By default, the OpenEmbedded build system disables components that have commercial or other special licensing requirements. Such requirements are defined on a recipe-by-recipe basis through the LICENSE_FLAGS variable definition in the affected recipe. For instance, the poky/meta/recipes-multimedia/gstreamer/gst-plugins-ugly recipe contains the following statement:

```
LICENSE_FLAGS = "commercial"
```

Here is a slightly more complicated example that contains both an explicit recipe name and version (after variable expansion):

```
LICENSE_FLAGS = "license_${PN}_${PV}"
```

In order for a component restricted by a LICENSE_FLAGS definition to be enabled and included in an image, it needs to have a matching entry in the global LICENSE_FLAGS_WHITELIST variable, which is a variable typically defined in your local.conf file. For example, to enable the poky/meta/recipes-multimedia/gstreamer/gst-plugins-ugly package, you could add either the string "commercial_gst-plugins-ugly" or the more general string "commercial" to LICENSE_FLAGS_WHITELIST. See the "License Flag Matching" section for a full explanation of how LICENSE_FLAGS matching works. Here is the example:

```
LICENSE_FLAGS_WHITELIST = "commercial_gst-plugins-ugly"
```

Likewise, to additionally enable the package built from the recipe containing LICENSE_FLAGS = "license_${PN}_${PV}", and assuming that the actual recipe name was emgd_1.10.bb, the following string would enable that package as well as the original gst-plugins-ugly package:

```
LICENSE_FLAGS_WHITELIST = "commercial_gst-plugins-ugly license_emgd_1.10"
```

As a convenience, you do not need to specify the complete license string in the whitelist for every package. You can use an abbreviated form, which consists of just the first portion or portions of the license string before the initial underscore character or characters. A partial string will match any license that contains the given string as the first portion of its license. For example, the following whitelist string will also match both of the packages previously mentioned as well as any other packages that have licenses starting with "commercial" or "license".

```
LICENSE_FLAGS_WHITELIST = "commercial license"
```

4.6.2.1. License Flag Matching

License flag matching allows you to control what recipes the OpenEmbedded build system includes in the build. Fundamentally, the build system attempts to match LICENSE_FLAGS strings found in recipes against LICENSE_FLAGS_WHITELIST strings found in the whitelist. A match causes the build system to include a recipe in the build, while failure to find a match causes the build system to exclude a recipe.

In general, license flag matching is simple. However, understanding some concepts will help you correctly and effectively use matching.

Before a flag defined by a particular recipe is tested against the contents of the whitelist, the expanded string _${PN} is appended to the flag. This expansion makes each LICENSE_FLAGS value recipe-specific. After expansion, the string is then matched against the whitelist. Thus, specifying LICENSE_FLAGS = "commercial" in recipe "foo", for example, results in the string "commercial_foo". And, to create a match, that string must appear in the whitelist.

Judicious use of the LICENSE_FLAGS strings and the contents of the LICENSE_FLAGS_WHITELIST variable allows you a lot of flexibility for including or excluding recipes based on licensing. For example, you can broaden the matching capabilities by using license flags string subsets in the whitelist.

Note
When using a string subset, be sure to use the part of the expanded string that precedes the appended underscore character (e.g. usethispart_1.3, usethispart_1.4, and so forth).

For example, simply specifying the string "commercial" in the whitelist matches any expanded LICENSE_FLAGS definition that starts with the string "commercial" such as "commercial_foo" and "commercial_bar", which are the strings the build system automatically generates for hypothetical recipes named "foo" and "bar" assuming those recipes simply specify the following:

```
LICENSE_FLAGS = "commercial"
```

Thus, you can choose to exhaustively enumerate each license flag in the whitelist and allow only specific recipes into the image, or you can use a string subset that causes a broader range of matches to allow a range of recipes into the image.

This scheme works even if the LICENSE_FLAGS string already has _${PN} appended. For example, the build system turns the license flag "commercial_1.2_foo" into "commercial_1.2_foo_foo" and would match both the general "commercial" and the specific "commercial_1.2_foo" strings found in the whitelist, as expected.

Here are some other scenarios:

- You can specify a versioned string in the recipe such as "commercial_foo_1.2" in a "foo" recipe. The build system expands this string to "commercial_foo_1.2_foo". Combine this license flag with a whitelist that has the string "commercial" and you match the flag along with any other flag that starts with the string "commercial".

- Under the same circumstances, you can use "commercial_foo" in the whitelist and the build system not only matches "commercial_foo_1.2" but also matches any license flag with the string "commercial_foo", regardless of the version.

- You can be very specific and use both the package and version parts in the whitelist (e.g. "commercial_foo_1.2") to specifically match a versioned recipe.

4.6.2.2. Other Variables Related to Commercial Licenses

Other helpful variables related to commercial license handling exist and are defined in the poky/meta/conf/distro/include/default-distrovars.inc file:

```
COMMERCIAL_AUDIO_PLUGINS ?= ""
COMMERCIAL_VIDEO_PLUGINS ?= ""
COMMERCIAL_QT = ""
```

If you want to enable these components, you can do so by making sure you have statements similar to the following in your local.conf configuration file:

```
COMMERCIAL_AUDIO_PLUGINS = "gst-plugins-ugly-mad \
    gst-plugins-ugly-mpegaudioparse"
COMMERCIAL_VIDEO_PLUGINS = "gst-plugins-ugly-mpeg2dec \
    gst-plugins-ugly-mpegstream gst-plugins-bad-mpegvideoparse"
COMMERCIAL_QT ?= "qmmp"
LICENSE_FLAGS_WHITELIST = "commercial_gst-plugins-ugly commercial_gst-plugins-bad commercia
```

Of course, you could also create a matching whitelist for those components using the more general "commercial" in the whitelist, but that would also enable all the other packages with LICENSE_FLAGS containing "commercial", which you may or may not want:

```
LICENSE_FLAGS_WHITELIST = "commercial"
```

Specifying audio and video plug-ins as part of the COMMERCIAL_AUDIO_PLUGINS and COMMERCIAL_VIDEO_PLUGINS statements or commercial Qt components as part of the COMMERCIAL_QT statement (along with the enabling LICENSE_FLAGS_WHITELIST) includes the plug-ins or components into built images, thus adding support for media formats or components.

Chapter 5. Migrating to a Newer Yocto Project Release

This chapter provides information you can use to migrate work to a newer Yocto Project release. You can find the same information in the release notes for a given release.

5.1. General Migration Considerations

Some considerations are not tied to a specific Yocto Project release. This section presents information you should consider when migrating to any new Yocto Project release.

- Dealing with Customized Recipes: Issues could arise if you take older recipes that contain customizations and simply copy them forward expecting them to work after you migrate to new Yocto Project metadata. For example, suppose you have a recipe in your layer that is a customized version of a core recipe copied from the earlier release, rather than through the use of an append file. When you migrate to a newer version of Yocto Project, the metadata (e.g. perhaps an include file used by the recipe) could have changed in a way that would break the build. Say, for example, a function is removed from an include file and the customized recipe tries to call that function.

  You could "forward-port" all your customizations in your recipe so that everything works for the new release. However, this is not the optimal solution as you would have to repeat this process with each new release if changes occur that give rise to problems.

  The better solution (where practical) is to use append files (*.bbappend) to capture any customizations you want to make to a recipe. Doing so, isolates your changes from the main recipe making them much more manageable. However, sometimes it is not practical to use an append file. A good example of this is when introducing a newer or older version of a recipe in another layer.

- Updating Append Files: Since append files generally only contain your customizations, they often do not need to be adjusted for new releases. However, if the .bbappend file is specific to a particular version of the recipe (i.e. its name does not use the % wildcard) and the version of the recipe to which it is appending has changed, then you will at a minimum need to rename the append file to match the name of the recipe file. A mismatch between an append file and its corresponding recipe file (.bb) will trigger an error during parsing.

  Depending on the type of customization the append file applies, other incompatibilities might occur when you upgrade. For example, if your append file applies a patch and the recipe to which it is appending is updated to a newer version, the patch might no longer apply. If this is the case and assuming the patch is still needed, you must modify the patch file so that it does apply.

5.2. Moving to the Yocto Project 1.3 Release

This section provides migration information for moving to the Yocto Project 1.3 Release from the prior release.

5.2.1. Local Configuration

Differences include changes for SSTATE_MIRRORS and bblayers.conf.

5.2.1.1. SSTATE_MIRRORS

The shared state cache (sstate-cache), as pointed to by SSTATE_DIR, by default now has two-character subdirectories to prevent issues arising from too many files in the same directory. Also, native sstate-cache packages will go into a subdirectory named using the distro ID string. If you copy the newly structured sstate-cache to a mirror location (either local or remote) and then point to it in SSTATE_MIRRORS, you need to append "PATH" to the end of the mirror URL so that the path used by BitBake before the mirror substitution is appended to the path used to access the mirror. Here is an example:

```
SSTATE_MIRRORS = "file://.* http://someserver.tld/share/sstate/PATH"
```

5.2.1.2. bblayers.conf

The meta-yocto layer consists of two parts that correspond to the Poky reference distribution and the reference hardware Board Support Packages (BSPs), respectively: meta-yocto and meta-yocto-bsp. When running BitBake or Hob for the first time after upgrading, your conf/bblayers.conf file will be updated to handle this change and you will be asked to re-run or restart for the changes to take effect.

5.2.2. Recipes

Differences include changes for the following:

• Python function whitespace

• proto= in SRC_URI

• nativesdk

• Task recipes

• IMAGE_FEATURES

• Removed recipes

5.2.2.1. Python Function Whitespace

All Python functions must now use four spaces for indentation. Previously, an inconsistent mix of spaces and tabs existed, which made extending these functions using _append or _prepend complicated given that Python treats whitespace as syntactically significant. If you are defining or extending any Python functions (e.g. populate_packages, do_unpack, do_patch and so forth) in custom recipes or classes, you need to ensure you are using consistent four-space indentation.

5.2.2.2. proto= in SRC_URI

Any use of proto= in SRC_URI needs to be changed to protocol=. In particular, this applies to the following URIs:

• svn://

• bzr://

• hg://

• osc://

Other URIs were already using protocol=. This change improves consistency.

5.2.2.3. nativesdk

The suffix nativesdk is now implemented as a prefix, which simplifies a lot of the packaging code for nativesdk recipes. All custom nativesdk recipes and any references need to be updated to use nativesdk-* instead of *-nativesdk.

5.2.2.4. Task Recipes

"Task" recipes are now known as "Package groups" and have been renamed from task-*.bb to packagegroup-*.bb. Existing references to the previous task-* names should work in most cases as there is an automatic upgrade path for most packages. However, you should update references in your own recipes and configurations as they could be removed in future releases. You should also rename any custom task-* recipes to packagegroup-*, and change them to inherit packagegroup instead of task, as well as taking the opportunity to remove anything now handled by packagegroup.bbclass, such as providing -dev and -dbg packages, setting LIC_FILES_CHKSUM, and so forth. See the "packagegroup.bbclass" section for further details.

5.2.2.5. IMAGE_FEATURES

Image recipes that previously included "apps-console-core" in IMAGE_FEATURES should now include "splash" instead to enable the boot-up splash screen. Retaining "apps-console-core" will still include the splash screen but generates a warning. The "apps-x11-core" and "apps-x11-games" IMAGE_FEATURES features have been removed.

5.2.2.6. Removed Recipes

The following recipes have been removed. For most of them, it is unlikely that you would have any references to them in your own Metadata [http://www.yoctoproject.org/docs/1.7.2/dev-manual/dev-manual.html#metadata]. However, you should check your metadata against this list to be sure:

- libx11-trim: Replaced by libx11, which has a negligible size difference with modern Xorg.

- xserver-xorg-lite: Use xserver-xorg, which has a negligible size difference when DRI and GLX modules are not installed.

- xserver-kdrive: Effectively unmaintained for many years.

- mesa-xlib: No longer serves any purpose.

- galago: Replaced by telepathy.

- gail: Functionality was integrated into GTK+ 2.13.

- eggdbus: No longer needed.

- gcc-*-intermediate: The build has been restructured to avoid the need for this step.

- libgsmd: Unmaintained for many years. Functionality now provided by ofono instead.

- contacts, dates, tasks, eds-tools: Largely unmaintained PIM application suite. It has been moved to meta-gnome in meta-openembedded.

In addition to the previously listed changes, the meta-demoapps directory has also been removed because the recipes in it were not being maintained and many had become obsolete or broken. Additionally, these recipes were not parsed in the default configuration. Many of these recipes are already provided in an updated and maintained form within the OpenEmbedded community layers such as meta-oe and meta-gnome. For the remainder, you can now find them in the meta-extras repository, which is in the Yocto Project Source Repositories [http://www.yoctoproject.org/docs/1.7.2/dev-manual/dev-manual.html#source-repositories].

5.2.3. Linux Kernel Naming

The naming scheme for kernel output binaries has been changed to now include PE as part of the filename:

```
KERNEL_IMAGE_BASE_NAME ?= "${KERNEL_IMAGETYPE}-${PE}-${PV}-${PR}-${MACHINE}-${DATETIME}"
```

Because the PE variable is not set by default, these binary files could result with names that include two dash characters. Here is an example:

```
bzImage--3.10.9+git0+cd502a8814_7144bcc4b8-r0-qemux86-64-20130830085431.bin
```

5.3. Moving to the Yocto Project 1.4 Release

This section provides migration information for moving to the Yocto Project 1.4 Release from the prior release.

5.3.1. BitBake

Differences include the following:

- Comment Continuation: If a comment ends with a line continuation (\) character, then the next line must also be a comment. Any instance where this is not the case, now triggers a warning. You must either remove the continuation character, or be sure the next line is a comment.

- Package Name Overrides: The runtime package specific variables RDEPENDS, RRECOMMENDS, RSUGGESTS, RPROVIDES, RCONFLICTS, RREPLACES, FILES, ALLOW_EMPTY, and the pre, post, install, and uninstall script functions pkg_preinst, pkg_postinst, pkg_prerm, and pkg_postrm should always have a package name override. For example, use RDEPENDS_${PN} for the main package instead of RDEPENDS. BitBake uses more strict checks when it parses recipes.

5.3.2. Build Behavior

Differences include the following:

- Shared State Code: The shared state code has been optimized to avoid running unnecessary tasks. For example, the following no longer populates the target sysroot since that is not necessary:

```
$ bitbake -c rootfs some-image
```

Instead, the system just needs to extract the output package contents, re-create the packages, and construct the root filesystem. This change is unlikely to cause any problems unless you have missing declared dependencies.

- Scanning Directory Names: When scanning for files in SRC_URI, the build system now uses FILESOVERRIDES instead of OVERRIDES for the directory names. In general, the values previously in OVERRIDES are now in FILESOVERRIDES as well. However, if you relied upon an additional value you previously added to OVERRIDES, you might now need to add it to FILESOVERRIDES unless you are already adding it through the MACHINEOVERRIDES or DISTROOVERRIDES variables, as appropriate. For more related changes, see the "Variables" section.

5.3.3. Proxies and Fetching Source

A new oe-git-proxy script has been added to replace previous methods of handling proxies and fetching source from Git. See the meta-yocto/conf/site.conf.sample file for information on how to use this script.

5.3.4. Custom Interfaces File (netbase change)

If you have created your own custom etc/network/interfaces file by creating an append file for the netbase recipe, you now need to create an append file for the init-ifupdown recipe instead, which you can find in the Source Directory [http://www.yoctoproject.org/docs/1.7.2/dev-manual/dev-manual.html#source-directory] at meta/recipes-core/init-ifupdown. For information on how to use append files, see the "Using .bbappend Files [http://www.yoctoproject.org/docs/1.7.2/dev-manual/dev-manual.html#using-bbappend-files]" in the Yocto Project Development Manual.

5.3.5. Remote Debugging

Support for remote debugging with the Eclipse IDE is now separated into an image feature (eclipse-debug) that corresponds to the packagegroup-core-eclipse-debug package group. Previously, the debugging feature was included through the tools-debug image feature, which corresponds to the packagegroup-core-tools-debug package group.

5.3.6. Variables

The following variables have changed:

- SANITY_TESTED_DISTROS: This variable now uses a distribution ID, which is composed of the host distributor ID followed by the release. Previously, SANITY_TESTED_DISTROS was composed of the description field. For example, "Ubuntu 12.10" becomes "Ubuntu-12.10". You do not need to worry about this change if you are not specifically setting this variable, or if you are specifically setting it to "".

- SRC_URI: The ${PN}, ${PF}, ${P}, and FILE_DIRNAME directories have been dropped from the default value of the FILESPATH variable, which is used as the search path for finding files referred to in SRC_URI. If you have a recipe that relied upon these directories, which would be unusual, then you will need to add the appropriate paths within the recipe or, alternatively, rearrange the files. The most common locations are still covered by ${BP}, ${BPN}, and "files", which all remain in the default value of FILESPATH.

5.3.7. Target Package Management with RPM

If runtime package management is enabled and the RPM backend is selected, Smart is now installed for package download, dependency resolution, and upgrades instead of Zypper. For more information on how to use Smart, run the following command on the target:

```
smart --help
```

5.3.8. Recipes Moved

The following recipes were moved from their previous locations because they are no longer used by anything in the OpenEmbedded-Core:

- clutter-box2d: Now resides in the meta-oe layer.

- evolution-data-server: Now resides in the meta-gnome layer.

- gthumb: Now resides in the meta-gnome layer.

- gtkhtml2: Now resides in the meta-oe layer.

- gupnp: Now resides in the meta-multimedia layer.

- gypsy: Now resides in the meta-oe layer.

- libcanberra: Now resides in the meta-gnome layer.

- libgdata: Now resides in the meta-gnome layer.

- libmusicbrainz: Now resides in the meta-multimedia layer.

- metacity: Now resides in the meta-gnome layer.

- polkit: Now resides in the meta-oe layer.

- zeroconf: Now resides in the meta-networking layer.

5.3.9. Removals and Renames

The following list shows what has been removed or renamed:

- evieext: Removed because it has been removed from xserver since 2008.

- Gtk+ DirectFB: Removed support because upstream Gtk+ no longer supports it as of version 2.18.

- libxfontcache / xfontcacheproto: Removed because they were removed from the Xorg server in 2008.

- libxp / libxprintapputil / libxprintutil / printproto: Removed because the XPrint server was removed from Xorg in 2008.

- libxtrap / xtrapproto: Removed because their functionality was broken upstream.

- linux-yocto 3.0 kernel: Removed with linux-yocto 3.8 kernel being added. The linux-yocto 3.2 and linux-yocto 3.4 kernels remain as part of the release.

- lsbsetup: Removed with functionality now provided by lsbtest.

- matchbox-stroke: Removed because it was never more than a proof-of-concept.

- `matchbox-wm-2` / `matchbox-theme-sato-2`: Removed because they are not maintained. However, `matchbox-wm` and `matchbox-theme-sato` are still provided.

- `mesa-dri`: Renamed to mesa.

- `mesa-xlib`: Removed because it was no longer useful.

- `mutter`: Removed because nothing ever uses it and the recipe is very old.

- `orinoco-conf`: Removed because it has become obsolete.

- `update-modules`: Removed because it is no longer used. The kernel module `postinstall` and `postrm` scripts can now do the same task without the use of this script.

- `web`: Removed because it is not maintained. Superseded by `web-webkit`.

- `xf86bigfontproto`: Removed because upstream it has been disabled by default since 2007. Nothing uses `xf86bigfontproto`.

- `xf86rushproto`: Removed because its dependency in `xserver` was spurious and it was removed in 2005.

- `zypper` / `libzypp` / `sat-solver`: Removed and been functionally replaced with Smart (`python-smartpm`) when RPM packaging is used and package management is enabled on the target.

5.4. Moving to the Yocto Project 1.5 Release

This section provides migration information for moving to the Yocto Project 1.5 Release from the prior release.

5.4.1. Host Dependency Changes

The OpenEmbedded build system now has some additional requirements on the host system:

- Python 2.7.3+

- Tar 1.24+

- Git 1.7.8+

- Patched version of Make if you are using 3.82. Most distributions that provide Make 3.82 use the patched version.

If the Linux distribution you are using on your build host does not provide packages for these, you can install and use the Buildtools tarball, which provides an SDK-like environment containing them.

For more information on this requirement, see the "Required Git, tar, and Python Versions" section.

5.4.2. `atom-pc` Board Support Package (BSP)

The `atom-pc` hardware reference BSP has been replaced by a `genericx86` BSP. This BSP is not necessarily guaranteed to work on all x86 hardware, but it will run on a wider range of systems than the `atom-pc` did.

Note
Additionally, a `genericx86-64` BSP has been added for 64-bit Atom systems.

5.4.3. BitBake

The following changes have been made that relate to BitBake:

- BitBake now supports a _remove operator. The addition of this operator means you will have to rename any items in recipe space (functions, variables) whose names currently contain _remove_ or end with _remove to avoid unexpected behavior.

- BitBake's global method pool has been removed. This method is not particularly useful and led to clashes between recipes containing functions that had the same name.

- The "none" server backend has been removed. The "process" server backend has been serving well as the default for a long time now.

- The `bitbake-runtask` script has been removed.

- ${P} and ${PF} are no longer added to PROVIDES by default in `bitbake.conf`. These version-specific PROVIDES items were seldom used. Attempting to use them could result in two versions being built simultaneously rather than just one version due to the way BitBake resolves dependencies.

5.4.4. QA Warnings

The following changes have been made to the package QA checks:

- If you have customized ERROR_QA or WARN_QA values in your configuration, check that they contain all of the issues that you wish to be reported. Previous Yocto Project versions contained a bug that meant that any item not mentioned in ERROR_QA or WARN_QA would be treated as a warning. Consequently, several important items were not already in the default value of WARN_QA. All of the possible QA checks are now documented in the "insane.bbclass" section.

- An additional QA check has been added to check if /usr/share/info/dir is being installed. Your recipe should delete this file within do_install if "make install" is installing it.

- If you are using the buildhistory class, the check for the package version going backwards is now controlled using a standard QA check. Thus, if you have customized your ERROR_QA or WARN_QA values and still wish to have this check performed, you should add "version-going-backwards" to your value for one or the other variables depending on how you wish it to be handled. See the documented QA checks in the "insane.bbclass" section.

5.4.5. Directory Layout Changes

The following directory changes exist:

- Output SDK installer files are now named to include the image name and tuning architecture through the SDK_NAME variable.

- Images and related files are now installed into a directory that is specific to the machine, instead of a parent directory containing output files for multiple machines. The DEPLOY_DIR_IMAGE variable continues to point to the directory containing images for the current MACHINE and should be used anywhere there is a need to refer to this directory. The runqemu script now uses this variable to find images and kernel binaries and will use BitBake to determine the directory. Alternatively, you can set the DEPLOY_DIR_IMAGE variable in the external environment.

- When buildhistory is enabled, its output is now written under the Build Directory [http://www.yoctoproject.org/docs/1.7.2/dev-manual/dev-manual.html#build-directory] rather than TMPDIR. Doing so makes it easier to delete TMPDIR and preserve the build history. Additionally, data for produced SDKs is now split by IMAGE_NAME.

- The pkgdata directory produced as part of the packaging process has been collapsed into a single machine-specific directory. This directory is located under sysroots and uses a machine-specific name (i.e. tmp/sysroots/machine/pkgdata).

5.4.6. Shortened Git**SRCREV** Values

BitBake will now shorten revisions from Git repositories from the normal 40 characters down to 10 characters within SRCPV for improved usability in path and file names. This change should be safe within contexts where these revisions are used because the chances of spatially close collisions is very low. Distant collisions are not a major issue in the way the values are used.

5.4.7. **IMAGE_FEATURES**

The following changes have been made that relate to IMAGE_FEATURES:

- The value of IMAGE_FEATURES is now validated to ensure invalid feature items are not added. Some users mistakenly add package names to this variable instead of using IMAGE_INSTALL in order to have the package added to the image, which does not work. This change is intended to catch those kinds of situations. Valid IMAGE_FEATURES are drawn from PACKAGE_GROUP definitions, COMPLEMENTARY_GLOB and a new "validitems" varflag on IMAGE_FEATURES. The "validitems" varflag change allows additional features to be added if they are not provided using the previous two mechanisms.

- The previously deprecated "apps-console-core" IMAGE_FEATURES item is no longer supported. Add "splash" to IMAGE_FEATURES if you wish to have the splash screen enabled, since this is all that apps-console-core was doing.

5.4.8. /run

The /run directory from the Filesystem Hierarchy Standard 3.0 has been introduced. You can find some of the implications for this change here [http://cgit.openembedded.org/openembedded-core/commit/?id=0e326280a15b0f2c4ef2ef4ec441f63f55b75873]. The change also means that recipes that install files to /var/run must be changed. You can find a guide on how to make these changes here [http://permalink.gmane.org/gmane.comp.handhelds.openembedded/58530].

5.4.9. Removal of Package Manager Database Within Image Recipes

The image core-image-minimal no longer adds remove_packaging_data_files to ROOTFS_POSTPROCESS_COMMAND. This addition is now handled automatically when "package-management" is not in IMAGE_FEATURES. If you have custom image recipes that make this addition, you should remove the lines, as they are not needed and might interfere with correct operation of postinstall scripts.

5.4.10. Images Now Rebuild Only on Changes Instead of Every Time

The do_rootfs and other related image construction tasks are no longer marked as "nostamp". Consequently, they will only be re-executed when their inputs have changed. Previous versions of the OpenEmbedded build system always rebuilt the image when requested rather when necessary.

5.4.11. Task Recipes

The previously deprecated task.bbclass has now been dropped. For recipes that previously inherited from this class, you should rename them from task-* to packagegroup-* and inherit packagegroup instead.

For more information, see the "packagegroup.bbclass" section.

5.4.12. BusyBox

By default, we now split BusyBox into two binaries: one that is suid root for those components that need it, and another for the rest of the components. Splitting BusyBox allows for optimization that eliminates the tinylogin recipe as recommended by upstream. You can disable this split by setting BUSYBOX_SPLIT_SUID to "0".

5.4.13. Automated Image Testing

A new automated image testing framework has been added through the testimage*.bbclass class. This framework replaces the older imagetest-qemu framework.

You can learn more about performing automated image tests in the "Performing Automated Runtime Testing [http://www.yoctoproject.org/docs/1.7.2/dev-manual/dev-manual.html#performing-automated-runtime-testing]" section.

5.4.14. Build History

Following are changes to Build History:

- Installed package sizes: `installed-package-sizes.txt` for an image now records the size of the files installed by each package instead of the size of each compressed package archive file.

- The dependency graphs (depends*.dot) now use the actual package names instead of replacing dashes, dots and plus signs with underscores.

- The `buildhistory-diff` and `buildhistory-collect-srcrevs` utilities have improved command-line handling. Use the ##help option for each utility for more information on the new syntax.

For more information on Build History, see the "Maintaining Build Output Quality" section.

5.4.15. **udev**

Following are changes to udev:

- udev no longer brings in `udev-extraconf` automatically through RRECOMMENDS, since this was originally intended to be optional. If you need the extra rules, then add `udev-extraconf` to your image.

- udev no longer brings in `pciutils-ids` or `usbutils-ids` through RRECOMMENDS. These are not needed by udev itself and removing them saves around 350KB.

5.4.16. Removed and Renamed Recipes

- The `linux-yocto` 3.2 kernel has been removed.

- `libtool-nativesdk` has been renamed to `nativesdk-libtool`.

- `tinylogin` has been removed. It has been replaced by a suid portion of Busybox. See the "BusyBox" section for more information.

- `external-python-tarball` has been renamed to `buildtools-tarball`.

- `web-webkit` has been removed. It has been functionally replaced by `midori`.

- `imake` has been removed. It is no longer needed by any other recipe.

- `transfig-native` has been removed. It is no longer needed by any other recipe.

- `anjuta-remote-run` has been removed. Anjuta IDE integration has not been officially supported for several releases.

5.4.17. Other Changes

Following is a list of short entries describing other changes:

- `run-postinsts`: Make this generic.

- `base-files`: Remove the unnecessary media/xxx directories.

- `alsa-state`: Provide an empty `asound.conf` by default.

- `classes/image`: Ensure BAD_RECOMMENDATIONS supports pre-renamed package names.

- `classes/rootfs_rpm`: Implement BAD_RECOMMENDATIONS for RPM.

- `systemd`: Remove systemd_unitdir if systemd is not in DISTRO_FEATURES.

- `systemd`: Remove init.d dir if systemd unit file is present and `sysvinit` is not a distro feature.

- `libpam`: Deny all services for the OTHER entries.

- `image.bbclass`: Move runtime_mapping_rename to avoid conflict with `multilib`. See YOCTO #4993 [https://bugzilla.yoctoproject.org/show_bug.cgi?id=4993] in Bugzilla for more information.

- `linux-dtb`: Use kernel build system to generate the dtb files.

- `kern-tools`: Switch from guilt to new `kgit-s2q` tool.

5.5. Moving to the Yocto Project 1.6 Release

This section provides migration information for moving to the Yocto Project 1.6 Release from the prior release.

5.5.1. `archiver` Class

The `archiver` class has been rewritten and its configuration has been simplified. For more details on the source archiver, see the "Maintaining Open Source License Compliance During Your Product's Lifecycle [http://www.yoctoproject.org/docs/1.7.2/dev-manual/dev-manual.html#maintaining-open-source-license-compliance-during-your-products-lifecycle]" section in the Yocto Project Development Manual.

5.5.2. Packaging Changes

The following packaging changes have been made:

- The binutils recipe no longer produces a `binutils-symlinks` package. `update-alternatives` is now used to handle the preferred `binutils` variant on the target instead.

- The tc (traffic control) utilities have been split out of the main `iproute2` package and put into the `iproute2-tc` package.

- The `gtk-engines` schemas have been moved to a dedicated `gtk-engines-schemas` package.

- The `armv7a` with thumb package architecture suffix has changed. The suffix for these packages with the thumb optimization enabled is "t2" as it should be. Use of this suffix was not the case in the 1.5 release. Architecture names will change within package feeds as a result.

5.5.3. BitBake

The following changes have been made to BitBake [http://www.yoctoproject.org/docs/1.7.2/dev-manual/dev-manual.html#bitbake-term].

5.5.3.1. Matching Branch Requirement for Git Fetching

When fetching source from a Git repository using SRC_URI, BitBake will now validate the SRCREV value against the branch. You can specify the branch using the following form:

```
SRC_URI = "git://server.name/repository;branch=branchname"
```

If you do not specify a branch, BitBake looks in the default "master" branch.

Alternatively, if you need to bypass this check (e.g. if you are fetching a revision corresponding to a tag that is not on any branch), you can add ";nobranch=1" to the end of the URL within SRC_URI.

5.5.3.2. Python Definition substitutions

BitBake had some previously deprecated Python definitions within its bb module removed. You should use their sub-module counterparts instead:

- bb.MalformedUrl: Use bb.fetch.MalformedUrl.

- bb.fetch.encodeurl: Use bb.fetch.encodeurl.

- bb.decodeurl: Use bb.fetch.decodeurl

- bb.mkdirhier: Use bb.utils.mkdirhier.

- bb.movefile: Use bb.utils.movefile.

- bb.copyfile: Use bb.utils.copyfile.

- bb.which: Use bb.utils.which.

- `bb.vercmp_string`: Use `bb.utils.vercmp_string`.

- `bb.vercmp`: Use `bb.utils.vercmp`.

5.5.3.3. SVK Fetcher

The SVK fetcher has been removed from BitBake.

5.5.3.4. Console Output Error Redirection

The BitBake console UI will now output errors to `stderr` instead of `stdout`. Consequently, if you are piping or redirecting the output of `bitbake` to somewhere else, and you wish to retain the errors, you will need to add 2>&1 (or something similar) to the end of your `bitbake` command line.

5.5.3.5. **task-taskname** Overrides

`task-taskname` overrides have been adjusted so that tasks whose names contain underscores have the underscores replaced by hyphens for the override so that they now function properly. For example, the task override for do_populate_sdk is `task-populate-sdk`.

5.5.4. Changes to Variables

The following variables have changed. For information on the OpenEmbedded build system variables, see the "Variables Glossary" Chapter.

5.5.4.1. **TMPDIR**

TMPDIR can no longer be on an NFS mount. NFS does not offer full POSIX locking and inode consistency and can cause unexpected issues if used to store TMPDIR.

The check for this occurs on startup. If TMPDIR is detected on an NFS mount, an error occurs.

5.5.4.2. **PRINC**

The PRINC variable has been deprecated and triggers a warning if detected during a build. For PR increments on changes, use the PR service instead. You can find out more about this service in the "Working With a PR Service [http://www.yoctoproject.org/docs/1.7.2/dev-manual/dev-manual.html#working-with-a-pr-service]" section in the Yocto Project Development Manual.

5.5.4.3. **IMAGE_TYPES**

The "sum.jffs2" option for IMAGE_TYPES has been replaced by the "jffs2.sum" option, which fits the processing order.

5.5.4.4. **COPY_LIC_MANIFEST**

The COPY_LIC_MANIFEST variable must now be set to "1" rather than any value in order to enable it.

5.5.4.5. **COPY_LIC_DIRS**

The COPY_LIC_DIRS variable must now be set to "1" rather than any value in order to enable it.

5.5.4.6. **PACKAGE_GROUP**

The PACKAGE_GROUP variable has been renamed to FEATURE_PACKAGES to more accurately reflect its purpose. You can still use PACKAGE_GROUP but the OpenEmbedded build system produces a warning message when it encounters the variable.

5.5.5. Directory Layout Changes

The meta-hob layer has been removed from the top-level of the Source Directory [http://www.yoctoproject.org/docs/1.7.2/dev-manual/dev-manual.html#source-directory]. The contents of this layer are no longer needed by the Hob user interface for building images and toolchains.

5.5.6. Package Test (ptest)

Package Tests (ptest) are built but not installed by default. For information on using Package Tests, see the "Setting up and running package test (ptest) [http://www.yoctoproject.org/docs/1.7.2/dev-manual/dev-manual.html#testing-packages-with-ptest]" section in the Yocto Project Development Manual. For information on the ptest class, see the "ptest.bbclass" section.

5.5.7. Build Changes

Separate build and source directories have been enabled by default for selected recipes where it is known to work (a whitelist) and for all recipes that inherit the cmake class. In future releases the autotools class will enable a separate build directory by default as well. Recipes building Autotools-based software that fails to build with a separate build directory should be changed to inherit from the autotools-brokensep class instead of the autotools class.

5.5.8. **qemu-native**

qemu-native now builds without SDL-based graphical output support by default. The following additional lines are needed in your local.conf to enable it:

```
PACKAGECONFIG_pn-qemu-native = "sdl"
ASSUME_PROVIDED += "libsdl-native"
```

Note
The default local.conf contains these statements. Consequently, if you are building a headless system and using a default local.conf file, you will need comment these two lines out.

5.5.9. **core-image-basic**

core-image-basic has been renamed to core-image-full-cmdline.

In addition to core-image-basic being renamed, packagegroup-core-basic has been renamed to packagegroup-core-full-cmdline to match.

5.5.10. Licensing

The top-level LICENSE file has been changed to better describe the license of the various components of OE-Core. However, the licensing itself remains unchanged.

Normally, this change would not cause any side-effects. However, some recipes point to this file within LIC_FILES_CHKSUM (as ${COREBASE}/LICENSE) and thus the accompanying checksum must be changed from 3f40d7994397109285ec7b81fdeb3b58 to 4d92cd373abda3937c2bc47fbc49d690. A better alternative is to have LIC_FILES_CHKSUM point to a file describing the license that is distributed with the source that the recipe is building, if possible, rather than pointing to ${COREBASE}/LICENSE.

5.5.11. **CFLAGS** Options

The "-fpermissive" option has been removed from the default CFLAGS value. You need to take action on individual recipes that fail when building with this option. You need to either patch the recipes to fix the issues reported by the compiler, or you need to add "-fpermissive" to CFLAGS in the recipes.

5.5.12. Custom Image Output Types

Custom image output types, as selected using IMAGE_FSTYPES, must declare their dependencies on other image types (if any) using a new IMAGE_TYPEDEP variable.

5.5.13. Tasks

The do_package_write task has been removed. The task is no longer needed.

5.5.14. **update-alternative** Provider

The default update-alternatives provider has been changed from opkg to opkg-utils. This change resolves some troublesome circular dependencies. The runtime package has also been renamed from update-alternatives-cworth to update-alternatives-opkg.

5.5.15. **virtclass** Overrides

The virtclass overrides are now deprecated. Use the equivalent class overrides instead (e.g. virtclass-native becomes class-native.)

5.5.16. Removed and Renamed Recipes

The following recipes have been removed:

- packagegroup-toolset-native - This recipe is largely unused.

- linux-yocto-3.8 - Support for the Linux yocto 3.8 kernel has been dropped. Support for the 3.10 and 3.14 kernels have been added with the linux-yocto-3.10 and linux-yocto-3.14 recipes.

- ocf-linux - This recipe has been functionally replaced using cryptodev-linux.

- genext2fs - genext2fs is no longer used by the build system and is unmaintained upstream.

- js - This provided an ancient version of Mozilla's javascript engine that is no longer needed.

- zaurusd - The recipe has been moved to the meta-handheld layer.

- eglibc 2.17 - Replaced by the eglibc 2.19 recipe.

- gcc 4.7.2 - Replaced by the now stable gcc 4.8.2.

- external-sourcery-toolchain - this recipe is now maintained in the meta-sourcery layer.

- linux-libc-headers-yocto 3.4+git - Now using version 3.10 of the linux-libc-headers by default.

- meta-toolchain-gmae - This recipe is obsolete.

- packagegroup-core-sdk-gmae - This recipe is obsolete.

- packagegroup-core-standalone-gmae-sdk-target - This recipe is obsolete.

5.5.17. Removed Classes

The following classes have become obsolete and have been removed:

- module_strip

- pkg_metainfo

- pkg_distribute

- image-empty

5.5.18. Reference Board Support Packages (BSPs)

The following reference BSPs changes occurred:

- The BeagleBoard (beagleboard) ARM reference hardware has been replaced by the BeagleBone (beaglebone) hardware.

- The RouterStation Pro (routerstationpro) MIPS reference hardware has been replaced by the EdgeRouter Lite (edgerouter) hardware.

The previous reference BSPs for the beagleboard and routerstationpro machines are still available in a new meta-yocto-bsp-old layer in the Source Repositories [http://git.yoctoproject.org] at http://git.yoctoproject.org/cgit/cgit.cgi/meta-yocto-bsp-old/.

5.6. Moving to the Yocto Project 1.7 Release

This section provides migration information for moving to the Yocto Project 1.7 Release from the prior release.

5.6.1. Changes to Setting QEMU**PACKAGECONFIG** Options in **local.conf**

The QEMU recipe now uses a number of PACKAGECONFIG options to enable various optional features. The method used to set defaults for these options means that existing local.conf files will need to be be modified to append to PACKAGECONFIG for qemu-native and nativesdk-qemu instead of setting it. In other words, to enable graphical output for QEMU, you should now have these lines in local.conf:

```
PACKAGECONFIG_append_pn-qemu-native = " sdl"
PACKAGECONFIG_append_pn-nativesdk-qemu = " sdl"
```

5.6.2. Minimum Git version

The minimum Git [http://www.yoctoproject.org/docs/1.7.2/dev-manual/dev-manual.html#git] version required on the build host is now 1.7.8 because the ##list option is now required by BitBake's Git fetcher. As always, if your host distribution does not provide a version of Git that meets this requirement, you can use the buildtools-tarball that does. See the "Required Git, tar, and Python Versions" section for more information.

5.6.3. Autotools Class Changes

The following autotools class changes occurred:

• A separate build directory is now used by default: The autotools class has been changed to use a directory for building (B), which is separate from the source directory (S). This is commonly referred to as B != S, or an out-of-tree build.

  If the software being built is already capable of building in a directory separate from the source, you do not need to do anything. However, if the software is not capable of being built in this manner, you will need to either patch the software so that it can build separately, or you will need to change the recipe to inherit the autotools-brokensep class instead of the autotools class.

• The ##foreign option is no longer passed to automake when running autoconf: This option tells automake that a particular software package does not follow the GNU standards and therefore should not be expected to distribute certain files such as ChangeLog, AUTHORS, and so forth. Because the majority of upstream software packages already tell automake to enable foreign mode themselves, the option is mostly superfluous. However, some recipes will need patches for this change. You can easily make the change by patching configure.ac so that it passes "foreign" to AM_INIT_AUTOMAKE(). See this commit [http://cgit.openembedded.org/openembedded-core/commit/?id=01943188f85ce6411717fb5bf702d609f55813f2] for an example showing how to make the patch.

5.6.4. Binary Configuration Scripts Disabled

Some of the core recipes that package binary configuration scripts now disable the scripts due to the scripts previously requiring error-prone path substitution. Software that links against these libraries using these scripts should use the much more robust pkg-config instead. The list of recipes changed in this version (and their configuration scripts) is as follows:

```
directfb (directfb-config)
freetype (freetype-config)
gpgme (gpgme-config)
libassuan (libassuan-config)
libcroco (croco-6.0-config)
libgcrypt (libgcrypt-config)
```

```
libgpg-error (gpg-error-config)
libksba (ksba-config)
libpcap (pcap-config)
libpcre (pcre-config)
libpng (libpng-config, libpng16-config)
libsdl (sdl-config)
libusb-compat (libusb-config)
libxml2 (xml2-config)
libxslt (xslt-config)
ncurses (ncurses-config)
neon (neon-config)
npth (npth-config)
pth (pth-config)
taglib (taglib-config)
```

Additionally, support for pkg-config has been added to some recipes in the previous list in the rare cases where the upstream software package does not already provide it.

5.6.5. `eglibc 2.19` Replaced with `glibc 2.20`

Because eglibc and glibc were already fairly close, this replacement should not require any significant changes to other software that links to eglibc. However, there were a number of minor changes in glibc 2.20 upstream that could require patching some software (e.g. the removal of the _BSD_SOURCE feature test macro).

glibc 2.20 requires version 2.6.32 or greater of the Linux kernel. Thus, older kernels will no longer be usable in conjunction with it.

For full details on the changes in glibc 2.20, see the upstream release notes here [https://sourceware.org/ml/libc-alpha/2014-09/msg00088.html].

5.6.6. Kernel Module Autoloading

The module_autoload_* variable is now deprecated and a new KERNEL_MODULE_AUTOLOAD variable should be used instead. Also, module_conf_* must now be used in conjunction with a new KERNEL_MODULE_PROBECONF variable. The new variables no longer require you to specify the module name as part of the variable name. This change not only simplifies usage but also allows the values of these variables to be appropriately incorporated into task signatures and thus trigger the appropriate tasks to re-execute when changed. You should replace any references to module_autoload_* with KERNEL_MODULE_AUTOLOAD, and add any modules for which module_conf_* is specified to KERNEL_MODULE_PROBECONF.

For more information, see the KERNEL_MODULE_AUTOLOAD and KERNEL_MODULE_PROBECONF variables.

5.6.7. QA Check Changes

The following changes have occurred to the QA check process:

- Additional QA checks file-rdeps and build-deps have been added in order to verify that file dependencies are satisfied (e.g. package contains a script requiring /bin/bash) and build-time dependencies are declared, respectively. For more information, please see the "QA Error and Warning Messages" chapter.

- Package QA checks are now performed during a new do_package_qa task rather than being part of the do_package task. This allows more parallel execution. This change is unlikely to be an issue except for highly customized recipes that disable packaging tasks themselves by marking them as noexec. For those packages, you will need to disable the do_package_qa task as well.

- Files being overwritten during the do_populate_sysroot task now trigger an error instead of a warning. Recipes should not be overwriting files written to the sysroot by other recipes. If you have these types of recipes, you need to alter them so that they do not overwrite these files.

  You might now receive this error after changes in configuration or metadata resulting in orphaned files being left in the sysroot. If you do receive this error, the way to resolve the issue is to delete your TMPDIR or to move it out of the way and then re-start the build. Anything that has been fully built up to that point and does not need rebuilding will be restored from the shared state cache and the rest of the build will be able to proceed as normal.

5.6.8. Removed Recipes

The following recipes have been removed:

- x-load: This recipe has been superseded by U-boot SPL for all Cortex-based TI SoCs. For legacy boards, the meta-ti layer, which contains a maintained recipe, should be used instead.

- ubootchart: This recipe is obsolete. A bootchart2 recipe has been added to functionally replace it.

- linux-yocto 3.4: Support for the linux-yocto 3.4 kernel has been dropped. Support for the 3.10 and 3.14 kernels remains, while support for version 3.17 has been added.

- eglibc has been removed in favor of glibc. See the "eglibc 2.19 Replaced with glibc 2.20" section for more information.

5.6.9. Miscellaneous Changes

The following miscellaneous change occurred:

- The build history feature now writes build-id.txt instead of build-id. Additionally, build-id.txt now contains the full build header as printed by BitBake upon starting the build. You should manually remove old "build-id" files from your existing build history repositories to avoid confusion. For information on the build history feature, see the "Maintaining Build Output Quality" section.

Chapter 6. Source Directory Structure

The Source Directory [http://www.yoctoproject.org/docs/1.7.2/dev-manual/dev-manual.html#source-directory] consists of several components. Understanding them and knowing where they are located is key to using the Yocto Project well. This chapter describes the Source Directory and gives information about the various files and directories.

For information on how to establish a local Source Directory on your development system, see the "Getting Set Up [http://www.yoctoproject.org/docs/1.7.2/dev-manual/dev-manual.html#getting-setup]" section in the Yocto Project Development Manual.

Note
The OpenEmbedded build system does not support file or directory names that contain spaces. Be sure that the Source Directory you use does not contain these types of names.

6.1. Top-Level Core Components

This section describes the top-level components of the Source Directory [http://www.yoctoproject.org/docs/1.7.2/dev-manual/dev-manual.html#source-directory].

6.1.1. `bitbake/`

This directory includes a copy of BitBake for ease of use. The copy usually matches the current stable BitBake release from the BitBake project. BitBake, a Metadata [http://www.yoctoproject.org/docs/1.7.2/dev-manual/dev-manual.html#metadata] interpreter, reads the Yocto Project Metadata and runs the tasks defined by that data. Failures are usually from the Metadata and not from BitBake itself. Consequently, most users do not need to worry about BitBake.

When you run the `bitbake` command, the main BitBake executable, which resides in the `bitbake/bin/` directory, starts. Sourcing an environment setup script (e.g. `oe-init-build-env` or `oe-init-build-env-memres`) places the `scripts` and `bitbake/bin` directories (in that order) into the shell's PATH environment variable.

For more information on BitBake, see the BitBake User Manual [http://www.yoctoproject.org/docs/1.7.2/bitbake-user-manual/bitbake-user-manual.html].

6.1.2. `build/`

This directory contains user configuration files and the output generated by the OpenEmbedded build system in its standard configuration where the source tree is combined with the output. The Build Directory [http://www.yoctoproject.org/docs/1.7.2/dev-manual/dev-manual.html#build-directory] is created initially when you `source` the OpenEmbedded build environment setup script (i.e. `oe-init-build-env` or `oe-init-build-env-memres`).

It is also possible to place output and configuration files in a directory separate from the Source Directory [http://www.yoctoproject.org/docs/1.7.2/dev-manual/dev-manual.html#source-directory] by providing a directory name when you `source` the setup script. For information on separating output from your local Source Directory files, see the "`oe-init-build-env` and "`oe-init-build-env-memres`" sections.

6.1.3. `documentation/`

This directory holds the source for the Yocto Project documentation as well as templates and tools that allow you to generate PDF and HTML versions of the manuals. Each manual is contained in a sub-folder. For example, the files for this manual reside in the `ref-manual/` directory.

6.1.4. `meta/`

This directory contains the OpenEmbedded Core metadata. The directory holds recipes, common classes, and machine configuration for emulated targets (qemux86, qemuarm, and so forth.)

6.1.5. `meta-yocto/`

This directory contains the configuration for the Poky reference distribution.

6.1.6. `meta-yocto-bsp/`

This directory contains the Yocto Project reference hardware Board Support Packages (BSPs). For more information on BSPs, see the Yocto Project Board Support Package (BSP) Developer's Guide [http://www.yoctoproject.org/docs/1.7.2/bsp-guide/bsp-guide.html].

6.1.7. `meta-selftest/`

This directory adds additional recipes and append files used by the OpenEmbedded selftests to verify the behavior of the build system.

You do not have to add this layer to your `bblayers.conf` file unless you want to run the selftests.

6.1.8. `meta-skeleton/`

This directory contains template recipes for BSP and kernel development.

6.1.9. `scripts/`

This directory contains various integration scripts that implement extra functionality in the Yocto Project environment (e.g. QEMU scripts). The `oe-init-build-env` and `oe-init-build-env-memres` scripts append this directory to the shell's PATH environment variable.

The `scripts` directory has useful scripts that assist in contributing back to the Yocto Project, such as `create-pull-request` and `send-pull-request`.

6.1.10. `oe-init-build-env`

This script is one of two scripts that set up the OpenEmbedded build environment. For information on the other script, see the "`oe-init-build-env-memres`" section.

Running this script with the `source` command in a shell makes changes to PATH and sets other core BitBake variables based on the current working directory. You need to run an environment setup script before running BitBake commands. The script uses other scripts within the `scripts` directory to do the bulk of the work.

When you run this script, your Yocto Project environment is set up, a Build Directory [http://www.yoctoproject.org/docs/1.7.2/dev-manual/dev-manual.html#build-directory] is created, your working directory becomes the Build Directory, and you are presented with a list of common BitBake targets. Here is an example:

```
$ source oe-init-build-env

### Shell environment set up for builds. ###

You can now run 'bitbake <target>'

Common targets are:
    core-image-minimal
    core-image-sato
    meta-toolchain
    adt-installer
    meta-ide-support

You can also run generated qemu images with a command like 'runqemu qemux86'
```

The script gets its default list of common targets from the `conf-notes.txt` file, which is found in the `meta-yocto` directory within the Source Directory [http://www.yoctoproject.org/docs/1.7.2/dev-manual/dev-manual.html#source-directory]. Should you have custom distributions, it is very easy to modify this configuration file to include your targets for your distribution. See the "Creating a Custom Template Configuration Directory [http://www.yoctoproject.org/docs/1.7.2/dev-manual/dev-manual.html#creating-a-custom-template-configuration-directory]" section in the Yocto Project Development Manual for more information.

By default, running this script without a Build Directory [http://www.yoctoproject.org/docs/1.7.2/dev-manual/dev-manual.html#build-directory] argument creates the build directory in your current working directory. If you provide a Build Directory argument when you source the script, you direct the OpenEmbedded build system to create a Build Directory of your choice. For example, the following command creates a Build Directory named mybuilds that is outside of the Source Directory [http://www.yoctoproject.org/docs/1.7.2/dev-manual/dev-manual.html#source-directory]:

```
$ source oe-init-build-env ~/mybuilds
```

The OpenEmbedded build system uses the template configuration files, which are found by default in the meta-yocto/conf directory in the Source Directory [http://www.yoctoproject.org/docs/1.7.2/dev-manual/dev-manual.html#source-directory]. See the "Creating a Custom Template Configuration Directory [http://www.yoctoproject.org/docs/1.7.2/dev-manual/dev-manual.html#creating-a-custom-template-configuration-directory]" section in the Yocto Project Development Manual for more information.

Note
The OpenEmbedded build system does not support file or directory names that contain spaces. If you attempt to run the oe-init-build-env script from a Source Directory that contains spaces in either the filenames or directory names, the script returns an error indicating no such file or directory. Be sure to use a Source Directory free of names containing spaces.

6.1.11. oe-init-build-env-memres

This script is one of two scripts that set up the OpenEmbedded build environment. Aside from setting up the environment, this script starts a memory-resident BitBake server. For information on the other setup script, see the "oe-init-build-env" section.

Memory-resident BitBake resides in memory until you specifically remove it using the following BitBake command:

```
$ bitbake -m
```

Running this script with the source command in a shell makes changes to PATH and sets other core BitBake variables based on the current working directory. One of these variables is the BBSERVER variable, which allows the OpenEmbedded build system to locate the server that is running BitBake.

You need to run an environment setup script before using BitBake commands. Following is the script syntax:

```
$ source oe-init-build-env-memres port_number build_dir
```

The script uses other scripts within the scripts directory to do the bulk of the work.

If you do not provide a port number with the script, the BitBake server at port "12345" is started.

When you run this script, your Yocto Project environment is set up, a Build Directory [http://www.yoctoproject.org/docs/1.7.2/dev-manual/dev-manual.html#build-directory] is created, your working directory becomes the Build Directory, and you are presented with a list of common BitBake targets. Here is an example:

```
$ source oe-init-build-env-memres
No port specified, using dynamically selected port

### Shell environment set up for builds. ###

You can now run 'bitbake <target>'

Common targets are:
    core-image-minimal
    core-image-sato
    meta-toolchain
    adt-installer
    meta-ide-support

You can also run generated qemu images with a command like 'runqemu qemux86'
Bitbake server started on demand as needed, use bitbake -m to shut it down
```

The script gets its default list of common targets from the conf-notes.txt file, which is found in the meta-yocto directory within the Source Directory [http://www.yoctoproject.org/docs/1.7.2/dev-manual/dev-manual.html#source-directory]. Should you have custom distributions, it is very easy to modify this configuration file to include your targets for your distribution. See the "Creating a Custom Template Configuration Directory [http://www.yoctoproject.org/docs/1.7.2/dev-manual/dev-manual.html#creating-a-custom-template-configuration-directory]" section in the Yocto Project Development Manual for more information.

By default, running this script without a Build Directory [http://www.yoctoproject.org/docs/1.7.2/dev-manual/dev-manual.html#build-directory] argument creates a build directory named build. If you provide a Build Directory argument when you source the script, the Build Directory is created using that name. For example, the following command starts the BitBake server using the default port "12345" and creates a Build Directory named mybuilds that is outside of the Source Directory [http://www.yoctoproject.org/docs/1.7.2/dev-manual/dev-manual.html#source-directory]:

```
$ source oe-init-build-env-memres ~/mybuilds
```

The OpenEmbedded build system uses the template configuration files, which are found by default in the meta-yocto/conf directory in the Source Directory [http://www.yoctoproject.org/docs/1.7.2/dev-manual/dev-manual.html#source-directory]. See the "Creating a Custom Template Configuration Directory [http://www.yoctoproject.org/docs/1.7.2/dev-manual/dev-manual.html#creating-a-custom-template-configuration-directory]" section in the Yocto Project Development Manual for more information.

Note

The OpenEmbedded build system does not support file or directory names that contain spaces. If you attempt to run the oe-init-build-env-memres script from a Source Directory that contains spaces in either the filenames or directory names, the script returns an error indicating no such file or directory. Be sure to use a Source Directory free of names containing spaces.

6.1.12. `LICENSE`, `README`, and `README.hardware`

These files are standard top-level files.

6.2. The Build Directory -`build/`

The OpenEmbedded build system creates the Build Directory [http://www.yoctoproject.org/docs/1.7.2/dev-manual/dev-manual.html#build-directory] when you run one of the build environment setup scripts (i.e. oe-init-build-env or oe-init-build-env-memres).

If you do not give the Build Directory a specific name when you run a setup script, the name defaults to build.

The TOPDIR variable points to the Build Directory.

6.2.1. **build/buildhistory**

The OpenEmbedded build system creates this directory when you enable the build history feature. The directory tracks build information into image, packages, and SDK subdirectories. For information on the build history feature, see the "Maintaining Build Output Quality" section.

6.2.2. **build/conf/local.conf**

This configuration file contains all the local user configurations for your build environment. The local.conf file contains documentation on the various configuration options. Any variable set here overrides any variable set elsewhere within the environment unless that variable is hard-coded within a file (e.g. by using '=' instead of '?='). Some variables are hard-coded for various reasons but these variables are relatively rare.

Edit this file to set the MACHINE for which you want to build, which package types you wish to use (PACKAGE_CLASSES), the location from which you want to access downloaded files (DL_DIR), and how you want your host machine to use resources (BB_NUMBER_THREADS and PARALLEL_MAKE).

If local.conf is not present when you start the build, the OpenEmbedded build system creates it from local.conf.sample when you source the top-level build environment setup script (i.e. oe-init-build-env or oe-init-build-env-memres).

The source local.conf.sample file used depends on the $TEMPLATECONF script variable, which defaults to meta-yocto/conf when you are building from the Yocto Project development environment and defaults to meta/conf when you are building from the OpenEmbedded Core environment. Because the script variable points to the source of the local.conf.sample file, this implies that you can configure your build environment from any layer by setting the variable in the top-level build environment setup script as follows:

```
TEMPLATECONF=your_layer/conf
```

Once the build process gets the sample file, it uses sed to substitute final ${OEROOT} values for all ##OEROOT## values.

Note

You can see how the TEMPLATECONF variable is used by looking at the scripts/oe-setup-builddir script in the Source Directory [http://www.yoctoproject.org/docs/1.7.2/dev-manual/dev-manual.html#source-directory]. You can find the Yocto Project version of the local.conf.sample file in the meta-yocto/conf directory.

6.2.3. **build/conf/bblayers.conf**

This configuration file defines layers [http://www.yoctoproject.org/docs/1.7.2/dev-manual/dev-manual.html#understanding-and-creating-layers], which are directory trees, traversed (or walked) by BitBake. The bblayers.conf file uses the BBLAYERS variable to list the layers BitBake tries to find, and uses the BBLAYERS_NON_REMOVABLE variable to list layers that must not be removed.

If bblayers.conf is not present when you start the build, the OpenEmbedded build system creates it from bblayers.conf.sample when you source the top-level build environment setup script (i.e. oe-init-build-env or oe-init-build-env-memres).

The source bblayers.conf.sample file used depends on the $TEMPLATECONF script variable, which defaults to meta-yocto/conf when you are building from the Yocto Project development environment and defaults to meta/conf when you are building from the OpenEmbedded Core environment. Because the script variable points to the source of the bblayers.conf.sample file, this implies that you can base your build from any layer by setting the variable in the top-level build environment setup script as follows:

```
TEMPLATECONF=your_layer/conf
```

Once the build process gets the sample file, it uses sed to substitute final ${OEROOT} values for all ##OEROOT## values.

Note
You can see how the TEMPLATECONF variable scripts/oe-setup-builddir script in the Source Directory [http://www.yoctoproject.org/docs/1.7.2/dev-manual/dev-manual.html#source-directory]. You can find the Yocto Project version of the bblayers.conf.sample file in the meta-yocto/conf directory.

6.2.4. build/conf/sanity_info

This file indicates the state of the sanity checks and is created during the build.

6.2.5. build/downloads/

This directory contains downloaded upstream source tarballs. You can reuse the directory for multiple builds or move the directory to another location. You can control the location of this directory through the DL_DIR variable.

6.2.6. build/sstate-cache/

This directory contains the shared state cache. You can reuse the directory for multiple builds or move the directory to another location. You can control the location of this directory through the SSTATE_DIR variable.

6.2.7. build/tmp/

The OpenEmbedded build system creates and uses this directory for all the build system's output. The TMPDIR variable points to this directory.

BitBake creates this directory if it does not exist. As a last resort, to clean up a build and start it from scratch (other than the downloads), you can remove everything in the tmp directory or get rid of the directory completely. If you do, you should also completely remove the build/sstate-cache directory.

6.2.8. build/tmp/buildstats/

This directory stores the build statistics.

6.2.9. build/tmp/cache/

When BitBake parses the metadata, it creates a cache file of the result that can be used when subsequently running commands. BitBake stores these results here on a per-machine basis.

6.2.10. build/tmp/deploy/

This directory contains any "end result" output from the OpenEmbedded build process. The DEPLOY_DIR variable points to this directory. For more detail on the contents of the deploy directory, see the "Images" and "Application Development SDK" sections.

6.2.11. build/tmp/deploy/deb/

This directory receives any .deb packages produced by the build process. The packages are sorted into feeds for different architecture types.

6.2.12. build/tmp/deploy/rpm/

This directory receives any .rpm packages produced by the build process. The packages are sorted into feeds for different architecture types.

6.2.13. `build/tmp/deploy/ipk/`

This directory receives `.ipk` packages produced by the build process.

6.2.14. `build/tmp/deploy/licenses/`

This directory receives package licensing information. For example, the directory contains sub-directories for bash, busybox, and glibc (among others) that in turn contain appropriate COPYING license files with other licensing information. For information on licensing, see the "Maintaining Open Source License Compliance During Your Product's Lifecycle [http://www.yoctoproject.org/docs/1.7.2/dev-manual/dev-manual.html#maintaining-open-source-license-compliance-during-your-products-lifecycle]" section.

6.2.15. `build/tmp/deploy/images/`

This directory receives complete filesystem images. If you want to flash the resulting image from a build onto a device, look here for the image.

Be careful when deleting files in this directory. You can safely delete old images from this directory (e.g. `core-image-*`, `hob-image-*`, etc.). However, the kernel (`*zImage*`, `*uImage*`, etc.), bootloader and other supplementary files might be deployed here prior to building an image. Because these files are not directly produced from the image, if you delete them they will not be automatically re-created when you build the image again.

If you do accidentally delete files here, you will need to force them to be re-created. In order to do that, you will need to know the target that produced them. For example, these commands rebuild and re-create the kernel files:

```
$ bitbake -c clean virtual/kernel
$ bitbake virtual/kernel
```

6.2.16. `build/tmp/deploy/sdk/`

The OpenEmbedded build system creates this directory to hold toolchain installer scripts, which when executed, install the sysroot that matches your target hardware. You can find out more about these installers in the "Optionally Building a Toolchain Installer [http://www.yoctoproject.org/docs/1.7.2/adt-manual/adt-manual.html#optionally-building-a-toolchain-installer]" section in the Yocto Project Application Developer's Guide.

6.2.17. `build/tmp/sstate-control/`

The OpenEmbedded build system uses this directory for the shared state manifest files. The shared state code uses these files to record the files installed by each sstate task so that the files can be removed when cleaning the recipe or when a newer version is about to be installed. The build system also uses the manifests to detect and produce a warning when files from one task are overwriting those from another.

6.2.18. `build/tmp/sysroots/`

This directory contains shared header files and libraries as well as other shared data. Packages that need to share output with other packages do so within this directory. The directory is subdivided by architecture so multiple builds can run within the one Build Directory.

6.2.19. `build/tmp/stamps/`

This directory holds information that BitBake uses for accounting purposes to track what tasks have run and when they have run. The directory is sub-divided by architecture, package name, and version. Following is an example:

```
stamps/all-poky-linux/distcc-config/1.0-r0.do_build-2fdd....2do
```

Although the files in the directory are empty of data, BitBake uses the filenames and timestamps for tracking purposes.

6.2.20. **build/tmp/log/**

This directory contains general logs that are not otherwise placed using the package's WORKDIR. Examples of logs are the output from the do_check_pkg or do_distro_check tasks. Running a build does not necessarily mean this directory is created.

6.2.21. **build/tmp/work/**

This directory contains architecture-specific work sub-directories for packages built by BitBake. All tasks execute from the appropriate work directory. For example, the source for a particular package is unpacked, patched, configured and compiled all within its own work directory. Within the work directory, organization is based on the package group and version for which the source is being compiled as defined by the WORKDIR.

It is worth considering the structure of a typical work directory. As an example, consider linux-yocto-kernel-3.0 on the machine qemux86 built within the Yocto Project. For this package, a work directory of tmp/work/qemux86-poky-linux/linux-yocto/3.0+git1+<.....>, referred to as the WORKDIR, is created. Within this directory, the source is unpacked to linux-qemux86-standard-build and then patched by Quilt. (See the "Using a Quilt Flow [http://www.yoctoproject.org/docs/1.7.2/dev-manual/dev-manual.html#using-a-quilt-workflow]" section in the Yocto Project Development Manual for more information.) Within the linux-qemux86-standard-build directory, standard Quilt directories linux-3.0/patches and linux-3.0/.pc are created, and standard Quilt commands can be used.

There are other directories generated within WORKDIR. The most important directory is WORKDIR/temp/, which has log files for each task (log.do_*.pid) and contains the scripts BitBake runs for each task (run.do_*.pid). The WORKDIR/image/ directory is where "make install" places its output that is then split into sub-packages within WORKDIR/packages-split/.

6.2.22. **build/tmp/work-shared/**

For efficiency, the OpenEmbedded build system creates and uses this directory to hold recipes that share a work directory with other recipes. In practice, this is only used for gcc and its variants (e.g. gcc-cross, libgcc, gcc-runtime, and so forth).

6.3. The Metadata -**meta/**

As mentioned previously, Metadata [http://www.yoctoproject.org/docs/1.7.2/dev-manual/dev-manual.html#metadata] is the core of the Yocto Project. Metadata has several important subdivisions:

6.3.1. **meta/classes/**

This directory contains the *.bbclass files. Class files are used to abstract common code so it can be reused by multiple packages. Every package inherits the base.bbclass file. Examples of other important classes are autotools.bbclass, which in theory allows any Autotool-enabled package to work with the Yocto Project with minimal effort. Another example is kernel.bbclass that contains common code and functions for working with the Linux kernel. Functions like image generation or packaging also have their specific class files such as image.bbclass, rootfs_*.bbclass and package*.bbclass.

For reference information on classes, see the "Classes" chapter.

6.3.2. **meta/conf/**

This directory contains the core set of configuration files that start from bitbake.conf and from which all other configuration files are included. See the include statements at the end of the bitbake.conf file and you will note that even local.conf is loaded from there. While bitbake.conf sets up the defaults, you can often override these by using the (local.conf) file, machine file or the distribution configuration file.

6.3.3. **meta/conf/machine/**

This directory contains all the machine configuration files. If you set MACHINE = "qemux86", the OpenEmbedded build system looks for a qemux86.conf file in this directory. The include directory contains various data common to multiple machines. If you want to add support for a new machine to the Yocto Project, look in this directory.

6.3.4. **meta/conf/distro/**

The contents of this directory controls any distribution-specific configurations. For the Yocto Project, the defaultsetup.conf is the main file here. This directory includes the versions and the SRCDATE definitions for applications that are configured here. An example of an alternative configuration might be poky-bleeding.conf. Although this file mainly inherits its configuration from Poky.

6.3.5. **meta/conf/machine-sdk/**

The OpenEmbedded build system searches this directory for configuration files that correspond to the value of SDKMACHINE. By default, 32-bit and 64-bit x86 files ship with the Yocto Project that support some SDK hosts. However, it is possible to extend that support to other SDK hosts by adding additional configuration files in this subdirectory within another layer.

6.3.6. **meta/files/**

This directory contains common license files and several text files used by the build system. The text files contain minimal device information and lists of files and directories with known permissions.

6.3.7. **meta/lib/**

This directory contains OpenEmbedded Python library code used during the build process.

6.3.8. **meta/recipes-bsp/**

This directory contains anything linking to specific hardware or hardware configuration information such as "u-boot" and "grub".

6.3.9. **meta/recipes-connectivity/**

This directory contains libraries and applications related to communication with other devices.

6.3.10. **meta/recipes-core/**

This directory contains what is needed to build a basic working Linux image including commonly used dependencies.

6.3.11. **meta/recipes-devtools/**

This directory contains tools that are primarily used by the build system. The tools, however, can also be used on targets.

6.3.12. **meta/recipes-extended/**

This directory contains non-essential applications that add features compared to the alternatives in core. You might need this directory for full tool functionality or for Linux Standard Base (LSB) compliance.

6.3.13. **meta/recipes-gnome/**

This directory contains all things related to the GTK+ application framework.

6.3.14. **meta/recipes-graphics/**

This directory contains X and other graphically related system libraries

6.3.15. **meta/recipes-kernel/**

This directory contains the kernel and generic applications and libraries that have strong kernel dependencies.

6.3.16. **meta/recipes-lsb4/**

This directory contains recipes specifically added to support the Linux Standard Base (LSB) version 4.x.

6.3.17. **meta/recipes-multimedia/**

This directory contains codecs and support utilities for audio, images and video.

6.3.18. **meta/recipes-qt/**

This directory contains all things related to the Qt application framework.

6.3.19. **meta/recipes-rt/**

This directory contains package and image recipes for using and testing the PREEMPT_RT kernel.

6.3.20. **meta/recipes-sato/**

This directory contains the Sato demo/reference UI/UX and its associated applications and configuration data.

6.3.21. **meta/recipes-support/**

This directory contains recipes used by other recipes, but that are not directly included in images (i.e. dependencies of other recipes).

6.3.22. **meta/site/**

This directory contains a list of cached results for various architectures. Because certain "autoconf" test results cannot be determined when cross-compiling due to the tests not able to run on a live system, the information in this directory is passed to "autoconf" for the various architectures.

6.3.23. **meta/recipes.txt**

This file is a description of the contents of recipes-*.

Chapter 7. Classes

Class files are used to abstract common functionality and share it amongst multiple recipe (.bb) files. To use a class file, you simply make sure the recipe inherits the class. In most cases, when a recipe inherits a class it is enough to enable its features. There are cases, however, where in the recipe you might need to set variables or override some default behavior.

Any Metadata [http://www.yoctoproject.org/docs/1.7.2/dev-manual/dev-manual.html#metadata] usually found in a recipe can also be placed in a class file. Class files are identified by the extension .bbclass and are usually placed in a classes/ directory beneath the meta*/ directory found in the Source Directory [http://www.yoctoproject.org/docs/1.7.2/dev-manual/dev-manual.html#source-directory]. Class files can also be pointed to by BUILDDIR (e.g. build/) in the same way as .conf files in the conf directory. Class files are searched for in BBPATH using the same method by which .conf files are searched.

This chapter discusses only the most useful and important classes. Other classes do exist within the meta/classes directory in the Source Directory [http://www.yoctoproject.org/docs/1.7.2/dev-manual/dev-manual.html#source-directory]. You can reference the .bbclass files directly for more information.

7.1. **allarch.bbclass**

The allarch class is inherited by recipes that do not produce architecture-specific output. The class disables functionality that is normally needed for recipes that produce executable binaries (such as building the cross-compiler and a C library as pre-requisites, and splitting out of debug symbols during packaging).

By default, all recipes inherit the base and package classes, which enable functionality needed for recipes that produce executable output. If your recipe, for example, only produces packages that contain configuration files, media files, or scripts (e.g. Python and Perl), then it should inherit the allarch class.

7.2. **archiver.bbclass**

The archiver class supports releasing source code and other materials with the binaries.

For more details on the source archiver, see the "Maintaining Open Source License Compliance During Your Product's Lifecycle [http://www.yoctoproject.org/docs/1.7.2/dev-manual/dev-manual.html#maintaining-open-source-license-compliance-during-your-products-lifecycle]" section in the Yocto Project Development Manual.

7.3. **autotools.bbclass**

The autotools class supports Autotooled packages.

The autoconf, automake, and libtool bring standardization. This class defines a set of tasks (configure, compile etc.) that work for all Autotooled packages. It should usually be enough to define a few standard variables and then simply inherit autotools. This class can also work with software that emulates Autotools. For more information, see the "Autotooled Package [http://www.yoctoproject.org/docs/1.7.2/dev-manual/dev-manual.html#new-recipe-autotooled-package]" section in the Yocto Project Development Manual.

By default, the autotools class uses out-of-tree builds (B != S). If the software being built by a recipe does not support using out-of-tree builds, you should have the recipe inherit the autotools-brokensep class.

It's useful to have some idea of how the tasks defined by this class work and what they do behind the scenes.

- do_configure # Regenerates the configure script (using autoreconf) and then launches it with a standard set of arguments used during cross-compilation. You can pass additional parameters to configure through the EXTRA_OECONF variable.

- do_compile # Runs make with arguments that specify the compiler and linker. You can pass additional arguments through the EXTRA_OEMAKE variable.

- do_install # Runs make install and passes in ${D} as DESTDIR.

7.4. **autotools-brokensep.bbclass**

The autotools-brokensep class behaves the same as the autotools class but builds with B == S. This method is useful when out-of-tree build support is either not present or is broken.

Note
It is recommended that out-of-tree support be fixed and used if at all possible.

7.5. **base.bbclass**

The base class is special in that every .bb file implicitly inherits the class. This class contains definitions for standard basic tasks such as fetching, unpacking, configuring (empty by default), compiling (runs any Makefile present), installing (empty by default) and packaging (empty by default). These classes are often overridden or extended by other classes such as the autotools class or the package class. The class also contains some commonly used functions such as oe_runmake.

7.6. **bin_package.bbclass**

The bin_package class is a helper class for recipes that extract the contents of a binary package (e.g. an RPM) and install those contents rather than building the binary from source. The binary package is extracted and new packages in the configured output package format are created. Extraction and installation of proprietary binaries is a good example use for this class.

Note
For RPMs and other packages that do not contain a subdirectory, you should specify a "subdir" parameter. Here is an example where ${BP} is used so that the files are extracted into the subdirectory expected by the default value of S:

```
SRC_URI = "http://example.com/downloads/somepackage.rpm;subdir=${BP}"
```

7.7. **binconfig.bbclass**

The binconfig class helps to correct paths in shell scripts.

Before pkg-config had become widespread, libraries shipped shell scripts to give information about the libraries and include paths needed to build software (usually named LIBNAME-config). This class assists any recipe using such scripts.

During staging, the OpenEmbedded build system installs such scripts into the sysroots/ directory. Inheriting this class results in all paths in these scripts being changed to point into the sysroots/ directory so that all builds that use the script use the correct directories for the cross compiling layout. See the BINCONFIG_GLOB variable for more information.

7.8. **binconfig-disabled.bbclass**

An alternative version of the binconfig class, which disables binary configuration scripts by making them return an error in favor of using pkg-config to query the information. The scripts to be disabled should be specified using the BINCONFIG variable within the recipe inheriting the class.

7.9. **blacklist.bbclass**

The blacklist class prevents the OpenEmbedded build system from building specific recipes (blacklists them). To use this class, inherit the class globally and set PNBLACKLIST for each recipe you wish to blacklist. Specify the PN value as a variable flag (varflag) and provide a reason, which is reported, if the package is requested to be built as the value. For example, if you want to blacklist a recipe called "exoticware", you add the following to your local.conf or distribution configuration:

```
INHERIT += "blacklist"
PNBLACKLIST[exoticware] = "Not supported by our organization."
```

7.10. `boot-directdisk.bbclass`

The boot-directdisk class creates an image that can be placed directly onto a hard disk using dd and then booted. The image uses SYSLINUX.

The end result is a 512 boot sector populated with a Master Boot Record (MBR) and partition table followed by an MSDOS FAT16 partition containing SYSLINUX and a Linux kernel completed by the ext2 and ext3 root filesystems.

7.11. `bootimg.bbclass`

The bootimg class creates a bootable image using SYSLINUX, your kernel, and an optional initial RAM disk (initrd).

When you use this class, two things happen:

- A .hddimg file is created. This file is an MSDOS filesystem that contains SYSLINUX, a kernel, an initrd, and a root filesystem image. All three of these can be written to hard drives directly and also booted on a USB flash disks using dd.

- A CD .iso image is created. When this file is booted, the initrd boots and processes the label selected in SYSLINUX. Actions based on the label are then performed (e.g. installing to a hard drive).

The bootimg class supports the INITRD, NOISO, NOHDD, and ROOTFS variables.

7.12. `bugzilla.bbclass`

The bugzilla class supports setting up an instance of Bugzilla in which you can automatically files bug reports in response to build failures. For this class to work, you need to enable the XML-RPC interface in the instance of Bugzilla.

7.13. `buildhistory.bbclass`

The buildhistory class records a history of build output metadata, which can be used to detect possible regressions as well as used for analysis of the build output. For more information on using Build History, see the "Maintaining Build Output Quality" section.

7.14. `buildstats.bbclass`

The buildstats class records performance statistics about each task executed during the build (e.g. elapsed time, CPU usage, and I/O usage).

When you use this class, the output goes into the BUILDSTATS_BASE directory, which defaults to ${TMPDIR}/buildstats/. You can analyze the elapsed time using scripts/pybootchartgui/pybootchartgui.py, which produces a cascading chart of the entire build process and can be useful for highlighting bottlenecks.

Collecting build statistics is enabled by default through the USER_CLASSES variable from your local.conf file. Consequently, you do not have to do anything to enable the class. However, if you want to disable the class, simply remove "buildstats" from the USER_CLASSES list.

7.15. `buildstats-summary.bbclass`

When inherited globally, prints statistics at the end of the build on sstate re-use. In order to function, this class requires the buildstats class be enabled.

7.16. **ccache.bbclass**

The ccache class enables the C/C++ Compiler Cache [http://ccache.samba.org/] for the build. This class is used to give a minor performance boost during the build. However, using the class can lead to unexpected side-effects. Thus, it is recommended that you do not use this class. See http://ccache.samba.org/ for information on the C/C++ Compiler Cache.

7.17. **chrpath.bbclass**

The chrpath class is a wrapper around the "chrpath" utility, which is used during the build process for nativesdk, cross, and cross-canadian recipes to change RPATH records within binaries in order to make them relocatable.

7.18. **clutter.bbclass**

The clutter class consolidates the major and minor version naming and other common items used by Clutter and related recipes.

Note
Unlike some other classes related to specific libraries, recipes building other software that uses Clutter do not need to inherit this class unless they use the same recipe versioning scheme that the Clutter and related recipes do.

7.19. **cmake.bbclass**

The cmake class allows for recipes that need to build software using the CMake build system. You can use the EXTRA_OECMAKE variable to specify additional configuration options to be passed on the cmake command line.

7.20. **cml1.bbclass**

The cml1 class provides basic support for the Linux kernel style build configuration system.

7.21. **compress_doc.bbclass**

Enables compression for man pages and info pages. This class is intended to be inherited globally. The default compression mechanism is gz (gzip) but you can select an alternative mechanism by setting the DOC_COMPRESS variable.

7.22. **copyleft_compliance.bbclass**

The copyleft_compliance class preserves source code for the purposes of license compliance. This class is an alternative to the archiver class and is still used by some users even though it has been deprecated in favor of the archiver class.

7.23. **copyleft_filter.bbclass**

A class used by the archiver and copyleft_compliance classes for filtering licenses. The copyleft_filter class is an internal class and is not intended to be used directly.

7.24. **core-image.bbclass**

The core-image class provides common definitions for the core-image-* image recipes, such as support for additional IMAGE_FEATURES.

7.25. **cpan.bbclass**

The cpan class supports Perl modules.

Recipes for Perl modules are simple. These recipes usually only need to point to the source's archive and then inherit the proper class file. Building is split into two methods depending on which method the module authors used.

- Modules that use old Makefile.PL-based build system require cpan.bbclass in their recipes.

- Modules that use Build.PL-based build system require using cpan_build.bbclass in their recipes.

7.26. cross.bbclass

The cross class provides support for the recipes that build the cross-compilation tools.

7.27. cross-canadian.bbclass

The cross-canadian class provides support for the recipes that build the Canadian Cross-compilation tools for SDKs. See the "Cross-Development Toolchain Generation" section for more discussion on these cross-compilation tools.

7.28. crosssdk.bbclass

The crosssdk class provides support for the recipes that build the cross-compilation tools used for building SDKs. See the "Cross-Development Toolchain Generation" section for more discussion on these cross-compilation tools.

7.29. debian.bbclass

The debian class renames output packages so that they follow the Debian naming policy (i.e. glibc becomes libc6 and glibc-devel becomes libc6-dev.) Renaming includes the library name and version as part of the package name.

If a recipe creates packages for multiple libraries (shared object files of .so type), use the LEAD_SONAME variable in the recipe to specify the library on which to apply the naming scheme.

7.30. deploy.bbclass

The deploy class handles deploying files to the DEPLOY_DIR_IMAGE directory. The main function of this class is to allow the deploy step to be accelerated by shared state. Recipes that inherit this class should define their own do_deploy function to copy the files to be deployed to DEPLOYDIR, and use addtask to add the task at the appropriate place, which is usually after do_compile or do_install. The class then takes care of staging the files from DEPLOYDIR to DEPLOY_DIR_IMAGE.

7.31. devshell.bbclass

The devshell class adds the do_devshell task. Distribution policy dictates whether to include this class. See the "Using a Development Shell [http://www.yoctoproject.org/docs/1.7.2/dev-manual/dev-manual.html#platdev-appdev-devshell]" section in the Yocto Project Development Manual for more information about using devshell.

7.32. distro_features_check.bbclass

The distro_features_check class allows individual recipes to check for required and conflicting DISTRO_FEATURES.

This class provides support for the REQUIRED_DISTRO_FEATURES and CONFLICT_DISTRO_FEATURES variables. If any conditions specified in the recipe using the above variables are not met, the recipe will be skipped.

7.33. distrodata.bbclass

The distrodata class provides for automatic checking for upstream recipe updates. The class creates a comma-separated value (CSV) spreadsheet that contains information about the recipes. The information provides the do_distrodata and do_distro_check tasks, which do upstream checking and also verify if a package is used in multiple major distributions.

The class is not included by default. To use it, you must include the following files and set the INHERIT variable:

```
include conf/distro/include/distro_alias.inc
include conf/distro/include/recipe_color.inc
include conf/distro/include/maintainers.inc
include conf/distro/include/upstream_tracking.inc
include conf/distro/include/package_regex.inc
INHERIT+= "distrodata"
```

7.34. **distutils.bbclass**

The distutils class supports recipes for Python version 2.x extensions, which are simple. These recipes usually only need to point to the source's archive and then inherit the proper class. Building is split into two methods depending on which method the module authors used.

- Extensions that use an Autotools-based build system require Autotools and distutils-based classes in their recipes.

- Extensions that use build systems based on distutils require the distutils class in their recipes.

- Extensions that use build systems based on setuptools require the setuptools class in their recipes.

7.35. **distutils3.bbclass**

The distutils3 class supports recipes for Python version 3.x extensions, which are simple. These recipes usually only need to point to the source's archive and then inherit the proper class. Building is split into two methods depending on which method the module authors used.

- Extensions that use an Autotools-based build system require Autotools and distutils-based classes in their recipes.

- Extensions that use distutils-based build systems require the distutils class in their recipes.

- Extensions that use build systems based on setuptools3 require the setuptools3 class in their recipes.

7.36. **externalsrc.bbclass**

The externalsrc class supports building software from source code that is external to the OpenEmbedded build system. Building software from an external source tree means that the build system's normal fetch, unpack, and patch process is not used.

By default, the OpenEmbedded build system uses the S and B variables to locate unpacked recipe source code and to build it, respectively. When your recipe inherits the externalsrc class, you use the EXTERNALSRC and EXTERNALSRC_BUILD variables to ultimately define S and B.

By default, this class expects the source code to support recipe builds that use the B variable to point to the directory in which the OpenEmbedded build system places the generated objects built from the recipes. By default, the B directory is set to the following, which is separate from the source directory (S):

```
${WORKDIR}/${BPN}/{PV}/
```

See these variables for more information: WORKDIR, BPN, and PV,

For more information on the externalsrc class, see the comments in meta/classes/externalsrc.bbclass in the Source Directory [http://www.yoctoproject.org/docs/1.7.2/dev-manual/

dev-manual.html#source-directory]. For information on how to use the externalsrc class, see the "Building Software from an External Source [http://www.yoctoproject.org/docs/1.7.2/dev-manual/dev-manual.html#building-software-from-an-external-source]" section in the Yocto Project Development Manual.

7.37. **extrausers.bbclass**

The extrausers class allows additional user and group configuration to be applied at the image level. Inheriting this class either globally or from an image recipe allows additional user and group operations to be performed using the EXTRA_USERS_PARAMS variable.

Note
The user and group operations added using the extrausers class are not tied to a specific recipe outside of the recipe for the image. Thus, the operations can be performed across the image as a whole. Use the useradd class to add user and group configuration to a specific recipe.

Here is an example that uses this class in an image recipe:

```
inherit extrausers
EXTRA_USERS_PARAMS = "\
    useradd -p '' tester; \
    groupadd developers; \
    userdel nobody; \
    groupdel -g video; \
    groupmod -g 1020 developers; \
    usermod -s /bin/sh tester; \
    "
```

Here is an example that adds two users named "tester-jim" and "tester-sue" and assigns passwords:

```
inherit extrausers
EXTRA_USERS_PARAMS = "\
    useradd -P tester01 tester-jim; \
    useradd -P tester01 tester-sue; \
    "
```

Finally, here is an example that sets the root password to "1876*18":

```
inherit extrausers
EXTRA_USERS_PARAMS = "\
    useradd -P 1876*18 root; \
    "
```

7.38. **fontcache.bbclass**

The fontcache class generates the proper post-install and post-remove (postinst and postrm) scriptlets for font packages. These scriptlets call fc-cache (part of Fontconfig) to add the fonts to the font information cache. Since the cache files are architecture-specific, fc-cache runs using QEMU if the postinst scriptlets need to be run on the build host during image creation.

If the fonts being installed are in packages other than the main package, set FONT_PACKAGES to specify the packages containing the fonts.

7.39. **gconf.bbclass**

The gconf class provides common functionality for recipes that need to install GConf schemas. The schemas will be put into a separate package (${PN}-gconf) that is created automatically when this class is inherited. This package uses the appropriate post-install and post-remove (postinst/postrm) scriptlets to register and unregister the schemas in the target image.

7.40. **gettext.bbclass**

The gettext class provides support for building software that uses the GNU gettext internationalization and localization system. All recipes building software that use gettext should inherit this class.

7.41. **gnome.bbclass**

The gnome class supports recipes that build software from the GNOME stack. This class inherits the gnomebase, gtk-icon-cache, gconf and mime classes. The class also disables GObject introspection where applicable.

7.42. **gnomebase.bbclass**

The gnomebase class is the base class for recipes that build software from the GNOME stack. This class sets SRC_URI to download the source from the GNOME mirrors as well as extending FILES with the typical GNOME installation paths.

7.43. **grub-efi.bbclass**

The grub-efi class provides grub-efi-specific functions for building bootable images.

This class supports several variables:

- INITRD: Indicates list of filesystem images to concatenate and use as an initial RAM disk (initrd) (optional).

- ROOTFS: Indicates a filesystem image to include as the root filesystem (optional).

- GRUB_GFXSERIAL: Set this to "1" to have graphics and serial in the boot menu.

- LABELS: A list of targets for the automatic configuration.

- APPEND: An override list of append strings for each LABEL.

- GRUB_OPTS: Additional options to add to the configuration (optional). Options are delimited using semi-colon characters (;).

- GRUB_TIMEOUT: Timeout before executing the default LABEL (optional).

7.44. **gsettings.bbclass**

The gsettings class provides common functionality for recipes that need to install GSettings (glib) schemas. The schemas are assumed to be part of the main package. Appropriate post-install and post-remove (postinst/postrm) scriptlets are added to register and unregister the schemas in the target image.

7.45. **gtk-doc.bbclass**

The gtk-doc class is a helper class to pull in the appropriate gtk-doc dependencies and disable gtk-doc.

7.46. **gtk-icon-cache.bbclass**

The gtk-icon-cache class generates the proper post-install and post-remove (postinst/postrm) scriptlets for packages that use GTK+ and install icons. These scriptlets call gtk-update-icon-cache to add the fonts to GTK+'s icon cache. Since the cache files are architecture-specific, gtk-update-icon-cache is run using QEMU if the postinst scriptlets need to be run on the build host during image creation.

7.47. **gtk-immodules-cache.bbclass**

The gtk-immodules-cache class generates the proper post-install and post-remove (postinst/postrm) scriptlets for packages that install GTK+ input method modules for virtual keyboards. These scriptlets call gtk-update-icon-cache to add the input method modules to the cache. Since the cache files are architecture-specific, gtk-update-icon-cache is run using QEMU if the postinst scriptlets need to be run on the build host during image creation.

If the input method modules being installed are in packages other than the main package, set GTKIMMODULES_PACKAGES to specify the packages containing the modules.

7.48. **gummiboot.bbclass**

The gummiboot class provides functions specific to the gummiboot bootloader for building bootable images. This is an internal class and is not intended to be used directly. Set the EFI_PROVIDER variable to "gummiboot" to use this class.

For information on more variables used and supported in this class, see the GUMMIBOOT_CFG, GUMMIBOOT_ENTRIES, and GUMMIBOOT_TIMEOUT variables.

You can also see the Gummiboot documentation [http://freedesktop.org/wiki/Software/gummiboot/] for more information.

7.49. **gzipnative.bbclass**

The gzipnative class enables the use of native versions of gzip and pigz rather than the versions of these tools from the build host.

7.50. **icecc.bbclass**

The icecc class supports Icecream [https://github.com/icecc/icecream], which facilitates taking compile jobs and distributing them among remote machines.

The class stages directories with symlinks from gcc and g++ to icecc, for both native and cross compilers. Depending on each configure or compile, the OpenEmbedded build system adds the directories at the head of the PATH list and then sets the ICECC_CXX and ICEC_CC variables, which are the paths to the g++ and gcc compilers, respectively.

For the cross compiler, the class creates a tar.gz file that contains the Yocto Project toolchain and sets ICECC_VERSION, which is the version of the cross-compiler used in the cross-development toolchain, accordingly.

The class handles all three different compile stages (i.e native ,cross-kernel and target) and creates the necessary environment tar.gz file to be used by the remote machines. The class also supports SDK generation.

If ICECC_PATH is not set in your local.conf file, then the class tries to locate the icecc binary using which. If ICECC_ENV_EXEC is set in your local.conf file, the variable should point to the icecc-create-env script provided by the user. If you do not point to a user-provided script, the build system uses the default script provided by the recipe icecc-create-env-native.bb.

Note
This script is a modified version and not the one that comes with icecc.

If you do not want the Icecream distributed compile support to apply to specific recipes or classes, you can effectively "blacklist" them by listing the recipes and classes using the ICECC_USER_PACKAGE_BL and ICECC_USER_CLASS_BL, variables, respectively, in your local.conf file. Doing so causes the OpenEmbedded build system to handle these compilations locally.

Additionally, you can list recipes using the ICECC_USER_PACKAGE_WL variable in your local.conf file to force icecc to be enabled for recipes using an empty PARALLEL_MAKE variable.

Inheriting the `icecc` class changes all sstate signatures. Consequently, if a development team has a dedicated build system that populates STATE_MIRRORS and they want to reuse sstate from STATE_MIRRORS, then all developers and the build system need to either inherit the `icecc` class or nobody should.

At the distribution level, you can inherit the `icecc` class to be sure that all builders start with the same sstate signatures. After inheriting the class, you can then disable the feature by setting the ICECC_DISABLED variable to "1" as follows:

```
INHERIT_DISTRO_append = " icecc"
ICECC_DISABLED ??= "1"
```

This practice makes sure everyone is using the same signatures but also requires individuals that do want to use Icecream to enable the feature individually as follows in your `local.conf` file:

```
ICECC_DISABLED = ""
```

7.51. `image.bbclass`

The image class helps support creating images in different formats. First, the root filesystem is created from packages using one of the `rootfs*.bbclass` files (depending on the package format used) and then one or more image files are created.

- The IMAGE_FSTYPES variable controls the types of images to generate.

- The IMAGE_INSTALL variable controls the list of packages to install into the image.

For information on customizing images, see the "Customizing Images [http://www.yoctoproject.org/docs/1.7.2/dev-manual/dev-manual.html#usingpoky-extend-customimage]" section in the Yocto Project Development Manual. For information on how images are created, see the "Images" section elsewhere in this manual.

7.52. `image_types.bbclass`

The `image_types` class defines all of the standard image output types that you can enable through the IMAGE_FSTYPES variable. You can use this class as a reference on how to add support for custom image output types.

By default, this class is enabled through the IMAGE_CLASSES variable in `image.bbclass`. If you define your own image types using a custom BitBake class and then use IMAGE_CLASSES to enable it, the custom class must either inherit image_types or image_types must also appear in IMAGE_CLASSES.

7.53. `image_types_uboot.bbclass`

The `image_types_uboot` class defines additional image types specifically for the U-Boot bootloader.

7.54. `image-live.bbclass`

The `image-live` class supports building "live" images.

Normally, you do not use this class directly. Instead, you add "live" to IMAGE_FSTYPES. For example, if you were building an ISO image, you would add "live" to IMAGE_FSTYPES, set the NOISO variable to "0" and the build system would use the `image-live` class to build the ISO image.

7.55. `image-mklibs.bbclass`

The `image-mklibs` class enables the use of the mklibs utility during the do_rootfs task, which optimizes the size of libraries contained in the image.

By default, the class is enabled in the `local.conf.template` using the USER_CLASSES variable as follows:

```
USER_CLASSES ?= "buildstats image-mklibs image-prelink"
```

7.56. `image-prelink.bbclass`

The `image-prelink` class enables the use of the `prelink` utility during the `do_rootfs` task, which optimizes the dynamic linking of shared libraries to reduce executable startup time.

By default, the class is enabled in the `local.conf.template` using the USER_CLASSES variable as follows:

```
USER_CLASSES ?= "buildstats image-mklibs image-prelink"
```

7.57. `image-swab.bbclass`

The `image-swab` class enables the Swabber [http://www.yoctoproject.org/tools-resources/projects/swabber] tool in order to detect and log accesses to the host system during the OpenEmbedded build process.

Note
This class is currently unmaintained.

7.58. `image-vmdk.bbclass`

The `image-vmdk` class supports building VMware VMDK images. Normally, you do not use this class directly. Instead, you add "vmdk" to IMAGE_FSTYPES.

7.59. `insane.bbclass`

The insane class adds a step to the package generation process so that output quality assurance checks are generated by the OpenEmbedded build system. A range of checks are performed that check the build's output for common problems that show up during runtime. Distribution policy usually dictates whether to include this class.

You can configure the sanity checks so that specific test failures either raise a warning or an error message. Typically, failures for new tests generate a warning. Subsequent failures for the same test would then generate an error message once the metadata is in a known and good condition. See the "QA Error and Warning Messages" Chapter for a list of all the warning and error messages you might encounter using a default configuration.

Use the WARN_QA and ERROR_QA variables to control the behavior of these checks at the global level (i.e. in your custom distro configuration). However, to skip one or more checks in recipes, you should use INSANE_SKIP. For example, to skip the check for symbolic link `.so` files in the main package of a recipe, add the following to the recipe. You need to realize that the package name override, in this example ${PN}, must be used:

```
INSANE_SKIP_${PN} += "dev-so"
```

Please keep in mind that the QA checks exist in order to detect real or potential problems in the packaged output. So exercise caution when disabling these checks.

The following list shows the tests you can list with the WARN_QA and ERROR_QA variables:

- `already-stripped`: Checks that produced binaries have not already been stripped prior to the build system extracting debug symbols. It is common for upstream software projects to default to stripping debug symbols for output binaries. In order for debugging to work on the target using -dbg packages, this stripping must be disabled.

- `arch`: Checks the Executable and Linkable Format (ELF) type, bit size, and endianness of any binaries to ensure they match the target architecture. This test fails if any binaries do not match the type since there would be an incompatibility. The test could indicate that the wrong compiler or compiler options have been used. Sometimes software, like bootloaders, might need to bypass this check.

- `buildpaths`: Checks for paths to locations on the build host inside the output files. Currently, this test triggers too many false positives and thus is not normally enabled.

- `build-deps`: Determines if a build-time dependency that is specified through DEPENDS, explicit RDEPENDS, or task-level dependencies exists to match any runtime dependency. This determination is particularly useful to discover where runtime dependencies are detected and added during packaging. If no explicit dependency has been specified within the metadata, at the packaging stage it is too late to ensure that the dependency is built, and thus you can end up with an error when the package is installed into the image during the do_rootfs task because the auto-detected dependency was not satisfied. An example of this would be where the update-rc.d class automatically adds a dependency on the initscripts-functions package to packages that install an initscript that refers to /etc/init.d/functions. The recipe should really have an explicit RDEPENDS for the package in question on initscripts-functions so that the OpenEmbedded build system is able to ensure that the initscripts recipe is actually built and thus the initscripts-functions package is made available.

- `compile-host-path`: Checks the do_compile log for indications that paths to locations on the build host were used. Using such paths might result in host contamination of the build output.

- `debug-deps`: Checks that all packages except -dbg packages do not depend on -dbg packages, which would cause a packaging bug.

- `debug-files`: Checks for .debug directories in anything but the -dbg package. The debug files should all be in the -dbg package. Thus, anything packaged elsewhere is incorrect packaging.

- `dep-cmp`: Checks for invalid version comparison statements in runtime dependency relationships between packages (i.e. in RDEPENDS, RRECOMMENDS, RSUGGESTS, RPROVIDES, RREPLACES, and RCONFLICTS variable values). Any invalid comparisons might trigger failures or undesirable behavior when passed to the package manager.

- `desktop`: Runs the desktop-file-validate program against any .desktop files to validate their contents against the specification for .desktop files.

- `dev-deps`: Checks that all packages except -dev or -staticdev packages do not depend on -dev packages, which would be a packaging bug.

- `dev-so`: Checks that the .so symbolic links are in the -dev package and not in any of the other packages. In general, these symlinks are only useful for development purposes. Thus, the -dev package is the correct location for them. Some very rare cases do exist for dynamically loaded modules where these symlinks are needed instead in the main package.

- `file-rdeps`: Checks that file-level dependencies identified by the OpenEmbedded build system at packaging time are satisfied. For example, a shell script might start with the line #!/bin/bash. This line would translate to a file dependency on /bin/bash. Of the three package managers that the OpenEmbedded build system supports, only RPM directly handles file-level dependencies, resolving them automatically to packages providing the files. However, the lack of that functionality in the other two package managers does not mean the dependencies do not still need resolving. This QA check attempts to ensure that explicitly declared RDEPENDS exist to handle any file-level dependency detected in packaged files.

- `files-invalid`: Checks for FILES variable values that contain "//", which is invalid.

- `incompatible-license`: Report when packages are excluded from being created due to being marked with a license that is in INCOMPATIBLE_LICENSE.

- `install-host-path`: Checks the do_install log for indications that paths to locations on the build host were used. Using such paths might result in host contamination of the build output.

- `installed-vs-shipped`: Reports when files have been installed within do_install but have not been included in any package by way of the FILES variable. Files that do not appear in any package cannot be present in an image later on in the build process. Ideally, all installed files should be packaged or not installed at all. These files can be deleted at the end of do_install if the files are not needed in any package.

- `la`: Checks .la files for any TMPDIR paths. Any .la file containing these paths is incorrect since libtool adds the correct sysroot prefix when using the files automatically itself.

- `ldflags`: Ensures that the binaries were linked with the LDFLAGS options provided by the build system. If this test fails, check that the LDFLAGS variable is being passed to the linker command.

- `libdir`: Checks for libraries being installed into incorrect (possibly hardcoded) installation paths. For example, this test will catch recipes that install /lib/bar.so when ${base_libdir} is "lib32". Another example is when recipes install /usr/lib64/foo.so when ${libdir} is "/usr/lib".

- `libexec`: Checks if a package contains files in /usr/libexec. This check is not performed if the libexecdir variable has been set explicitly to /usr/libexec.

- `packages-list`: Checks for the same package being listed multiple times through the PACKAGES variable value. Installing the package in this manner can cause errors during packaging.

- `perm-config`: Reports lines in fs-perms.txt that have an invalid format.

- `perm-line`: Reports lines in fs-perms.txt that have an invalid format.

- `perm-link`: Reports lines in fs-perms.txt that specify 'link' where the specified target already exists.

- `perms`: Currently, this check is unused but reserved.

- `pkgconfig`: Checks .pc files for any TMPDIR/WORKDIR paths. Any .pc file containing these paths is incorrect since pkg-config itself adds the correct sysroot prefix when the files are accessed.

- `pkgname`: Checks that all packages in PACKAGES have names that do not contain invalid characters (i.e. characters other than 0-9, a-z, ., +, and -).

- `pkgv-undefined`: Checks to see if the PKGV variable is undefined during do_package.

- `pkgvarcheck`: Checks through the variables RDEPENDS, RRECOMMENDS, RSUGGESTS, RCONFLICTS, RPROVIDES, RREPLACES, FILES, ALLOW_EMPTY, pkg_preinst, pkg_postinst, pkg_prerm and pkg_postrm, and reports if there are variable sets that are not package-specific. Using these variables without a package suffix is bad practice, and might unnecessarily complicate dependencies of other packages within the same recipe or have other unintended consequences.

- `pn-overrides`: Checks that a recipe does not have a name (PN) value that appears in OVERRIDES. If a recipe is named such that its PN value matches something already in OVERRIDES (e.g. PN happens to be the same as MACHINE or DISTRO), it can have unexpected consequences. For example, assignments such as FILES_${PN} = "xyz" effectively turn into FILES = "xyz".

- `rpaths`: Checks for rpaths in the binaries that contain build system paths such as TMPDIR. If this test fails, bad -rpath options are being passed to the linker commands and your binaries have potential security issues.

- `split-strip`: Reports that splitting or stripping debug symbols from binaries has failed.

- `staticdev`: Checks for static library files (*.a) in non-staticdev packages.

- `symlink-to-sysroot`: Checks for symlinks in packages that point into TMPDIR on the host. Such symlinks will work on the host, but are clearly invalid when running on the target.

- `textrel`: Checks for ELF binaries that contain relocations in their .text sections, which can result in a performance impact at runtime.

- `unsafe-references-in-binaries`: Reports when a binary installed in ${base_libdir}, ${base_bindir}, or ${base_sbindir}, depends on another binary installed under ${exec_prefix}. This dependency is a concern if you want the system to remain basically operable if /usr is mounted separately and is not mounted.

Note

Defaults for binaries installed in ${base_libdir}, ${base_bindir}, and ${base_sbindir} are /lib, /bin, and /sbin, respectively. The default for a binary installed under ${exec_prefix} is /usr.

- unsafe-references-in-scripts: Reports when a script file installed in ${base_libdir}, ${base_bindir}, or ${base_sbindir}, depends on files installed under ${exec_prefix}. This dependency is a concern if you want the system to remain basically operable if /usr is mounted separately and is not mounted.

  Note

  Defaults for binaries installed in ${base_libdir}, ${base_bindir}, and ${base_sbindir} are /lib, /bin, and /sbin, respectively. The default for a binary installed under ${exec_prefix} is /usr.

- useless-rpaths: Checks for dynamic library load paths (rpaths) in the binaries that by default on a standard system are searched by the linker (e.g. /lib and /usr/lib). While these paths will not cause any breakage, they do waste space and are unnecessary.

- var-undefined: Reports when variables fundamental to packaging (i.e. WORKDIR, DEPLOY_DIR, D, PN, and PKGD) are undefined during do_package.

- version-going-backwards: If Build History is enabled, reports when a package being written out has a lower version than the previously written package under the same name. If you are placing output packages into a feed and upgrading packages on a target system using that feed, the version of a package going backwards can result in the target system not correctly upgrading to the "new" version of the package.

  Note

  If you are not using runtime package management on your target system, then you do not need to worry about this situation.

- xorg-driver-abi: Checks that all packages containing Xorg drivers have ABI dependencies. The xserver-xorg recipe provides driver ABI names. All drivers should depend on the ABI versions that they have been built against. Driver recipes that include xorg-driver-input.inc or xorg-driver-video.inc will automatically get these versions. Consequently, you should only need to explicitly add dependencies to binary driver recipes.

7.60. **insserv.bbclass**

The insserv class uses the insserv utility to update the order of symbolic links in /etc/rc?.d/ within an image based on dependencies specified by LSB headers in the init.d scripts themselves.

7.61. **kernel.bbclass**

The kernel class handles building Linux kernels. The class contains code to build all kernel trees. All needed headers are staged into the STAGING_KERNEL_DIR directory to allow out-of-tree module builds using the module class.

This means that each built kernel module is packaged separately and inter-module dependencies are created by parsing the modinfo output. If all modules are required, then installing the kernel-modules package installs all packages with modules and various other kernel packages such as kernel-vmlinux.

Various other classes are used by the kernel and module classes internally including the kernel-arch, module-base, and linux-kernel-base classes.

7.62. **kernel-arch.bbclass**

The kernel-arch class sets the ARCH environment variable for Linux kernel compilation (including modules).

7.63. **kernel-module-split.bbclass**

The kernel-module-split class provides common functionality for splitting Linux kernel modules into separate packages.

7.64. **kernel-yocto.bbclass**

The kernel-yocto class provides common functionality for building from linux-yocto style kernel source repositories.

7.65. **lib_package.bbclass**

The lib_package class supports recipes that build libraries and produce executable binaries, where those binaries should not be installed by default along with the library. Instead, the binaries are added to a separate ${PN}-bin package to make their installation optional.

7.66. **license.bbclass**

The license class provides license manifest creation and license exclusion. This class is enabled by default using the default value for the INHERIT_DISTRO variable.

7.67. **linux-kernel-base.bbclass**

The linux-kernel-base class provides common functionality for recipes that build out of the Linux kernel source tree. These builds goes beyond the kernel itself. For example, the Perf recipe also inherits this class.

7.68. **logging.bbclass**

The logging class provides the standard shell functions used to log messages for various BitBake severity levels (i.e. bbplain, bbnote, bbwarn, bberror, bbfatal, and bbdebug).

This class is enabled by default since it is inherited by the base class.

7.69. **meta.bbclass**

The meta class is inherited by recipes that do not build any output packages themselves, but act as a "meta" target for building other recipes.

7.70. **metadata_scm.bbclass**

The metadata_scm class provides functionality for querying the branch and revision of a Source Code Manager (SCM) repository.

The base class uses this class to print the revisions of each layer before starting every build. The metadata_scm class is enabled by default because it is inherited by the base class.

7.71. **mime.bbclass**

The mime class generates the proper post-install and post-remove (postinst/postrm) scriptlets for packages that install MIME type files. These scriptlets call update-mime-database to add the MIME types to the shared database.

7.72. **mirrors.bbclass**

The mirrors class sets up some standard MIRRORS entries for source code mirrors. These mirrors provide a fall-back path in case the upstream source specified in SRC_URI within recipes is unavailable.

This class is enabled by default since it is inherited by the base class.

7.73. `module.bbclass`

The `module` class provides support for building out-of-tree Linux kernel modules. The class inherits the `module-base` and `kernel-module-split` classes, and implements the `do_compile` and `do_install` tasks. The class provides everything needed to build and package a kernel module.

For general information on out-of-tree Linux kernel modules, see the "Incorporating Out-of-Tree Modules [http://www.yoctoproject.org/docs/1.7.2/kernel-manual/kernel-manual.html#incorporating-out-of-tree-modules]" section in the Yocto Project Linux Kernel Development Manual.

7.74. `module-base.bbclass`

The `module-base` class provides the base functionality for building Linux kernel modules. Typically, a recipe that builds software that includes one or more kernel modules and has its own means of building the module inherits this class as opposed to inheriting the `module` class.

7.75. `multilib*.bbclass`

The `multilib*` classes provide support for building libraries with different target optimizations or target architectures and installing them side-by-side in the same image.

For more information on using the Multilib feature, see the "Combining Multiple Versions of Library Files into One Image [http://www.yoctoproject.org/docs/1.7.2/dev-manual/dev-manual.html#combining-multiple-versions-library-files-into-one-image]" section in the Yocto Project Development Manual.

7.76. `native.bbclass`

The `native` class provides common functionality for recipes that wish to build tools to run on the build host (i.e. tools that use the compiler or other tools from the build host).

You can create a recipe that builds tools that run natively on the host a couple different ways:

- Create a `myrecipe-native.bb` that inherits the `native` class. If you use this method, you must order the inherit statement in the recipe after all other inherit statements so that the `native` class is inherited last.

- Create or modify a target recipe that contains the following:

      BBCLASSEXTEND = "native"

  Inside the recipe, use `_class-native` and `_class-target` overrides to specify any functionality specific to the respective native or target case.

Although applied differently, the `native` class is used with both methods. The advantage of the second method is that you do not need to have two separate recipes (assuming you need both) for native and target. All common parts of the recipe are automatically shared.

7.77. `nativesdk.bbclass`

The `nativesdk` class provides common functionality for recipes that wish to build tools to run as part of an SDK (i.e. tools that run on `SDKMACHINE`).

You can create a recipe that builds tools that run on the SDK machine a couple different ways:

- Create a `myrecipe-nativesdk.bb` recipe that inherits the `nativesdk` class. If you use this method, you must order the inherit statement in the recipe after all other inherit statements so that the `nativesdk` class is inherited last.

- Create a `nativesdk` variant of any recipe by adding the following:

```
BBCLASSEXTEND = "nativesdk"
```

Inside the recipe, use `_class-nativesdk` and `_class-target` overrides to specify any functionality specific to the respective SDK machine or target case.

Although applied differently, the `nativesdk` class is used with both methods. The advantage of the second method is that you do not need to have two separate recipes (assuming you need both) for the SDK machine and the target. All common parts of the recipe are automatically shared.

7.78. `oelint.bbclass`

The `oelint` class is an obsolete lint checking tool that exists in `meta/classes` in the Source Directory [http://www.yoctoproject.org/docs/1.7.2/dev-manual/dev-manual.html#source-directory].

A number of classes exist that are could be generally useful in OE-Core but are never actually used within OE-Core itself. The `oelint` class is one such example. However, being aware of this class can reduce the proliferation of different versions of similar classes across multiple layers.

7.79. `own-mirrors.bbclass`

The `own-mirrors` class makes it easier to set up your own PREMIRRORS from which to first fetch source before attempting to fetch it from the upstream specified in SRC_URI within each recipe.

To use this class, inherit it globally and specify SOURCE_MIRROR_URL. Here is an example:

```
INHERIT += "own-mirrors"
SOURCE_MIRROR_URL = "http://example.com/my-source-mirror"
```

You can specify only a single URL in SOURCE_MIRROR_URL.

7.80. `package.bbclass`

The package class supports generating packages from a build's output. The core generic functionality is in `package.bbclass`. The code specific to particular package types resides in these package-specific classes: `package_deb`, `package_rpm`, `package_ipk`, and `package_tar`.

You can control the list of resulting package formats by using the PACKAGE_CLASSES variable defined in your `conf/local.conf` configuration file, which is located in the Build Directory [http://www.yoctoproject.org/docs/1.7.2/dev-manual/dev-manual.html#build-directory]. When defining the variable, you can specify one or more package types. Since images are generated from packages, a packaging class is needed to enable image generation. The first class listed in this variable is used for image generation.

If you take the optional step to set up a repository (package feed) on the development host that can be used by Smart, you can install packages from the feed while you are running the image on the target (i.e. runtime installation of packages). For more information, see the "Using Runtime Package Management [http://www.yoctoproject.org/docs/1.7.2/dev-manual/dev-manual.html#using-runtime-package-management]" section in the Yocto Project Development Manual.

The package-specific class you choose can affect build-time performance and has space ramifications. In general, building a package with IPK takes about thirty percent less time as compared to using RPM to build the same or similar package. This comparison takes into account a complete build of the package with all dependencies previously built. The reason for this discrepancy is because the RPM package manager creates and processes more Metadata [http://www.yoctoproject.org/docs/1.7.2/dev-manual/dev-manual.html#metadata] than the IPK package manager. Consequently, you might consider setting PACKAGE_CLASSES to "package_ipk" if you are building smaller systems.

Before making your package manager decision, however, you should consider some further things about using RPM:

- RPM starts to provide more abilities than IPK due to the fact that it processes more Metadata. For example, this information includes individual file types, file checksum generation and evaluation on install, sparse file support, conflict detection and resolution for Multilib systems, ACID style upgrade, and repackaging abilities for rollbacks.

- For smaller systems, the extra space used for the Berkeley Database and the amount of metadata when using RPM can affect your ability to perform on-device upgrades.

You can find additional information on the effects of the package class at these two Yocto Project mailing list links:

- https://lists.yoctoproject.org/pipermail/poky/2011-May/006362.html   [http://lists.yoctoproject.org/pipermail/poky/2011-May/006362.html]

- https://lists.yoctoproject.org/pipermail/poky/2011-May/006363.html   [http://lists.yoctoproject.org/pipermail/poky/2011-May/006363.html]

7.81. **package_deb.bbclass**

The package_deb class provides support for creating packages that use the .deb file format. The class ensures the packages are written out to the ${DEPLOY_DIR}/deb directory in a .deb file format.

This class inherits the package class and is enabled through the PACKAGE_CLASSES variable in the local.conf file.

7.82. **package_ipk.bbclass**

The package_ipk class provides support for creating packages that use the .ipk file format. The class ensures the packages are written out to the ${DEPLOY_DIR}/ipk directory in a .ipk file format.

This class inherits the package class and is enabled through the PACKAGE_CLASSES variable in the local.conf file.

7.83. **package_rpm.bbclass**

The package_rpm class provides support for creating packages that use the .rpm file format. The class ensures the packages are written out to the ${DEPLOY_DIR}/rpm directory in a .rpm file format.

This class inherits the package class and is enabled through the PACKAGE_CLASSES variable in the local.conf file.

7.84. **package_tar.bbclass**

The package_tar class provides support for creating packages that use the .tar file format. The class ensures the packages are written out to the ${DEPLOY_DIR}/tar directory in a .tar file format.

This class inherits the package class and is enabled through the PACKAGE_CLASSES variable in the local.conf file.

Note
You cannot specify the package_tar class first using the PACKAGE_CLASSES variable. You must use .deb, .ipk, or .rpm file formats for your image or SDK.

7.85. **packagedata.bbclass**

The packagedata class provides common functionality for reading pkgdata files found in PKGDATA_DIR. These files contain information about each output package produced by the OpenEmbedded build system.

This class is enabled by default because it is inherited by the package class.

7.86. **packagegroup.bbclass**

The packagegroup class sets default values appropriate for package group recipes (e.g. PACKAGES, PACKAGE_ARCH, ALLOW_EMPTY, and so forth). It is highly recommended that all package group recipes inherit this class.

For information on how to use this class, see the "Customizing Images Using Custom Package Groups [http://www.yoctoproject.org/docs/1.7.2/dev-manual/dev-manual.html#usingpoky-extend-customimage-customtasks]" section in the Yocto Project Development Manual.

Previously, this class was called the task class.

7.87. **packageinfo.bbclass**

The packageinfo class gives a BitBake user interface the ability to retrieve information about output packages from the pkgdata files.

This class is enabled automatically when using the Hob [http://www.yoctoproject.org/tools-resources/projects/hob] user interface.

7.88. **patch.bbclass**

The patch class provides all functionality for applying patches during the do_patch task.

This class is enabled by default because it is inherited by the base class.

7.89. **perlnative.bbclass**

When inherited by a recipe, the perlnative class supports using the native version of Perl built by the build system rather than using the version provided by the build host.

7.90. **pixbufcache.bbclass**

The pixbufcache class generates the proper post-install and post-remove (postinst/postrm) scriptlets for packages that install pixbuf loaders, which are used with gdk-pixbuf. These scriptlets call update_pixbuf_cache to add the pixbuf loaders to the cache. Since the cache files are architecture-specific, update_pixbuf_cache is run using QEMU if the postinst scriptlets need to be run on the build host during image creation.

If the pixbuf loaders being installed are in packages other than the recipe's main package, set PIXBUF_PACKAGES to specify the packages containing the loaders.

7.91. **pkgconfig.bbclass**

The pkg-config class provides a standard way to get header and library information. This class aims to smooth integration of pkg-config into libraries that use it.

During staging, BitBake installs pkg-config data into the sysroots/ directory. By making use of sysroot functionality within pkg-config, this class no longer has to manipulate the files.

7.92. **populate_sdk.bbclass**

The populate_sdk class provides support for SDK-only recipes. For information on advantages gained when building a cross-development toolchain using the do_populate_sdk task, see the "Optionally Building a Toolchain Installer [http://www.yoctoproject.org/docs/1.7.2/adt-manual/adt-manual.html#optionally-building-a-toolchain-installer]" section in the Yocto Project Application Developer's Guide.

7.93. **populate_sdk_*.bbclass**

The populate_sdk_* classes support SDK creation and consist of the following classes:

- populate_sdk_base: The base class supporting SDK creation under all package managers (i.e. DEB, RPM, and opkg).

- populate_sdk_deb: Supports creation of the SDK given the Debian package manager.

- populate_sdk_rpm: Supports creation of the SDK given the RPM package manager.

- populate_sdk_ipk: Supports creation of the SDK given the opkg (IPK format) package manager.

The populate_sdk_base class inherits the appropriate populate_sdk_* (i.e. deb, rpm, and ipk) based on IMAGE_PKGTYPE.

The base class ensures all source and destination directories are established and then populates the SDK. After populating the SDK, the populate_sdk_base class constructs two sysroots: ${SDK_ARCH}-nativesdk, which contains the cross-compiler and associated tooling, and the target, which contains a target root filesystem that is configured for the SDK usage. These two images reside in SDK_OUTPUT, which consists of the following:

```
${SDK_OUTPUT}/${SDK_ARCH}-nativesdk-pkgs
${SDK_OUTPUT}/${SDKTARGETSYSROOT}/target-pkgs
```

Finally, the base populate SDK class creates the toolchain environment setup script, the tarball of the SDK, and the installer.

The respective populate_sdk_deb, populate_sdk_rpm, and populate_sdk_ipk classes each support the specific type of SDK. These classes are inherited by and used with the populate_sdk_base class.

For more information on the cross-development toolchain generation, see the "Cross-Development Toolchain Generation" section. For information on advantages gained when building a cross-development toolchain using the do_populate_sdk task, see the "Optionally Building a Toolchain Installer [http://www.yoctoproject.org/docs/1.7.2/adt-manual/adt-manual.html#optionally-building-a-toolchain-installer]" section in the Yocto Project Application Developer's Guide.

7.94. **prexport.bbclass**

The prexport class provides functionality for exporting PR values.

Note

This class is not intended to be used directly. Rather, it is enabled when using "bitbake-prserv-tool export".

7.95. **primport.bbclass**

The primport class provides functionality for importing PR values.

Note

This class is not intended to be used directly. Rather, it is enabled when using "bitbake-prserv-tool import".

7.96. **prserv.bbclass**

The prserv class provides functionality for using a PR service [http://www.yoctoproject.org/docs/1.7.2/dev-manual/dev-manual.html#working-with-a-pr-service] in order to automatically manage the incrementing of the PR variable for each recipe.

This class is enabled by default because it is inherited by the package class. However, the OpenEmbedded build system will not enable the functionality of this class unless PRSERV_HOST has been set.

7.97. **ptest.bbclass**

The ptest class provides functionality for packaging and installing runtime tests for recipes that build software that provides these tests.

This class is intended to be inherited by individual recipes. However, the class' functionality is largely disabled unless "ptest" appears in DISTRO_FEATURES. See the "Testing Packages With ptest [http://www.yoctoproject.org/docs/1.7.2/dev-manual/dev-manual.html#testing-packages-with-ptest]" section in the Yocto Project Development Manual for more information on ptest.

7.98. ptest-gnome.bbclass

Enables package tests (ptests) specifically for GNOME packages, which have tests intended to be executed with gnome-desktop-testing.

For information on setting up and running ptests, see the "Testing Packages With ptest [http://www.yoctoproject.org/docs/1.7.2/dev-manual/dev-manual.html#testing-packages-with-ptest]" section in the Yocto Project Development Manual.

7.99. python-dir.bbclass

The python-dir class provides the base version, location, and site package location for Python.

7.100. pythonnative.bbclass

When inherited by a recipe, the pythonnative class supports using the native version of Python built by the build system rather than using the version provided by the build host.

7.101. qemu.bbclass

The qemu class provides functionality for recipes that either need QEMU or test for the existence of QEMU. Typically, this class is used to run programs for a target system on the build host using QEMU's application emulation mode.

7.102. qmake*.bbclass

The qmake* classes support recipes that need to build software that uses Qt's qmake build system and are comprised of the following:

• qmake_base: Provides base functionality for all versions of qmake.

• qmake2: Extends base functionality for qmake 2.x as used by Qt 4.x.

If you need to set any configuration variables or pass any options to qmake, you can add these to the EXTRA_QMAKEVARS_PRE or EXTRA_QMAKEVARS_POST variables, depending on whether the arguments need to be before or after the .pro file list on the command line, respectively.

By default, all .pro files are built. If you want to specify your own subset of .pro files to be built, specify them in the QMAKE_PROFILES variable.

7.103. qt4*.bbclass

The qt4* classes support recipes that need to build software that uses the Qt development framework version 4.x and consist of the following:

• qt4e: Supports building against Qt/Embedded, which uses the framebuffer for graphical output.

• qt4x11: Supports building against Qt/X11.

The classes inherit the qmake2 class.

7.104. relocatable.bbclass

The relocatable class enables relocation of binaries when they are installed into the sysroot.

This class makes use of the chrpath class and is used by both the cross and native classes.

7.105. **report-error.bbclass**

The report-error class supports enabling the error reporting tool [http://www.yoctoproject.org/docs/1.7.2/dev-manual/dev-manual.html#using-the-error-reporting-tool], which allows you to submit build error information to a central database.

The class collects debug information for recipe, recipe version, task, machine, distro, build system, target system, host distro, branch, commit, and log. From the information, report files using a JSON format are created and stored in ${LOG_DIR}/error-report.

7.106. **rm_work.bbclass**

The rm_work class supports deletion of temporary workspace, which can ease your hard drive demands during builds.

The OpenEmbedded build system can use a substantial amount of disk space during the build process. A portion of this space is the work files under the ${TMPDIR}/work directory for each recipe. Once the build system generates the packages for a recipe, the work files for that recipe are no longer needed. However, by default, the build system preserves these files for inspection and possible debugging purposes. If you would rather have these files deleted to save disk space as the build progresses, you can enable rm_work by adding the following to your local.conf file, which is found in the Build Directory [http://www.yoctoproject.org/docs/1.7.2/dev-manual/dev-manual.html#build-directory].

```
INHERIT += "rm_work"
```

If you are modifying and building source code out of the work directory for a recipe, enabling rm_work will potentially result in your changes to the source being lost. To exclude some recipes from having their work directories deleted by rm_work, you can add the names of the recipe or recipes you are working on to the RM_WORK_EXCLUDE variable, which can also be set in your local.conf file. Here is an example:

```
RM_WORK_EXCLUDE += "busybox glibc"
```

7.107. **rootfs*.bbclass**

The rootfs* classes support creating the root filesystem for an image and consist of the following classes:

- The rootfs_deb class, which supports creation of root filesystems for images built using .deb packages.

- The rootfs_rpm class, which supports creation of root filesystems for images built using .rpm packages.

- The rootfs_ipk class, which supports creation of root filesystems for images built using .ipk packages.

The root filesystem is created from packages using one of the rootfs*.bbclass files as determined by the PACKAGE_CLASSES variable.

For information on how root filesystem images are created, see the "Image Generation" section.

7.108. **sanity.bbclass**

The sanity class checks to see if prerequisite software is present on the host system so that users can be notified of potential problems that might affect their build. The class also performs basic user configuration checks from the local.conf configuration file to prevent common mistakes that cause build failures. Distribution policy usually determines whether to include this class.

7.109. **scons.bbclass**

The scons class supports recipes that need to build software that uses the SCons build system. You can use the EXTRA_OESCONS variable to specify additional configuration options you want to pass SCons command line.

7.110. **sdl.bbclass**

The sdl class supports recipes that need to build software that uses the Simple DirectMedia Layer (SDL) library.

7.111. **setuptools.bbclass**

The setuptools class supports Python version 2.x extensions that use build systems based on setuptools. If your recipe uses these build systems, the recipe needs to inherit the setuptools class.

7.112. **setuptools3.bbclass**

The setuptools3 class supports Python version 3.x extensions that use build systems based on setuptools3. If your recipe uses these build systems, the recipe needs to inherit the setuptools3 class.

7.113. **sip.bbclass**

The sip class supports recipes that build or package SIP-based Python bindings.

7.114. **siteconfig.bbclass**

The siteconfig class provides functionality for handling site configuration. The class is used by the autotools class to accelerate the do_configure task.

7.115. **siteinfo.bbclass**

The siteinfo class provides information about the targets that might be needed by other classes or recipes.

As an example, consider Autotools, which can require tests that must execute on the target hardware. Since this is not possible in general when cross compiling, site information is used to provide cached test results so these tests can be skipped over but still make the correct values available. The meta/site directory contains test results sorted into different categories such as architecture, endianness, and the libc used. Site information provides a list of files containing data relevant to the current build in the CONFIG_SITE variable that Autotools automatically picks up.

The class also provides variables like SITEINFO_ENDIANNESS and SITEINFO_BITS that can be used elsewhere in the metadata.

Because the base class includes the siteinfo class, it is always active.

7.116. **spdx.bbclass**

The spdx class integrates real-time license scanning, generation of SPDX standard output, and verification of license information during the build.

Note
This class is currently at the prototype stage in the 1.6 release.

7.117. **sstate.bbclass**

The sstate class provides support for Shared State (sstate). By default, the class is enabled through the INHERIT_DISTRO variable's default value.

For more information on sstate, see the "Shared State Cache" section.

7.118. **staging.bbclass**

The staging class provides support for staging files into the sysroot during the do_populate_sysroot task. The class is enabled by default because it is inherited by the base class.

7.119. **syslinux.bbclass**

The syslinux class provides syslinux-specific functions for building bootable images.

The class supports the following variables:

- INITRD: Indicates list of filesystem images to concatenate and use as an initial RAM disk (initrd). This variable is optional.

- ROOTFS: Indicates a filesystem image to include as the root filesystem. This variable is optional.

- AUTO_SYSLINUXMENU: Enables creating an automatic menu when set to "1".

- LABELS: Lists targets for automatic configuration.

- APPEND: Lists append string overrides for each label.

- SYSLINUX_OPTS: Lists additional options to add to the syslinux file. Semicolon characters separate multiple options.

- SYSLINUX_SPLASH: Lists a background for the VGA boot menu when you are using the boot menu.

- SYSLINUX_DEFAULT_CONSOLE: Set to "console=ttyX" to change kernel boot default console.

- SYSLINUX_SERIAL: Sets an alternate serial port. Or, turns off serial when the variable is set with an empty string.

- SYSLINUX_SERIAL_TTY: Sets an alternate "console=tty..." kernel boot argument.

7.120. **systemd.bbclass**

The systemd class provides support for recipes that install systemd unit files.

The functionality for this class is disabled unless you have "systemd" in DISTRO_FEATURES.

Under this class, the recipe or Makefile (i.e. whatever the recipe is calling during the do_install task) installs unit files into ${D}${systemd_unitdir}/system. If the unit files being installed go into packages other than the main package, you need to set SYSTEMD_PACKAGES in your recipe to identify the packages in which the files will be installed.

You should set SYSTEMD_SERVICE to the name of the service file. You should also use a package name override to indicate the package to which the value applies. If the value applies to the recipe's main package, use ${PN}. Here is an example from the connman recipe:

```
SYSTEMD_SERVICE_${PN} = "connman.service"
```

Services are set up to start on boot automatically unless you have set SYSTEMD_AUTO_ENABLE to "disable".

For more information on systemd, see the "Selecting an Initialization Manager [http://www.yoctoproject.org/docs/1.7.2/dev-manual/dev-manual.html#selecting-an-initialization-manager]" section in the Yocto Project Development Manual.

7.121. `terminal.bbclass`

The `terminal` class provides support for starting a terminal session. The `OE_TERMINAL` variable controls which terminal emulator is used for the session.

Other classes use the `terminal` class anywhere a separate terminal session needs to be started. For example, the `patch` class assuming `PATCHRESOLVE` is set to "user", the `cml1` class, and the `devshell` class all use the `terminal` class.

7.122. `testimage.bbclass`

The `testimage` class supports running automated tests against images using QEMU and on actual hardware. The class handles loading the tests and starting the image.

To use the class, you need to perform steps to set up the environment. The tests are commands that run on the target system over `ssh`. they are written in Python and make use of the `unittest` module.

For information on how to enable, run, and create new tests, see the "Performing Automated Runtime Testing [http://www.yoctoproject.org/docs/1.7.2/dev-manual/dev-manual.html#performing-automated-runtime-testing]" section.

7.123. `texinfo.bbclass`

This class should be inherited by recipes whose upstream packages invoke the texinfo utilities at build-time. Native and cross recipes are made to use the dummy scripts provided by `texinfo-dummy-native`, for improved performance. Target architecture recipes use the genuine Texinfo utilities. By default, they use the Texinfo utilities on the host system.

Note
If you want to use the Texinfo recipe shipped with the build system, you can remove "texinfo-native" from `ASSUME_PROVIDED` and makeinfo from `SANITY_REQUIRED_UTILITIES`.

7.124. `tinderclient.bbclass`

The `tinderclient` class submits build results to an external Tinderbox instance.

Note
This class is currently unmaintained.

7.125. `toaster.bbclass`

The `toaster` class collects information about packages and images and sends them as events that the BitBake user interface can receive. The class is enabled when the Toaster user interface is running.

This class is not intended to be used directly.

7.126. `toolchain-scripts.bbclass`

The `toolchain-scripts` class provides the scripts used for setting up the environment for installed SDKs.

7.127. `typecheck.bbclass`

The `typecheck` class provides support for validating the values of variables set at the configuration level against their defined types. The OpenEmbedded build system allows you to define the type of a variable using the "type" varflag. Here is an example:

```
IMAGE_FEATURES[type] = "list"
```

7.128. **uboot-config.bbclass**

The uboot-config class provides support for U-Boot configuration for a machine. Specify the machine in your recipe as follows:

```
UBOOT_CONFIG ??= <default>
UBOOT_CONFIG[foo] = "config,images"
```

You can also specify the machine using this method:

```
UBOOT_MACHINE = "config"
```

See the UBOOT_CONFIG and UBOOT_MACHINE variables for additional information.

7.129. **uninative.bbclass**

Provides a means of reusing native/cross over multiple distros.

Note
Currently, the method used by the uninative class is experimental.
For more information, see the commit message here [http://cgit.openembedded.org/openembedded-core/commit/?id=e66c96ae9c7ba21ebd04a4807390f0031238a85a].

7.130. **update-alternatives.bbclass**

The update-alternatives class helps the alternatives system when multiple sources provide the same command. This situation occurs when several programs that have the same or similar function are installed with the same name. For example, the ar command is available from the busybox, binutils and elfutils packages. The update-alternatives class handles renaming the binaries so that multiple packages can be installed without conflicts. The ar command still works regardless of which packages are installed or subsequently removed. The class renames the conflicting binary in each package and symlinks the highest priority binary during installation or removal of packages.

To use this class, you need to define a number of variables:

• ALTERNATIVE

• ALTERNATIVE_LINK_NAME

• ALTERNATIVE_TARGET

• ALTERNATIVE_PRIORITY

These variables list alternative commands needed by a package, provide pathnames for links, default links for targets, and so forth. For details on how to use this class, see the comments in the update-alternatives.bbclass [http://git.yoctoproject.org/cgit/cgit.cgi/poky/tree/meta/classes/update-alternatives.bbclass].

Note
You can use the update-alternatives command directly in your recipes. However, this class simplifies things in most cases.

7.131. **update-rc.d.bbclass**

The update-rc.d class uses update-rc.d to safely install an initialization script on behalf of the package. The OpenEmbedded build system takes care of details such as making sure the script is stopped before a package is removed and started when the package is installed.

Three variables control this class: INITSCRIPT_PACKAGES, INITSCRIPT_NAME and INITSCRIPT_PARAMS. See the variable links for details.

7.132. **useradd.bbclass**

The useradd class supports the addition of users or groups for usage by the package on the target. For example, if you have packages that contain system services that should be run under their own user or group, you can use this class to enable creation of the user or group. The meta-skeleton/recipes-skeleton/useradd/useradd-example.bb recipe in the Source Directory [http://www.yoctoproject.org/docs/1.7.2/dev-manual/dev-manual.html#source-directory] provides a simple example that shows how to add three users and groups to two packages. See the useradd-example.bb recipe for more information on how to use this class.

The useradd class supports the USERADD_PACKAGES, USERADD_PARAM, GROUPADD_PARAM, and GROUPMEMS_PARAM variables.

7.133. **useradd-staticids.bbclass**

The useradd-staticids class supports the addition of users or groups that have static user identification (uid) and group identification (gid) values.

The default behavior of the OpenEmbedded build system for assigning uid and gid values when packages add users and groups during package install time is to add them dynamically. This works fine for programs that do not care what the values of the resulting users and groups become. In these cases, the order of the installation determines the final uid and gid values. However, if non-deterministic uid and gid values are a problem, you can override the default, dynamic application of these values by setting static values. When you set static values, the OpenEmbedded build system looks in BBPATH for files/passwd and files/group files for the values.

To use static uid and gid values, you need to set some variables. See the USERADDEXTENSION, USERADD_UID_TABLES, USERADD_GID_TABLES, and USERADD_ERROR_DYNAMIC variables. You can also see the useradd class for additional information.

Notes

You do not use this class directly. You either enable or disable the class by setting the USERADDEXTENSION variable. If you enable or disable the class in a configured system, TMPDIR might contain incorrect uid and gid values. Deleting the TMPDIR directory will correct this condition.

7.134. **utility-tasks.bbclass**

The utility-tasks class provides support for various "utility" type tasks that are applicable to all recipes, such as do_clean and do_listtasks.

This class is enabled by default because it is inherited by the base class.

7.135. **utils.bbclass**

The utils class provides some useful Python functions that are typically used in inline Python expressions (e.g. ${@...}). One example use is for bb.utils.contains().

This class is enabled by default because it is inherited by the base class.

7.136. **vala.bbclass**

The vala class supports recipes that need to build software written using the Vala programming language.

7.137. **waf.bbclass**

The waf class supports recipes that need to build software that uses the Waf build system. You can use the EXTRA_OECONF variable to specify additional configuration options to be passed on the Waf command line.

Chapter 8. Tasks

Tasks are units of execution for BitBake. Recipes (.bb files) use tasks to complete configuring, compiling, and packaging software. This chapter provides a reference of the tasks defined in the OpenEmbedded build system.

8.1. Normal Recipe Build Tasks

The following sections describe normal tasks associated with building a recipe.

8.1.1. **do_build**

The default task for all recipes. This task depends on all other normal tasks required to build a recipe.

8.1.2. **do_compile**

Compiles the source in the compilation directory, which is pointed to by the B variable.

8.1.3. **do_compile_ptest_base**

Compiles the runtime test suite included in the software being built.

8.1.4. **do_configure**

Configures the source by enabling and disabling any build-time and configuration options for the software being built.

8.1.5. **do_configure_ptest_base**

Configures the runtime test suite included in the software being built.

8.1.6. **do_deploy**

Writes output files that are to be deployed to the deploy directory, which is defined by the DEPLOYDIR variable.

The do_deploy task is a shared state (sstate) task, which means that the task can be accelerated through sstate use. Realize also that if the task is re-executed, any previous output is removed (i.e. "cleaned").

8.1.7. **do_fetch**

Fetches the source code. This task uses the SRC_URI variable and the argument's prefix to determine the correct fetcher module.

8.1.8. **do_install**

Copies files from the compilation directory, which is defined by the B variable, to a holding area defined by the D variable.

8.1.9. **do_install_ptest_base**

Copies the runtime test suite files from the compilation directory to a holding area.

8.1.10. **do_package**

Analyzes the content of the holding area and splits it into subsets based on available packages and files.

8.1.11. **do_package_qa**

Runs QA checks on packaged files. For more information on these checks, see the insane class.

8.1.12. **do_package_write_deb**

Creates the actual DEB packages and places them in the Package Feeds area.

8.1.13. **do_package_write_ipk**

Creates the actual IPK packages and places them in the Package Feeds area.

8.1.14. **do_package_write_rpm**

Creates the actual RPM packages and places them in the Package Feeds area.

8.1.15. **do_package_write_tar**

Creates tar archives for packages and places them in the Package Feeds area.

8.1.16. **do_packagedata**

Creates package metadata used by the build system to generate the final packages.

8.1.17. **do_patch**

Locates patch files and applies them to the source code. See the "Patching" section for more information.

8.1.18. **do_populate_lic**

Writes license information for the recipe that is collected later when the image is constructed.

8.1.19. **do_populate_sdk**

Creates the file and directory structure for an installable SDK. See the "SDK Generation" section for more information.

8.1.20. **do_populate_sysroot**

Copies a subset of files installed by the do_install task into the sysroot in order to make them available to other recipes.

The do_populate_sysroot task is a shared state (sstate) task, which means that the task can be accelerated through sstate use. Realize also that if the task is re-executed, any previous output is removed (i.e. "cleaned").

8.1.21. **do_rm_work**

Removes work files after the OpenEmbedded build system has finished with them. You can learn more by looking at the "rm_work.bbclass" section.

8.1.22. **do_rm_work_all**

Top-level task for removing work files after the build system has finished with them.

8.1.23. **do_unpack**

Unpacks the source code into a working directory pointed to by ${WORKDIR}. The S variable also plays a role in where unpacked source files ultimately reside. For more information on how source files are unpacked, see the "Source Fetching" section and the WORKDIR and S variable descriptions.

8.2. Manually Called Tasks

These tasks are typically manually triggered (e.g. by using the `bitbake -c` command-line option):

8.2.1. **do_checkuri**

Validates the SRC_URI value.

8.2.2. **do_checkuriall**

Validates the SRC_URI value for all recipes required to build a target.

8.2.3. **do_clean**

Removes all output files for a target from the do_unpack task forward (i.e. do_unpack, do_configure, do_compile, do_install, and do_package).

You can run this task using BitBake as follows:

```
$ bitbake -c clean recipe
```

Running this task does not remove the sstate) cache files. Consequently, if no changes have been made and the recipe is rebuilt after cleaning, output files are simply restored from the sstate cache. If you want to remove the sstate cache files for the recipe, you need to use the do_cleansstate task instead (i.e. bitbake -c cleansstate recipe).

8.2.4. **do_cleanall**

Removes all output files, shared state (sstate) cache, and downloaded source files for a target (i.e. the contents of DL_DIR). Essentially, the do_cleanall task is identical to the do_cleansstate task with the added removal of downloaded source files.

You can run this task using BitBake as follows:

```
$ bitbake -c cleanall recipe
```

Typically, you would not normally use the cleanall task. Do so only if you want to start fresh with the do_fetch task.

8.2.5. **do_cleansstate**

Removes all output files and shared state (sstate) cache for a target. Essentially, the do_cleansstate task is identical to the do_clean task with the added removal of shared state (sstate) cache.

You can run this task using BitBake as follows:

```
$ bitbake -c cleansstate recipe
```

When you run the do_cleansstate task, the OpenEmbedded build system no longer uses any sstate. Consequently, building the recipe from scratch is guaranteed.

Note
The do_cleansstate task cannot remove sstate from a remote sstate mirror. If you need to build a target from scratch using remote mirrors, use the "-f" option as follows:

```
$ bitbake -f -c do_cleansstate target
```

8.2.6. **do_devshell**

Starts a shell whose environment is set up for development, debugging, or both. See the "Using a Development Shell [http://www.yoctoproject.org/docs/1.7.2/dev-manual/dev-manual.html#platdev-appdev-devshell]" section in the Yocto Project Development Manual for more information about using devshell.

8.2.7. **do_fetchall**

Fetches all remote sources required to build a target.

8.2.8. **do_listtasks**

Lists all defined tasks for a target.

8.2.9. **do_package_index**

Creates or updates the index in the Package Feeds area.

> ### Note
> This task is not triggered with the bitbake -c command-line option as are the other tasks in this section. Because this task is specifically for the package-index recipe, you run it using bitbake package-index.

8.3. Image-Related Tasks

The following tasks are applicable to image recipes.

8.3.1. **do_bootimg**

Creates a bootable live image. See the IMAGE_FSTYPES variable for additional information on live image types.

8.3.2. **do_bundle_initramfs**

Combines an initial RAM disk (initramfs) image and kernel together to form a single image. The CONFIG_INITRAMFS_SOURCE variable has some more information about these types of images.

8.3.3. **do_rootfs**

Creates the root filesystem (file and directory structure) for an image. See the "Image Generation" section for more information on how the root filesystem is created.

8.3.4. **do_testimage**

Boots an image and performs runtime tests within the image. For information on automatically testing images, see the "Performing Automated Runtime Testing [http://www.yoctoproject.org/docs/1.7.2/dev-manual/dev-manual.html#performing-automated-runtime-testing]" section in the Yocto Project Development Manual.

8.3.5. **do_testimage_auto**

Boots an image and performs runtime tests within the image immediately after it has been built. This task is enabled when you set TEST_IMAGE equal to "1".

For information on automatically testing images, see the "Performing Automated Runtime Testing [http://www.yoctoproject.org/docs/1.7.2/dev-manual/dev-manual.html#performing-automated-runtime-testing]" section in the Yocto Project Development Manual.

8.3.6. **do_vmdkimg**

Creates a .vmdk image for use with VMware [http://www.vmware.com/] and compatible virtual machine hosts.

8.4. Kernel-Related Tasks

The following tasks are applicable to kernel recipes. Some of these tasks (e.g. the do_menuconfig task) are also applicable to recipes that use Linux kernel style configuration such as the BusyBox recipe.

8.4.1. **do_compile_kernelmodules**

Compiles loadable modules for the Linux kernel.

8.4.2. **do_diffconfig**

Compares the old and new config files after running the do_menuconfig task for the kernel.

8.4.3. **do_kernel_checkout**

Checks out source/meta branches for a linux-yocto style kernel.

8.4.4. **do_kernel_configcheck**

Validates the kernel configuration for a linux-yocto style kernel.

8.4.5. **do_kernel_configme**

Assembles the kernel configuration for a linux-yocto style kernel.

8.4.6. **do_kernel_link_vmlinux**

Creates a symbolic link in arch/$arch/boot for vmlinux kernel images.

8.4.7. **do_menuconfig**

Runs make menuconfig for the kernel. For information on menuconfig, see the "Using menuconfig [http://www.yoctoproject.org/docs/1.7.2/dev-manual/dev-manual.html#using-menuconfig]" section in the Yocto Project Development Manual.

8.4.8. **do_savedefconfig**

Creates a minimal Linux kernel configuration file.

8.4.9. **do_sizecheck**

Checks the size of the kernel image against KERNEL_IMAGE_MAXSIZE when set.

8.4.10. **do_strip**

Strips unneeded sections out of the Linux kernel image.

8.4.11. **do_uboot_mkimage**

Creates a uImage file from the kernel for the U-Boot bootloader.

8.4.12. **do_validate_branches**

Ensures that the source, metadata (or both) branches are on the locations specified by their SRCREV values for a linux-yocto style kernel.

8.5. Miscellaneous Tasks

The following sections describe miscellaneous tasks.

8.5.1. **do_generate_qt_config_file**

Writes a qt.conf configuration file used for building a Qt-based application.

8.5.2. **do_spdx**

A build stage that takes the source code and scans it on a remote FOSSOLOGY server in order to produce an SPDX document. This task applies only to the spdx class.

Chapter 9. QA Error and Warning Messages

9.1. Introduction

When building a recipe, the OpenEmbedded build system performs various QA checks on the output to ensure that common issues are detected and reported. Sometimes when you create a new recipe to build new software, it will build with no problems. When this is not the case, or when you have QA issues building any software, it could take a little time to resolve them.

While it is tempting to ignore a QA message or even to disable QA checks, it is best to try and resolve any reported QA issues. This chapter provides a list of the QA messages and brief explanations of the issues you could encounter so that you can properly resolve problems.

The next section provides a list of all QA error and warning messages based on a default configuration. Each entry provides the message or error form along with an explanation.

Notes

- At the end of each message, the name of the associated QA test (as listed in the "`insane.bbclass`" section) appears within square brackets.

- As mentioned, this list of error and warning messages is for QA checks only. The list does not cover all possible build errors or warnings you could encounter.

- Because some QA checks are disabled by default, this list does not include all possible QA check errors and warnings.

9.2. Errors and Warnings

- `<packagename>: <path> is using libexec please relocate to <libexecdir> [libexec]`

  The specified package contains files in /usr/libexec. By default, `libexecdir` is set to "`${libdir}/${BPN}`" rather than to "/usr/libexec". Thus, installing to /usr/libexec is likely not desirable.

- `package <packagename> contains bad RPATH <rpath> in file <file> [rpaths]`

  The specified binary produced by the recipe contains dynamic library load paths (rpaths) that contain build system paths such as TMPDIR, which are incorrect for the target and could potentially be a security issue. Check for bad -rpath options being passed to the linker in your do_compile log. Depending on the build system used by the software being built, there might be a configure option to disable rpath usage completely within the build of the software.

- `<packagename>: <file> contains probably-redundant RPATH <rpath> [useless-rpaths]`

  The specified binary produced by the recipe contains dynamic library load paths (rpaths) that on a standard system are searched by default by the linker (e.g. /lib and /usr/lib). While these paths will not cause any breakage, they do waste space and are unnecessary. Depending on the build system used by the software being built, there might be a configure option to disable rpath usage completely within the build of the software.

- `<packagename> requires <files>, but no providers in its RDEPENDS [file-rdeps]`

  A file-level dependency has been identified from the specified package on the specified files, but there is no explicit corresponding entry in RDEPENDS. If particular files are required at runtime then RDEPENDS should be declared in the recipe to ensure the packages providing them are built.

- `<packagename1> rdepends on <packagename2>`, but it isn't a build dependency? `[build-deps]`

  A runtime dependency exists between the two specified packages, but there is nothing explicit within the recipe to enable the OpenEmbedded build system to ensure that dependency is satisfied. This condition is usually triggered by an RDEPENDS value being added at the packaging stage rather than up front, which is usually automatic based on the contents of the package. In most cases, you should change the recipe to add an explicit RDEPENDS for the dependency.

- `non -dev/-dbg/-nativesdk package contains symlink .so: <packagename> path '<path>' [dev-so]`

  Symlink `.so` files are for development only, and should therefore go into the -dev package. This situation might occur if you add `*.so*` rather than `*.so.*` to a non-dev package. Change FILES (and possibly PACKAGES) such that the specified `.so` file goes into an appropriate -dev package.

- `non -staticdev package contains static .a library: <packagename> path '<path>' [staticdev]`

  Static `.a` library files should go into a -staticdev package. Change FILES (and possibly PACKAGES) such that the specified `.a` file goes into an appropriate -staticdev package.

- `<packagename>: found library in wrong location [libdir]`

  The specified file may have been installed into an incorrect (possibly hardcoded) installation path. For example, this test will catch recipes that install `/lib/bar.so` when `${base_libdir}` is "lib32". Another example is when recipes install `/usr/lib64/foo.so` when `${libdir}` is "/usr/lib". False positives occasionally exist. For these cases add "libdir" to INSANE_SKIP for the package.

- `non debug package contains .debug directory: <packagename> path <path> [debug-files]`

  The specified package contains a `.debug` directory, which should not appear in anything but the -dbg package. This situation might occur if you add a path which contains a `.debug` directory and do not explicitly add the `.debug` directory to the -dbg package. If this is the case, add the `.debug` directory explicitly to FILES_${PN}-dbg. See FILES for additional information on FILES.

- `Architecture did not match (<machine_arch> to <file_arch>) on <file> [arch]`

  By default, the OpenEmbedded build system checks the Executable and Linkable Format (ELF) type, bit size, and endianness of any binaries to ensure they match the target architecture. This test fails if any binaries do not match the type since there would be an incompatibility. The test could indicate that the wrong compiler or compiler options have been used. Sometimes software, like bootloaders, might need to bypass this check. If the file you receive the error for is firmware that is not intended to be executed within the target operating system or is intended to run on a separate processor within the device, you can add "arch" to INSANE_SKIP for the package. Another option is to check the do_compile log and verify that the compiler options being used are correct.

- `Bit size did not match (<machine_bits> to <file_bits>) <recipe> on <file> [arch]`

  By default, the OpenEmbedded build system checks the Executable and Linkable Format (ELF) type, bit size, and endianness of any binaries to ensure they match the target architecture. This test fails if any binaries do not match the type since there would be an incompatibility. The test could indicate that the wrong compiler or compiler options have been used. Sometimes software, like bootloaders, might need to bypass this check. If the file you receive the error for is firmware that is not intended to be executed within the target operating system or is intended to run on a separate processor within the device, you can add "arch" to INSANE_SKIP for the package. Another option is to check the do_compile log and verify that the compiler options being used are correct.

- Endianness did not match (<machine_endianness> to <file_endianness>) on <file> [arch]

By default, the OpenEmbedded build system checks the Executable and Linkable Format (ELF) type, bit size, and endianness of any binaries to ensure they match the target architecture. This test fails if any binaries do not match the type since there would be an incompatibility. The test could indicate that the wrong compiler or compiler options have been used. Sometimes software, like bootloaders, might need to bypass this check. If the file you receive the error for is firmware that is not intended to be executed within the target operating system or is intended to run on a separate processor within the device, you can add "arch" to INSANE_SKIP for the package. Another option is to check the do_compile log and verify that the compiler options being used are correct.

- ELF binary '<file>' has relocations in .text [textrel]

The specified ELF binary contains relocations in its .text sections. This situation can result in a performance impact at runtime.

- No GNU_HASH in the elf binary: '<file>' [ldflags]

This indicates that binaries produced when building the recipe have not been linked with the LDFLAGS options provided by the build system. Check to be sure that the LDFLAGS variable is being passed to the linker command. A common workaround for this situation is to pass in LDFLAGS using TARGET_CC_ARCH within the recipe as follows:

```
TARGET_CC_ARCH += "${LDFLAGS}"
```

- Package <packagename> contains Xorg driver (<driver>) but no xorg-abi- dependencies [xorg-driver-abi]

The specified package contains an Xorg driver, but does not have a corresponding ABI package dependency. The xserver-xorg recipe provides driver ABI names. All drivers should depend on the ABI versions that they have been built against. Driver recipes that include xorg-driver-input.inc or xorg-driver-video.inc will automatically get these versions. Consequently, you should only need to explicitly add dependencies to binary driver recipes.

- The /usr/share/info/dir file is not meant to be shipped in a particular package. [infodir]

The /usr/share/info/dir should not be packaged. Add the following line to your do_install task or to your do_install_append within the recipe as follows:

```
rm ${D}${infodir}/dir
```

- Symlink <path> in <packagename> points to TMPDIR [symlink-to-sysroot]

The specified symlink points into TMPDIR on the host. Such symlinks will work on the host. However, they are clearly invalid when running on the target. You should either correct the symlink to use a relative path or remove the symlink.

- `<file> failed sanity test (workdir) in path <path> [la]`

  The specified `.la` file contains TMPDIR paths. Any `.la` file containing these paths is incorrect since `libtool` adds the correct sysroot prefix when using the files automatically itself.

- `<file> failed sanity test (tmpdir) in path <path> [pkgconfig]`

  The specified `.pc` file contains TMPDIR/WORKDIR paths. Any `.pc` file containing these paths is incorrect since `pkg-config` itself adds the correct sysroot prefix when the files are accessed.

- `<packagename> rdepends on <debug_packagename> [debug-deps]`

  A dependency exists between the specified non-dbg package (i.e. a package whose name does not end in `-dbg`) and a package that is a dbg package. The dbg packages contain debug symbols and are brought in using several different methods:

  - Using the dbg-pkgs IMAGE_FEATURES value.

  - Using IMAGE_INSTALL.

  - As a dependency of another dbg package that was brought in using one of the above methods. The dependency might have been automatically added because the dbg package erroneously contains files that it should not contain (e.g. a non-symlink `.so` file) or it might have been added manually (e.g. by adding to RDEPENDS).

- `<packagename> rdepends on <dev_packagename> [dev-deps]`

  A dependency exists between the specified non-dev package (a package whose name does not end in `-dev`) and a package that is a dev package. The dev packages contain development headers and are usually brought in using several different methods:

  - Using the dev-pkgs IMAGE_FEATURES value.

  - Using IMAGE_INSTALL.

  - As a dependency of another dev package that was brought in using one of the above methods. The dependency might have been automatically added (because the dev package erroneously contains files that it should not have (e.g. a non-symlink `.so` file) or it might have been added manually (e.g. by adding to RDEPENDS).

- `<var>_<packagename> is invalid: <comparison> (<value>) only comparisons <, =, >, <=, and >= are allowed [dep-cmp]`

  If you are adding a versioned dependency relationship to one of the dependency variables (RDEPENDS, RRECOMMENDS, RSUGGESTS, RPROVIDES, RREPLACES, or RCONFLICTS), you must only use the named comparison operators. Change the versioned dependency values you are adding to match those listed in the message.

- `<recipename>: The compile log indicates that host include and/or library paths were used. Please check the log '<logfile>' for more information. [compile-host-path]`

  The log for the do_compile task indicates that paths on the host were searched for files, which is not appropriate when cross-compiling. Look for "is unsafe for cross-compilation" or "CROSS COMPILE Badness" in the specified log file.

- `<recipename>: The install log indicates that host include and/or library paths were used. Please check the log '<logfile>' for more information. [install-host-path]`

The log for the do_install task indicates that paths on the host were searched for files, which is not appropriate when cross-compiling. Look for "is unsafe for cross-compilation" or "CROSS COMPILE Badness" in the specified log file.

- This autoconf log indicates errors, it looked at host include and/or library paths while determining system capabilities. Rerun configure task after fixing this. The path was '<path>'

The log for the do_configure task indicates that paths on the host were searched for files, which is not appropriate when cross-compiling. Look for "is unsafe for cross-compilation" or "CROSS COMPILE Badness" in the specified log file.

- <packagename> doesn't match the [a-z0-9.+-]+ regex [pkgname]

The convention within the OpenEmbedded build system (sometimes enforced by the package manager itself) is to require that package names are all lower case and to allow a restricted set of characters. If your recipe name does not match this, or you add packages to PACKAGES that do not conform to the convention, then you will receive this error. Rename your recipe. Or, if you have added a non-conforming package name to PACKAGES, change the package name appropriately.

- <recipe>: configure was passed unrecognized options: <options> [unknown-configure-option]

The configure script is reporting that the specified options are unrecognized. This situation could be because the options were previously valid but have been removed from the configure script. Or, there was a mistake when the options were added and there is another option that should be used instead. If you are unsure, consult the upstream build documentation, the ./configure ##help output, and the upstream change log or release notes. Once you have worked out what the appropriate change is, you can update EXTRA_OECONF or the individual PACKAGECONFIG option values accordingly.

- Recipe <recipefile> has PN of "<recipename>" which is in OVERRIDES, this can result in unexpected behavior. [pn-overrides]

The specified recipe has a name (PN) value that appears in OVERRIDES. If a recipe is named such that its PN value matches something already in OVERRIDES (e.g. PN happens to be the same as MACHINE or DISTRO), it can have unexpected consequences. For example, assignments such as FILES_${PN} = "xyz" effectively turn into FILES = "xyz". Rename your recipe (or if PN is being set explicitly, change the PN value) so that the conflict does not occur. See FILES for additional information.

- <recipefile>: Variable <variable> is set as not being package specific, please fix this. [pkgvarcheck]

Certain variables (RDEPENDS, RRECOMMENDS, RSUGGESTS, RCONFLICTS, RPROVIDES, RREPLACES, FILES, pkg_preinst, pkg_postinst, pkg_prerm, pkg_postrm, and ALLOW_EMPTY) should always be set specific to a package (i.e. they should be set with a package name override such as RDEPENDS_${PN} = "value" rather than RDEPENDS = "value"). If you receive this error, correct any assignments to these variables within your recipe.

- File '<file>' from <recipename> was already stripped, this will prevent future debugging! [already-stripped]

Produced binaries have already been stripped prior to the build system extracting debug symbols. It is common for upstream software projects to default to stripping debug symbols for output binaries. In order for debugging to work on the target using -dbg packages, this stripping must be disabled.

Depending on the build system used by the software being built, disabling this stripping could be as easy as specifying an additional configure option. If not, disabling stripping might involve patching the build scripts. In the latter case, look for references to "strip" or "STRIP", or the "-s" or "-S" command-line options being specified on the linker command line (possibly through the compiler command line if preceded with "-Wl,").

Note

Disabling stripping here does not mean that the final packaged binaries will be unstripped. Once the OpenEmbedded build system splits out debug symbols to the -dbg package, it will then strip the symbols from the binaries.

- `<packagename>` is listed in `PACKAGES` multiple times, this leads to packaging errors. `[packages-list]`

  Package names must appear only once in the PACKAGES variable. You might receive this error if you are attempting to add a package to PACKAGES that is already in the variable's value.

- `FILES` variable for package `<packagename>` contains `'//'` which is invalid. Attempting to fix this but you should correct the metadata. `[files-invalid]`

  The string "//" is invalid in a Unix path. Correct all occurrences where this string appears in a FILES variable so that there is only a single "/".

- `<recipename>`: Files/directories were installed but not shipped `[installed-vs-shipped]`

  Files have been installed within the do_install task but have not been included in any package by way of the FILES variable. Files that do not appear in any package cannot be present in an image later on in the build process. You need to do one of the following:

  - Add the files to FILES for the package you want them to appear in (e.g. FILES_${PN} for the main package).

  - Delete the files at the end of the do_install task if the files are not needed in any package.

- `<oldpackage>-<oldpkgversion>` was registered as shlib provider for `<library>`, changing it to `<newpackage>-<newpkgversion>` because it was built later

  This message means that both <oldpackage> and <newpackage> provide the specified shared library. You can expect this message when a recipe has been renamed. However, if that is not the case, the message might indicate that a private version of a library is being erroneously picked up as the provider for a common library. If that is the case, you should add the library's .so file name to PRIVATE_LIBS in the recipe that provides the private version of the library.

9.3. Configuring and Disabling QA Checks

You can configure the QA checks globally so that specific check failures either raise a warning or an error message, using the WARN_QA and ERROR_QA variables, respectively. You can also disable checks within a particular recipe using INSANE_SKIP. For information on how to work with the QA checks, see the "insane.bbclass" section.

Tip

Please keep in mind that the QA checks exist in order to detect real or potential problems in the packaged output. So exercise caution when disabling these checks.

Chapter 10. Images

The OpenEmbedded build system provides several example images to satisfy different needs. When you issue the bitbake command you provide a "top-level" recipe that essentially begins the build for the type of image you want.

Note

Building an image without GNU General Public License Version 3 (GPLv3), GNU Lesser General Public License Version 3 (LGPLv3), and the GNU Affero General Public License Version 3 (AGPL-3.0) components is only supported for minimal and base images. Furthermore, if you are going to build an image using non-GPLv3 and similarly licensed components, you must make the following changes in the local.conf file before using the BitBake command to build the minimal or base image:

1. Comment out the EXTRA_IMAGE_FEATURES line
2. Set INCOMPATIBLE_LICENSE = "GPL-3.0 LGPL-3.0 AGPL-3.0"

From within the poky Git repository, you can use the following command to display the list of directories within the Source Directory [http://www.yoctoproject.org/docs/1.7.2/dev-manual/dev-manual.html#source-directory] that containe image recipe files:

```
$ ls meta*/recipes*/images/*.bb
```

Following is a list of supported recipes:

- build-appliance-image: An example virtual machine that contains all the pieces required to run builds using the build system as well as the build system itself. You can boot and run the image using either the VMware Player [http://www.vmware.com/products/player/overview.html] or VMware Workstation [http://www.vmware.com/products/workstation/overview.html]. For more information on this image, see the Build Appliance [http://www.yoctoproject.org/documentation/build-appliance] page on the Yocto Project website.

- core-image-base: A console-only image that fully supports the target device hardware.

- core-image-clutter: An image with support for the Open GL-based toolkit Clutter, which enables development of rich and animated graphical user interfaces.

- core-image-directfb: An image that uses directfb instead of X11.

- core-image-full-cmdline: A console-only image with more full-featured Linux system functionality installed.

- core-image-lsb: An image that conforms to the Linux Standard Base (LSB) specification. This image requires a distribution configuration that enables LSB compliance (e.g. poky-lsb). If you build core-image-lsb without that configuration, the image will not be LSB-compliant.

- core-image-lsb-dev: A core-image-lsb image that is suitable for development work using the host. The image includes headers and libraries you can use in a host development environment. This image requires a distribution configuration that enables LSB compliance (e.g. poky-lsb). If you build core-image-lsb-dev without that configuration, the image will not be LSB-compliant.

- core-image-lsb-sdk: A core-image-lsb that includes everything in meta-toolchain but also includes development headers and libraries to form a complete standalone SDK. This image requires a distribution configuration that enables LSB compliance (e.g. poky-lsb). If you build core-image-lsb-sdk without that configuration, the image will not be LSB-compliant. This image is suitable for development using the target.

- core-image-minimal: A small image just capable of allowing a device to boot.

- core-image-minimal-dev: A core-image-minimal image suitable for development work using the host. The image includes headers and libraries you can use in a host development environment.

- `core-image-minimal-initramfs`: A `core-image-minimal` image that has the Minimal RAM-based Initial Root Filesystem (initramfs) as part of the kernel, which allows the system to find the first "init" program more efficiently. See the `PACKAGE_INSTALL` variable for additional information helpful when working with initramfs images.

- `core-image-minimal-mtdutils`: A `core-image-minimal` image that has support for the Minimal MTD Utilities, which let the user interact with the MTD subsystem in the kernel to perform operations on flash devices.

- `core-image-rt`: A `core-image-minimal` image plus a real-time test suite and tools appropriate for real-time use.

- `core-image-rt-sdk`: A `core-image-rt` image that includes everything in `meta-toolchain`. The image also includes development headers and libraries to form a complete stand-alone SDK and is suitable for development using the target.

- `core-image-sato`: An image with Sato support, a mobile environment and visual style that works well with mobile devices. The image supports X11 with a Sato theme and applications such as a terminal, editor, file manager, media player, and so forth.

- `core-image-sato-dev`: A `core-image-sato` image suitable for development using the host. The image includes libraries needed to build applications on the device itself, testing and profiling tools, and debug symbols. This image was formerly `core-image-sdk`.

- `core-image-sato-sdk`: A `core-image-sato` image that includes everything in meta-toolchain. The image also includes development headers and libraries to form a complete standalone SDK and is suitable for development using the target.

- `core-image-testmaster`: A "master" image designed to be used for automated runtime testing. Provides a "known good" image that is deployed to a separate partition so that you can boot into it and use it to deploy a second image to be tested. You can find more information about runtime testing in the "Performing Automated Runtime Testing [http://www.yoctoproject.org/docs/1.7.2/dev-manual/dev-manual.html#performing-automated-runtime-testing]" section in the Yocto Project Development Manual.

- `core-image-testmaster-initramfs`: A RAM-based Initial Root Filesystem (initramfs) image tailored for use with the `core-image-testmaster` image.

- `core-image-weston`: A very basic Wayland image with a terminal. This image provides the Wayland protocol libraries and the reference Weston compositor. For more information, see the "Wayland" section.

- `core-image-x11`: A very basic X11 image with a terminal.

- `qt4e-demo-image`: An image that launches into the demo application for the embedded (not based on X11) version of Qt.

Chapter 11. Features

This chapter provides a reference of shipped machine and distro features you can include as part of your image, a reference on image features you can select, and a reference on feature backfilling.

Features provide a mechanism for working out which packages should be included in the generated images. Distributions can select which features they want to support through the DISTRO_FEATURES variable, which is set or appended to in a distribution's configuration file such as poky.conf, poky-tiny.conf, poky-lsb.conf and so forth. Machine features are set in the MACHINE_FEATURES variable, which is set in the machine configuration file and specifies the hardware features for a given machine.

These two variables combine to work out which kernel modules, utilities, and other packages to include. A given distribution can support a selected subset of features so some machine features might not be included if the distribution itself does not support them.

One method you can use to determine which recipes are checking to see if a particular feature is contained or not is to grep through the Metadata [http://www.yoctoproject.org/docs/1.7.2/dev-manual/dev-manual.html#metadata] for the feature. Here is an example that discovers the recipes whose build is potentially changed based on a given feature:

```
$ cd poky
$ git grep 'contains.*MACHINE_FEATURES.*feature'
```

11.1. Machine Features

The items below are features you can use with MACHINE_FEATURES. Features do not have a one-to-one correspondence to packages, and they can go beyond simply controlling the installation of a package or packages. Sometimes a feature can influence how certain recipes are built. For example, a feature might determine whether a particular configure option is specified within the do_configure task for a particular recipe.

This feature list only represents features as shipped with the Yocto Project metadata:

- acpi: Hardware has ACPI (x86/x86_64 only)

- alsa: Hardware has ALSA audio drivers

- apm: Hardware uses APM (or APM emulation)

- bluetooth: Hardware has integrated BT

- efi: Support for booting through EFI

- ext2: Hardware HDD or Microdrive

- irda: Hardware has IrDA support

- keyboard: Hardware has a keyboard

- pcbios: Support for booting through BIOS

- pci: Hardware has a PCI bus

- pcmcia: Hardware has PCMCIA or CompactFlash sockets

- phone: Mobile phone (voice) support

- qvga: Machine has a QVGA (320x240) display

- rtc: Machine has a Real-Time Clock

- screen: Hardware has a screen

- serial: Hardware has serial support (usually RS232)

- touchscreen: Hardware has a touchscreen

- usbgadget: Hardware is USB gadget device capable

- usbhost: Hardware is USB Host capable

- vfat: FAT file system support

- wifi: Hardware has integrated WiFi

11.2. Distro Features

The items below are features you can use with DISTRO_FEATURES to enable features across your distribution. Features do not have a one-to-one correspondence to packages, and they can go beyond simply controlling the installation of a package or packages. In most cases, the presence or absence of a feature translates to the appropriate option supplied to the configure script during the do_configure task for the recipes that optionally support the feature.

Some distro features are also machine features. These select features make sense to be controlled both at the machine and distribution configuration level. See the COMBINED_FEATURES [http://www.yoctoproject.org/docs/1.7.2/ref-manual/ref-manual.html#var-COMBINED_FEATURES] variable for more information.

This list only represents features as shipped with the Yocto Project metadata:

- alsa: Include ALSA support (OSS compatibility kernel modules installed if available).

- bluetooth: Include bluetooth support (integrated BT only).

- cramfs: Include CramFS support.

- directfb: Include DirectFB support.

- ext2: Include tools for supporting for devices with internal HDD/Microdrive for storing files (instead of Flash only devices).

- ipsec: Include IPSec support.

- ipv6: Include IPv6 support.

- irda: Include IrDA support.

- keyboard: Include keyboard support (e.g. keymaps will be loaded during boot).

- nfs: Include NFS client support (for mounting NFS exports on device).

- opengl: Include the Open Graphics Library, which is a cross-language, multi-platform application programming interface used for rendering two and three-dimensional graphics.

- pci: Include PCI bus support.

- pcmcia: Include PCMCIA/CompactFlash support.

- ppp: Include PPP dialup support.

- smbfs: Include SMB networks client support (for mounting Samba/Microsoft Windows shares on device).

- systemd: Include support for this init manager, which is a full replacement of for init with parallel starting of services, reduced shell overhead, and other features. This init manager is used by many distributions.

- usbgadget: Include USB Gadget Device support (for USB networking/serial/storage).

- usbhost: Include USB Host support (allows to connect external keyboard, mouse, storage, network etc).

- wayland: Include the Wayland display server protocol and the library that supports it.

- wifi: Include WiFi support (integrated only).

- x11: Include the X server and libraries.

11.3. Image Features

The contents of images generated by the OpenEmbedded build system can be controlled by the IMAGE_FEATURES and EXTRA_IMAGE_FEATURES variables that you typically configure in your image recipes. Through these variables, you can add several different predefined packages such as development utilities or packages with debug information needed to investigate application problems or profile applications.

The following image features are available for all images:

- dbg-pkgs: Installs debug symbol packages for all packages installed in a given image.

- debug-tweaks: Makes an image suitable for development (e.g. allows root logins without passwords).

- dev-pkgs: Installs development packages (headers and extra library links) for all packages installed in a given image.

- doc-pkgs: Installs documentation packages for all packages installed in a given image.

- package-management: Installs package management tools and preserves the package manager database.

- ptest-pkgs: Installs ptest packages for all ptest-enabled recipes.

- read-only-rootfs: Creates an image whose root filesystem is read-only. See the "Creating a Read-Only Root Filesystem [http://www.yoctoproject.org/docs/1.7.2/dev-manual/dev-manual.html#creating-a-read-only-root-filesystem]" section in the Yocto Project Development Manual for more information.

- splash: Enables showing a splash screen during boot. By default, this screen is provided by psplash, which does allow customization. If you prefer to use an alternative splash screen package, you can do so by setting the SPLASH variable to a different package name (or names) within the image recipe or at the distro configuration level.

- staticdev-pkgs: Installs static development packages, which are static libraries (i.e. *.a files), for all packages installed in a given image.

Some image features are available only when you inherit the core-image class. The current list of these valid features is as follows:

- eclipse-debug: Provides Eclipse remote debugging support.

- hwcodecs: Installs hardware acceleration codecs.

- nfs-server: Installs an NFS server.

- qt4-pkgs: Supports Qt4/X11 and demo applications.

- ssh-server-dropbear: Installs the Dropbear minimal SSH server.

- ssh-server-openssh: Installs the OpenSSH SSH server, which is more full-featured than Dropbear. Note that if both the OpenSSH SSH server and the Dropbear minimal SSH server are present in IMAGE_FEATURES, then OpenSSH will take precedence and Dropbear will not be installed.

- tools-debug: Installs debugging tools such as strace and gdb. For information on GDB, see the "Debugging With the GNU Project Debugger (GDB) Remotely [http://www.yoctoproject.org/docs/1.7.2/dev-manual/dev-manual.html#platdev-gdb-remotedebug]" section in the Yocto Project Development Manual. For information on tracing and profiling, see the Yocto Project Profiling and Tracing Manual [http://www.yoctoproject.org/docs/1.7.2/profile-manual/profile-manual.html].

- tools-profile: Installs profiling tools such as oprofile, exmap, and LTTng. For general information on user-space tools, see the "User-Space Tools [http://www.yoctoproject.org/docs/1.7.2/adt-manual/adt-manual.html#user-space-tools]" section in the Yocto Project Application Developer's Guide.

- tools-sdk: Installs a full SDK that runs on the device.

- tools-testapps: Installs device testing tools (e.g. touchscreen debugging).

- x11: Installs the X server.

- x11-base: Installs the X server with a minimal environment.

- x11-sato: Installs the OpenedHand Sato environment.

11.4. Feature Backfilling

Sometimes it is necessary in the OpenEmbedded build system to extend MACHINE_FEATURES or DISTRO_FEATURES to control functionality that was previously enabled and not able to be disabled. For these cases, we need to add an additional feature item to appear in one of these variables, but we do not want to force developers who have existing values of the variables in their configuration to add the new feature in order to retain the same overall level of functionality. Thus, the OpenEmbedded build system has a mechanism to automatically "backfill" these added features into existing distro or machine configurations. You can see the list of features for which this is done by finding the DISTRO_FEATURES_BACKFILL and MACHINE_FEATURES_BACKFILL variables in the meta/conf/bitbake.conf file.

Because such features are backfilled by default into all configurations as described in the previous paragraph, developers who wish to disable the new features need to be able to selectively prevent the backfilling from occurring. They can do this by adding the undesired feature or features to the DISTRO_FEATURES_BACKFILL_CONSIDERED or MACHINE_FEATURES_BACKFILL_CONSIDERED variables for distro features and machine features respectively.

Here are two examples to help illustrate feature backfilling:

- The "pulseaudio" distro feature option: Previously, PulseAudio support was enabled within the Qt and GStreamer frameworks. Because of this, the feature is backfilled and thus enabled for all distros through the DISTRO_FEATURES_BACKFILL variable in the meta/conf/bitbake.conf file. However, your distro needs to disable the feature. You can disable the feature without affecting other existing distro configurations that need PulseAudio support by adding "pulseaudio" to DISTRO_FEATURES_BACKFILL_CONSIDERED in your distro's .conf file. Adding the feature to this variable when it also exists in the DISTRO_FEATURES_BACKFILL variable prevents the build system from adding the feature to your configuration's DISTRO_FEATURES, effectively disabling the feature for that particular distro.

- The "rtc" machine feature option: Previously, real time clock (RTC) support was enabled for all target devices. Because of this, the feature is backfilled and thus enabled for all machines through the MACHINE_FEATURES_BACKFILL variable in the meta/conf/bitbake.conf file. However, your target device does not have this capability. You can disable RTC support for your device without affecting other machines that need RTC support by adding the feature to your machine's MACHINE_FEATURES_BACKFILL_CONSIDERED list in the machine's .conf file. Adding the feature to this variable when it also exists in the MACHINE_FEATURES_BACKFILL variable prevents the build system from adding the feature to your configuration's MACHINE_FEATURES, effectively disabling RTC support for that particular machine.

Chapter 12. Variables Glossary

This chapter lists common variables used in the OpenEmbedded build system and gives an overview of their function and contents.

Glossary

A B C D E F G H I K L M O P Q R S T U W

A

ABIEXTENSION

Extension to the Application Binary Interface (ABI) field of the GNU canonical architecture name (e.g. "eabi").

ABI extensions are set in the machine include files. For example, the meta/conf/machine/include/arm/arch-arm.inc file sets the following extension:

```
ABIEXTENSION = "eabi"
```

ALLOW_EMPTY

Specifies if an output package should still be produced if it is empty. By default, BitBake does not produce empty packages. This default behavior can cause issues when there is an RDEPENDS or some other hard runtime requirement on the existence of the package.

Like all package-controlling variables, you must always use them in conjunction with a package name override, as in:

```
ALLOW_EMPTY_${PN} = "1"
ALLOW_EMPTY_${PN}-dev = "1"
ALLOW_EMPTY_${PN}-staticdev = "1"
```

ALTERNATIVE

Lists commands in a package that need an alternative binary naming scheme. Sometimes the same command is provided in multiple packages. When this occurs, the OpenEmbedded build system needs to use the alternatives system to create a different binary naming scheme so the commands can co-exist.

To use the variable, list out the package's commands that also exist as part of another package. For example, if the busybox package has four commands that also exist as part of another package, you identify them as follows:

```
ALTERNATIVE_busybox = "sh sed test bracket"
```

For more information on the alternatives system, see the "update-alternatives.bbclass" section.

ALTERNATIVE_LINK_NAME

Used by the alternatives system to map duplicated commands to actual locations. For example, if the bracket command provided by the busybox package is duplicated through another package, you must use the ALTERNATIVE_LINK_NAME variable to specify the actual location:

```
ALTERNATIVE_LINK_NAME[bracket] = "/usr/bin/["
```

In this example, the binary for the bracket command (i.e. [ ) from the busybox package resides in /usr/bin/.

Note
If `ALTERNATIVE_LINK_NAME` is not defined, it defaults to `${bindir}/name`.

For more information on the alternatives system, see the "update-alternatives.bbclass" section.

ALTERNATIVE_PRIORITY

Used by the alternatives system to create default priorities for duplicated commands. You can use the variable to create a single default regardless of the command name or package, a default for specific duplicated commands regardless of the package, or a default for specific commands tied to particular packages. Here are the available syntax forms:

```
ALTERNATIVE_PRIORITY = "priority"
ALTERNATIVE_PRIORITY[name] = "priority"
ALTERNATIVE_PRIORITY_pkg[name] = "priority"
```

For more information on the alternatives system, see the "update-alternatives.bbclass" section.

ALTERNATIVE_TARGET

Used by the alternatives system to create default link locations for duplicated commands. You can use the variable to create a single default location for all duplicated commands regardless of the command name or package, a default for specific duplicated commands regardless of the package, or a default for specific commands tied to particular packages. Here are the available syntax forms:

```
ALTERNATIVE_TARGET = "target"
ALTERNATIVE_TARGET[name] = "target"
ALTERNATIVE_TARGET_pkg[name] = "target"
```

Note

If `ALTERNATIVE_TARGET` is not defined, it inherits the value from the `ALTERNATIVE_LINK_NAME` variable.

If `ALTERNATIVE_LINK_NAME` and `ALTERNATIVE_TARGET` are the same, the target for `ALTERNATIVE_TARGET` has ".{BPN}" appended to it.

Finally, if the file referenced has not been renamed, the alternatives system will rename it to avoid the need to rename alternative files in the do_install task while retaining support for the command if necessary.

For more information on the alternatives system, see the "update-alternatives.bbclass" section.

APPEND

An override list of append strings for each LABEL.

See the grub-efi class for more information on how this variable is used.

ASSUME_PROVIDED

Lists recipe names (PN values) BitBake does not attempt to build. Instead, BitBake assumes these recipes have already been built.

In OpenEmbedded Core, ASSUME_PROVIDED mostly specifies native tools that should not be built. An example is git-native, which when specified, allows for the Git binary from the host to be used rather than building git-native.

AUTHOR

The email address used to contact the original author or authors in order to send patches and forward bugs.

AUTO_SYSLINUXMENU

Enables creating an automatic menu. You must set this in your recipe. The syslinux class checks this variable.

AUTOREV

When SRCREV is set to the value of this variable, it specifies to use the latest source revision in the repository. Here is an example:

```
SRCREV = "${AUTOREV}"
```

AVAILTUNES

The list of defined CPU and Application Binary Interface (ABI) tunings (i.e. "tunes") available for use by the OpenEmbedded build system.

The list simply presents the tunes that are available. Not all tunes may be compatible with a particular machine configuration, or with each other in a Multilib [http://www.yoctoproject.org/docs/1.7.2/dev-manual/dev-manual.html#combining-multiple-versions-library-files-into-one-image] configuration.

To add a tune to the list, be sure to append it with spaces using the "+=" BitBake operator. Do not simply replace the list by using the "=" operator. See the "Basic Syntax [http://www.yoctoproject.org/docs/1.7.2/bitbake-user-manual/bitbake-user-manual.html#basic-syntax]" section in the BitBake User Manual for more information.

B

B

The directory within the Build Directory [http://www.yoctoproject.org/docs/1.7.2/dev-manual/dev-manual.html#build-directory] in which the OpenEmbedded build system places generated objects during a recipe's build process. By default, this directory is the same as the S directory, which is defined as:

```
S = "${WORKDIR}/${BP}/"
```

You can separate the (S) directory and the directory pointed to by the B variable. Most Autotools-based recipes support separating these directories. The build system defaults to using separate directories for gcc and some kernel recipes.

BAD_RECOMMENDATIONS

Lists "recommended-only" packages to not install. Recommended-only packages are packages installed only through the RRECOMMENDS variable. You can prevent any of these "recommended" packages from being installed by listing them with the BAD_RECOMMENDATIONS variable:

```
BAD_RECOMMENDATIONS = "package_name package_name package_name .
```

You can set this variable globally in your local.conf file or you can attach it to a specific image recipe by using the recipe name override:

```
BAD_RECOMMENDATIONS_pn-target_image = "package_name"
```

It is important to realize that if you choose to not install packages using this variable and some other packages are dependent on them (i.e. listed in a recipe's RDEPENDS variable), the OpenEmbedded build system ignores your request and will install the packages to avoid dependency errors.

Support for this variable exists only when using the IPK and RPM packaging backend. Support does not exist for DEB.

See the NO_RECOMMENDATIONS and the PACKAGE_EXCLUDE variables for related information.

BASE_LIB

The library directory name for the CPU or Application Binary Interface (ABI) tune. The BASE_LIB applies only in the Multilib context. See the "Combining Multiple Versions of Library Files into One Image [http://www.yoctoproject.org/docs/1.7.2/dev-manual/dev-manual.html#combining-multiple-versions-library-files-into-one-image]" section in the Yocto Project Development Manual for information on Multilib.

The BASE_LIB variable is defined in the machine include files in the Source Directory [http://www.yoctoproject.org/docs/1.7.2/dev-manual/dev-manual.html#source-directory]. If Multilib is not being used, the value defaults to "lib".

BB_DANGLINGAPPENDS_WARNONLY Defines how BitBake handles situations where an append file (.bbappend) has no corresponding recipe file (.bb). This condition often occurs when layers get out of sync (e.g. oe-core bumps a recipe version and the old recipe no longer exists and the other layer has not been updated to the new version of the recipe yet).

The default fatal behavior is safest because it is the sane reaction given something is out of sync. It is important to realize when your changes are no longer being applied.

You can change the default behavior by setting this variable to "1", "yes", or "true" in your local.conf file, which is located in the Build Directory [http://www.yoctoproject.org/docs/1.7.2/dev-manual/dev-manual.html#build-directory]: Here is an example:

```
BB_DANGLINGAPPENDS_WARNONLY = "1"
```

BB_DISKMON_DIRS

Monitors disk space and available inodes during the build and allows you to control the build based on these parameters.

Disk space monitoring is disabled by default. To enable monitoring, add the BB_DISKMON_DIRS variable to your conf/local.conf file found in the Build Directory [http://www.yoctoproject.org/docs/1.7.2/dev-manual/dev-manual.html#build-directory]. Use the following form:

```
BB_DISKMON_DIRS = "action,dir,threshold [...]"

where:

    action is:
       ABORT:     Immediately abort the build when
                  a threshold is broken.
       STOPTASKS: Stop the build after the currently
```

executing tasks have finished when
a threshold is broken.

WARN: Issue a warning but continue the
build when a threshold is broken.
Subsequent warnings are issued as
defined by the
BB_DISKMON_WARNINTERVAL variable,
which must be defined in the
conf/local.conf file.

dir is:
Any directory you choose. You can specify one or
more directories to monitor by separating the
groupings with a space. If two directories are
on the same device, only the first directory
is monitored.

threshold is:
Either the minimum available disk space,
the minimum number of free inodes, or
both. You must specify at least one. To
omit one or the other, simply omit the value.
Specify the threshold using G, M, K for Gbytes,
Mbytes, and Kbytes, respectively. If you do
not specify G, M, or K, Kbytes is assumed by
default. Do not use GB, MB, or KB.

Here are some examples:

```
BB_DISKMON_DIRS = "ABORT,${TMPDIR},1G,100K WARN,${SSTATE_DIR},1G
BB_DISKMON_DIRS = "STOPTASKS,${TMPDIR},1G"
BB_DISKMON_DIRS = "ABORT,${TMPDIR},,100K"
```

The first example works only if you also provide the
BB_DISKMON_WARNINTERVAL variable in the conf/local.conf. This
example causes the build system to immediately abort when either
the disk space in ${TMPDIR} drops below 1 Gbyte or the available
free inodes drops below 100 Kbytes. Because two directories are
provided with the variable, the build system also issue a warning
when the disk space in the ${SSTATE_DIR} directory drops below
1 Gbyte or the number of free inodes drops below 100 Kbytes.
Subsequent warnings are issued during intervals as defined by the
BB_DISKMON_WARNINTERVAL variable.

The second example stops the build after all currently executing tasks
complete when the minimum disk space in the ${TMPDIR} directory
drops below 1 Gbyte. No disk monitoring occurs for the free inodes
in this case.

The final example immediately aborts the build when the number of
free inodes in the ${TMPDIR} directory drops below 100 Kbytes. No
disk space monitoring for the directory itself occurs in this case.

BB_DISKMON_WARNINTERVAL   Defines the disk space and free inode warning intervals. To set these
intervals, define the variable in your conf/local.conf file in the
Build Directory [http://www.yoctoproject.org/docs/1.7.2/dev-manual/
dev-manual.html#build-directory].

If you are going to use the BB_DISKMON_WARNINTERVAL variable, you
must also use the BB_DISKMON_DIRS variable and define its action as
"WARN". During the build, subsequent warnings are issued each time

disk space or number of free inodes further reduces by the respective interval.

If you do not provide a BB_DISKMON_WARNINTERVAL variable and you do use BB_DISKMON_DIRS with the "WARN" action, the disk monitoring interval defaults to the following:

```
BB_DISKMON_WARNINTERVAL = "50M,5K"
```

When specifying the variable in your configuration file, use the following form:

```
BB_DISKMON_WARNINTERVAL = "disk_space_interval,disk_inode_interva
```

where:

```
disk_space_interval is:
    An interval of memory expressed in either
    G, M, or K for Gbytes, Mbytes, or Kbytes,
    respectively. You cannot use GB, MB, or KB.

disk_inode_interval is:
    An interval of free inodes expressed in either
    G, M, or K for Gbytes, Mbytes, or Kbytes,
    respectively. You cannot use GB, MB, or KB.
```

Here is an example:

```
BB_DISKMON_DIRS = "WARN,${SSTATE_DIR},1G,100K"
BB_DISKMON_WARNINTERVAL = "50M,5K"
```

These variables cause the OpenEmbedded build system to issue subsequent warnings each time the available disk space further reduces by 50 Mbytes or the number of free inodes further reduces by 5 Kbytes in the ${SSTATE_DIR} directory. Subsequent warnings based on the interval occur each time a respective interval is reached beyond the initial warning (i.e. 1 Gbytes and 100 Kbytes).

BB_GENERATE_MIRROR_TARBALLS Causes tarballs of the Git repositories, including the Git metadata, to be placed in the DL_DIR directory.

For performance reasons, creating and placing tarballs of the Git repositories is not the default action by the OpenEmbedded build system.

```
BB_GENERATE_MIRROR_TARBALLS = "1"
```

Set this variable in your local.conf file in the Build Directory [http://www.yoctoproject.org/docs/1.7.2/dev-manual/dev-manual.html#build-directory].

BB_NUMBER_THREADS The maximum number of tasks BitBake should run in parallel at any one time. If your host development system supports multiple cores, a good rule of thumb is to set this variable to twice the number of cores.

The default value for BB_NUMBER_THREADS is equal to the number of cores your build system has.

BBCLASSEXTEND	Allows you to extend a recipe so that it builds variants of the software. Common variants for recipes exist such as "natives" like `quilt-native`, which is a copy of Quilt built to run on the build system; "crosses" such as `gcc-cross`, which is a compiler built to run on the build machine but produces binaries that run on the target MACHINE; "nativesdk", which targets the SDK machine instead of MACHINE; and "mulitlibs" in the form "`multilib:multilib_name`".

To build a different variant of the recipe with a minimal amount of code, it usually is as simple as adding the following to your recipe:

```
BBCLASSEXTEND =+ "native nativesdk"
BBCLASSEXTEND =+ "multilib:multilib_name"
```

BBFILE_COLLECTIONS	Lists the names of configured layers. These names are used to find the other BBFILE_* variables. Typically, each layer will append its name to this variable in its `conf/layer.conf` file.
BBFILE_PATTERN	Variable that expands to match files from BBFILES in a particular layer. This variable is used in the `conf/layer.conf` file and must be suffixed with the name of the specific layer (e.g. BBFILE_PATTERN_emenlow).
BBFILE_PRIORITY	Assigns the priority for recipe files in each layer.

This variable is useful in situations where the same recipe appears in more than one layer. Setting this variable allows you to prioritize a layer against other layers that contain the same recipe - effectively letting you control the precedence for the multiple layers. The precedence established through this variable stands regardless of a recipe's version (PV variable). For example, a layer that has a recipe with a higher PV value but for which the BBFILE_PRIORITY is set to have a lower precedence still has a lower precedence.

A larger value for the BBFILE_PRIORITY variable results in a higher precedence. For example, the value 6 has a higher precedence than the value 5. If not specified, the BBFILE_PRIORITY variable is set based on layer dependencies (see the LAYERDEPENDS variable for more information. The default priority, if unspecified for a layer with no dependencies, is the lowest defined priority + 1 (or 1 if no priorities are defined).

Tip
You can use the command `bitbake-layers show-layers` to list all configured layers along with their priorities.

BBFILES	List of recipe files used by BitBake to build software.
BBINCLUDELOGS	Variable that controls how BitBake displays logs on build failure.
BBLAYERS	Lists the layers to enable during the build. This variable is defined in the bblayers.conf configuration file in the Build Directory [http://www.yoctoproject.org/docs/1.7.2/dev-manual/dev-manual.html#build-directory]. Here is an example:

```
BBLAYERS = " \
  /home/scottrif/poky/meta \
  /home/scottrif/poky/meta-yocto \
  /home/scottrif/poky/meta-yocto-bsp \
  /home/scottrif/poky/meta-mykernel \
  "

BBLAYERS_NON_REMOVABLE ?= " \
  /home/scottrif/poky/meta \
```

```
  /home/scottrif/poky/meta-yocto \
  "
```

This example enables four layers, one of which is a custom, user-defined layer named meta-mykernel.

BBLAYERS_NON_REMOVABLE   Lists core layers that cannot be removed from the bblayers.conf file during a build using the Hob [https://www.yoctoproject.org/tools-resources/projects/hob].

Note

When building an image outside of Hob, this variable is ignored.

In order for BitBake to build your image using Hob, your bblayers.conf file must include the meta and meta-yocto core layers. Here is an example that shows these two layers listed in the BBLAYERS_NON_REMOVABLE statement:

```
BBLAYERS = " \
  /home/scottrif/poky/meta \
  /home/scottrif/poky/meta-yocto \
  /home/scottrif/poky/meta-yocto-bsp \
  /home/scottrif/poky/meta-mykernel \
  "

BBLAYERS_NON_REMOVABLE ?= " \
  /home/scottrif/poky/meta \
  /home/scottrif/poky/meta-yocto \
  "
```

BBMASK   Prevents BitBake from processing recipes and recipe append files. Use the BBMASK variable from within the conf/local.conf file found in the Build Directory [http://www.yoctoproject.org/docs/1.7.2/dev-manual/dev-manual.html#build-directory].

You can use the BBMASK variable to "hide" these .bb and .bbappend files. BitBake ignores any recipe or recipe append files that match the expression. It is as if BitBake does not see them at all. Consequently, matching files are not parsed or otherwise used by BitBake.

The value you provide is passed to Python's regular expression compiler. The expression is compared against the full paths to the files. For complete syntax information, see Python's documentation at http://docs.python.org/release/2.3/lib/re-syntax.html.

The following example uses a complete regular expression to tell BitBake to ignore all recipe and recipe append files in the meta-ti/recipes-misc/ directory:

```
BBMASK = "meta-ti/recipes-misc/"
```

If you want to mask out multiple directories or recipes, use the vertical bar to separate the regular expression fragments. This next example masks out multiple directories and individual recipes:

```
BBMASK = "meta-ti/recipes-misc/|meta-ti/recipes-ti/packagegroup/"
BBMASK .= "|.*meta-oe/recipes-support/"
BBMASK .= "|.*openldap"
BBMASK .= "|.*opencv"
BBMASK .= "|.*lzma"
```

Notice how the vertical bar is used to append the fragments.

Note

When specifying a directory name, use the trailing slash character to ensure you match just that directory name.

BBPATH

Used by BitBake to locate .bbclass and configuration files. This variable is analogous to the PATH variable.

Note

If you run BitBake from a directory outside of the Build Directory [http://www.yoctoproject.org/docs/1.7.2/dev-manual/dev-manual.htmlbuild-directory], you must be sure to set BBPATH to point to the Build Directory. Set the variable as you would any environment variable and then run BitBake:

```
$ BBPATH = "build_directory"
$ export BBPATH
$ bitbake target
```

BBSERVER

Points to the server that runs memory-resident BitBake. This variable is set by the oe-init-build-env-memres setup script and should not be hand-edited. The variable is only used when you employ memory-resident BitBake. The setup script exports the value as follows:

```
export BBSERVER=localhost:$port
```

For more information on how the BBSERVER is used, see the oe-init-build-env-memres script, which is located in the Source Directory [http://www.yoctoproject.org/docs/1.7.2/dev-manual/dev-manual.html#source-directory].

BINCONFIG

When inheriting the binconfig-disabled class, this variable specifies binary configuration scripts to disable in favor of using pkg-config to query the information. The binconfig-disabled class will modify the specified scripts to return an error so that calls to them can be easily found and replaced.

To add multiple scripts, separate them by spaces. Here is an example from the libpng recipe:

```
BINCONFIG = "${bindir}/libpng-config ${bindir}/libpng16-config"
```

BINCONFIG_GLOB

When inheriting the binconfig class, this variable specifies a wildcard for configuration scripts that need editing. The scripts are edited to correct any paths that have been set up during compilation so that they are correct for use when installed into the sysroot and called by the build processes of other recipes.

For more information on how this variable works, see meta/classes/binconfig.bbclass in the Source Directory [http://www.yoctoproject.org/docs/1.7.2/dev-manual/dev-manual.html#source-directory]. You can also find general information on the class in the "binconfig.bbclass" section.

BP

The base recipe name and version but without any special recipe name suffix (i.e. -native, lib64-, and so forth). BP is comprised of the following:

$${BPN}-${PV}

BPN	The bare name of the recipe. This variable is a version of the PN variable but removes common suffixes such as "-native" and "-cross" as well as removes common prefixes such as multilib's "lib64-" and "lib32-". The exact list of suffixes removed is specified by the SPECIAL_PKGSUFFIX variable. The exact list of prefixes removed is specified by the MLPREFIX variable. Prefixes are removed for multilib and nativesdk cases.
BUGTRACKER	Specifies a URL for an upstream bug tracking website for a recipe. The OpenEmbedded build system does not use this variable. Rather, the variable is a useful pointer in case a bug in the software being built needs to be manually reported.
BUILD_CFLAGS	Specifies the flags to pass to the C compiler when building for the build host. When building in the -native context, CFLAGS is set to the value of this variable by default.
BUILD_CPPFLAGS	Specifies the flags to pass to the C pre-processor (i.e. to both the C and the C++ compilers) when building for the build host. When building in the native context, CPPFLAGS is set to the value of this variable by default.
BUILD_CXXFLAGS	Specifies the flags to pass to the C++ compiler when building for the build host. When building in the native context, CXXFLAGS is set to the value of this variable by default.
BUILD_LDFLAGS	Specifies the flags to pass to the linker when building for the build host. When building in the -native context, LDFLAGS is set to the value of this variable by default.
BUILD_OPTIMIZATION	Specifies the optimization flags passed to the C compiler when building for the build host or the SDK. The flags are passed through the BUILD_CFLAGS and BUILDSDK_CFLAGS default values.
	The default value of the BUILD_OPTIMIZATION variable is "-O2 -pipe".
BUILDDIR	Points to the location of the Build Directory [http://www.yoctoproject.org/docs/1.7.2/dev-manual/dev-manual.html#build-directory]. You can define this directory indirectly through the oe-init-build-env and oe-init-build-env-memres scripts by passing in a Build Directory path when you run the scripts. If you run the scripts and do not provide a Build Directory path, the BUILDDIR defaults to build in the current directory.
BUILDHISTORY_COMMIT	When inheriting the buildhistory class, this variable specifies whether or not to commit the build history output in a local Git repository. If set to "1", this local repository will be maintained automatically by the buildhistory class and a commit will be created on every build for changes to each top-level subdirectory of the build history output (images, packages, and sdk). If you want to track changes to build history over time, you should set this value to "1".
	By default, the buildhistory class does not commit the build history output in a local Git repository:
	BUILDHISTORY_COMMIT ?= "0"
BUILDHISTORY_COMMIT_AUTHOR	When inheriting the buildhistory class, this variable specifies the author to use for each Git commit. In order

for the BUILDHISTORY_COMMIT_AUTHOR variable to work, the BUILDHISTORY_COMMIT variable must be set to "1".

Git requires that the value you provide for the BUILDHISTORY_COMMIT_AUTHOR variable takes the form of "name <email@host>". Providing an email address or host that is not valid does not produce an error.

By default, the buildhistory class sets the variable as follows:

```
BUILDHISTORY_COMMIT_AUTHOR ?= "buildhistory <buildhistory@${DIS
```

BUILDHISTORY_DIR

When inheriting the buildhistory class, this variable specifies the directory in which build history information is kept. For more information on how the variable works, see the buildhistory.class.

By default, the buildhistory class sets the directory as follows:

```
BUILDHISTORY_DIR ?= "${TOPDIR}/buildhistory"
```

BUILDHISTORY_FEATURES

When inheriting the buildhistory class, this variable specifies the build history features to be enabled. For more information on how build history works, see the "Maintaining Build Output Quality" section.

You can specify three features in the form of a space-separated list:

- image: Analysis of the contents of images, which includes the list of installed packages among other things.

- package: Analysis of the contents of individual packages.

- sdk: Analysis of the contents of the software development kit (SDK).

By default, the buildhistory class enables all three features:

```
BUILDHISTORY_FEATURES ?= "image package sdk"
```

BUILDHISTORY_IMAGE_FILES

When inheriting the buildhistory class, this variable specifies a list of paths to files copied from the image contents into the build history directory under an "image-files" directory in the directory for the image, so that you can track the contents of each file. The default is to copy /etc/passwd and /etc/group, which allows you to monitor for changes in user and group entries. You can modify the list to include any file. Specifying an invalid path does not produce an error. Consequently, you can include files that might not always be present.

By default, the buildhistory class provides paths to the following files:

```
BUILDHISTORY_IMAGE_FILES ?= "/etc/passwd /etc/group"
```

BUILDHISTORY_PUSH_REPO

When inheriting the buildhistory class, this variable optionally specifies a remote repository to which build history pushes Git changes. In order for BUILDHISTORY_PUSH_REPO to work, BUILDHISTORY_COMMIT must be set to "1".

The repository should correspond to a remote address that specifies a repository as understood by Git, or alternatively to a remote name that you have set up manually using `git` remote within the local repository.

By default, the `buildhistory` class sets the variable as follows:

```
BUILDHISTORY_PUSH_REPO ?= ""
```

BUILDSDK_CFLAGS

Specifies the flags to pass to the C compiler when building for the SDK. When building in the `nativesdk` context, CFLAGS is set to the value of this variable by default.

BUILDSDK_CPPFLAGS

Specifies the flags to pass to the C pre-processor (i.e. to both the C and the C++ compilers) when building for the SDK. When building in the `nativesdk` context, CPPFLAGS is set to the value of this variable by default.

BUILDSDK_CXXFLAGS

Specifies the flags to pass to the C++ compiler when building for the SDK. When building in the `nativesdk` context, CXXFLAGS is set to the value of this variable by default.

BUILDSDK_LDFLAGS

Specifies the flags to pass to the linker when building for the SDK. When building in the `nativesdk-` context, LDFLAGS is set to the value of this variable by default.

BUILDSTATS_BASE

Points to the location of the directory that holds build statistics when you use and enable the `buildstats` class. The BUILDSTATS_BASE directory defaults to ${TMPDIR}/buildstats/.

BUSYBOX_SPLIT_SUID

For the BusyBox recipe, specifies whether to split the output executable file into two parts: one for features that require `setuid` root, and one for the remaining features (i.e. those that do not require `setuid` root).

The BUSYBOX_SPLIT_SUID variable defaults to "1", which results in a single output executable file. Set the variable to "0" to split the output file.

C

CFLAGS

Specifies the flags to pass to the C compiler. This variable is exported to an environment variable and thus made visible to the software being built during the compilation step.

Default initialization for CFLAGS varies depending on what is being built:

- TARGET_CFLAGS when building for the target

- BUILD_CFLAGS when building for the build host (i.e. -native)

- BUILDSDK_CFLAGS when building for an SDK (i.e. nativesdk-)

CLASSOVERRIDE

An internal variable specifying the special class override that should currently apply (e.g. "class-target", "class-native", and so forth). The classes that use this variable set it to appropriate values.

You do not normally directly interact with this variable. The value for the CLASSOVERRIDE variable goes into OVERRIDES and then can be used as an override. Here is an example where "python-native" is added to DEPENDS only when building for the native case:

```
DEPENDS_append_class-native = " python-native"
```

COMBINED_FEATURES

Provides a list of hardware features that are enabled in both MACHINE_FEATURES and DISTRO_FEATURES. This select list of features contains features that make sense to be controlled both at the machine and distribution configuration level. For example, the "bluetooth" feature requires hardware support but should also be optional at the distribution level, in case the hardware supports Bluetooth but you do not ever intend to use it.

For more information, see the MACHINE_FEATURES and DISTRO_FEATURES variables.

COMMON_LICENSE_DIR

Points to meta/files/common-licenses in the Source Directory [http://www.yoctoproject.org/docs/1.7.2/dev-manual/dev-manual.html#source-directory], which is where generic license files reside.

COMPATIBLE_HOST

A regular expression that resolves to one or more hosts (when the recipe is native) or one or more targets (when the recipe is non-native) with which a recipe is compatible. The regular expression is matched against HOST_SYS. You can use the variable to stop recipes from being built for classes of systems with which the recipes are not compatible. Stopping these builds is particularly useful with kernels. The variable also helps to increase parsing speed since the build system skips parsing recipes not compatible with the current system.

COMPATIBLE_MACHINE

A regular expression that resolves to one or more target machines with which a recipe is compatible. The regular expression is matched against MACHINEOVERRIDES. You can use the variable to stop recipes from being built for machines with which the recipes are not compatible. Stopping these builds is particularly useful with kernels. The variable also helps to increase parsing speed since the build system skips parsing recipes not compatible with the current machine.

COMPLEMENTARY_GLOB

Defines wildcards to match when installing a list of complementary packages for all the packages explicitly (or implicitly) installed in an image. The resulting list of complementary packages is associated with an item that can be added to IMAGE_FEATURES. An example usage of this is the "dev-pkgs" item that when added to IMAGE_FEATURES will install -dev packages (containing headers and other development files) for every package in the image.

To add a new feature item pointing to a wildcard, use a variable flag to specify the feature item name and use the value to specify the wildcard. Here is an example:

```
COMPLEMENTARY_GLOB[dev-pkgs] = '*-dev'
```

CONFFILES

Identifies editable or configurable files that are part of a package. If the Package Management System (PMS) is being used to update packages on the target system, it is possible that configuration files you have changed after the original installation and that you now want to remain unchanged are overwritten. In other words, editable files might exist in the package that you do not want reset as part of the package update process. You can use the CONFFILES variable to list the files in the package that you wish to prevent the PMS from overwriting during this update process.

To use the CONFFILES variable, provide a package name override that identifies the resulting package. Then, provide a space-separated list of files. Here is an example:

```
CONFFILES_${PN} += "${sysconfdir}/file1 \
    ${sysconfdir}/file2 ${sysconfdir}/file3"
```

A relationship exists between the CONFFILES and FILES variables. The files listed within CONFFILES must be a subset of the files listed within FILES. Because the configuration files you provide with CONFFILES are simply being identified so that the PMS will not overwrite them, it makes sense that the files must already be included as part of the package through the FILES variable.

Note

When specifying paths as part of the CONFFILES variable, it is good practice to use appropriate path variables. For example, ${sysconfdir} rather than /etc or ${bindir} rather than /usr/bin. You can find a list of these variables at the top of the meta/conf/bitbake.conf file in the Source Directory [http://www.yoctoproject.org/docs/1.7.2/dev-manual/dev-manual.html#source-directory].

CONFIG_INITRAMFS_SOURCE

Identifies the initial RAM disk (initramfs) source files. The OpenEmbedded build system receives and uses this kernel Kconfig variable as an environment variable. By default, the variable is set to null ("").

The CONFIG_INITRAMFS_SOURCE can be either a single cpio archive with a .cpio suffix or a space-separated list of directories and files for building the initramfs image. A cpio archive should contain a filesystem archive to be used as an initramfs image. Directories should contain a filesystem layout to be included in the initramfs image. Files should contain entries according to the format described by the usr/gen_init_cpio program in the kernel tree.

If you specify multiple directories and files, the initramfs image will be the aggregate of all of them.

CONFIG_SITE

A list of files that contains autoconf test results relevant to the current build. This variable is used by the Autotools utilities when running configure.

CONFLICT_DISTRO_FEATURES

When inheriting the distro_features_check class, this variable identifies distribution features that would be in conflict should the recipe be built. In other words, if the CONFLICT_DISTRO_FEATURES variable lists a feature that also appears in DISTRO_FEATURES within the current configuration, an error occurs and the build stops.

COPY_LIC_DIRS

If set to "1" along with the COPY_LIC_MANIFEST variable, the OpenEmbedded build system copies into the image the license files, which are located in /usr/share/common-licenses, for each package. The license files are placed in directories within the image itself.

COPY_LIC_MANIFEST

If set to "1", the OpenEmbedded build system copies the license manifest for the image to /usr/share/common-licenses/license.manifest within the image itself.

CORE_IMAGE_EXTRA_INSTALL

Specifies the list of packages to be added to the image. You should only set this variable in the local.conf configuration file found in the Build Directory [http://www.yoctoproject.org/docs/1.7.2/dev-manual/dev-manual.html#build-directory].

This variable replaces POKY_EXTRA_INSTALL, which is no longer supported.

COREBASE

Specifies the parent directory of the OpenEmbedded Core Metadata layer (i.e. meta).

It is an important distinction that COREBASE points to the parent of this layer and not the layer itself. Consider an example where you have cloned the Poky Git repository and retained the poky name for your local copy of the repository. In this case, COREBASE points to the poky folder because it is the parent directory of the poky/meta layer.

CPPFLAGS

Specifies the flags to pass to the C pre-processor (i.e. to both the C and the C++ compilers). This variable is exported to an environment variable and thus made visible to the software being built during the compilation step.

Default initialization for CPPFLAGS varies depending on what is being built:

- TARGET_CPPFLAGS when building for the target

- BUILD_CPPFLAGS when building for the build host (i.e. -native)

- BUILDSDK_CPPFLAGS when building for an SDK (i.e. nativesdk-)

CXXFLAGS

Specifies the flags to pass to the C++ compiler. This variable is exported to an environment variable and thus made visible to the software being built during the compilation step.

Default initialization for CXXFLAGS varies depending on what is being built:

- TARGET_CXXFLAGS when building for the target

- BUILD_CXXFLAGS when building for the build host (i.e. -native)

- BUILDSDK_CXXFLAGS when building for an SDK (i.e. nativesdk)

D

D

The destination directory. The location in the Build Directory [http://www.yoctoproject.org/docs/1.7.2/dev-manual/dev-manual.html#build-directory] where components are installed by the do_install task. This location defaults to:

${WORKDIR}/image

DATETIME

The date and time on which the current build started. The format is suitable for timestamps.

DEBUG_BUILD

Specifies to build packages with debugging information. This influences the value of the SELECTED_OPTIMIZATION variable.

DEBUG_OPTIMIZATION

The options to pass in TARGET_CFLAGS and CFLAGS when compiling a system for debugging. This variable defaults to "-O -fno-omit-frame-pointer ${DEBUG_FLAGS} -pipe".

DEFAULT_PREFERENCE

Specifies a weak bias for recipe selection priority.

The most common usage of this is variable is to set it to "-1" within a recipe for a development version of a piece of software. Using the variable in this way causes the stable version of the recipe to build by default in the absence of PREFERRED_VERSION being used to build the development version.

Note
The bias provided by DEFAULT_PREFERENCE is weak and is overridden by BBFILE_PRIORITY if that variable is different

between two layers that contain different versions of the same recipe.

DEFAULTTUNE

The default CPU and Application Binary Interface (ABI) tunings (i.e. the "tune") used by the OpenEmbedded build system. The DEFAULTTUNE helps define TUNE_FEATURES.

The default tune is either implicitly or explicitly set by the machine (MACHINE). However, you can override the setting using available tunes as defined with AVAILTUNES.

DEPENDS

Lists a recipe's build-time dependencies (i.e. other recipe files). The system ensures that all the dependencies listed have been built and have their contents in the appropriate sysroots before the recipe's configure task is executed.

Consider this simple example for two recipes named "a" and "b" that produce similarly named packages. In this example, the DEPENDS statement appears in the "a" recipe:

```
DEPENDS = "b"
```

Here, the dependency is such that the do_configure task for recipe "a" depends on the do_populate_sysroot task of recipe "b". This means anything that recipe "b" puts into sysroot is available when recipe "a" is configuring itself.

For information on runtime dependencies, see the RDEPENDS variable.

DEPLOY_DIR

Points to the general area that the OpenEmbedded build system uses to place images, packages, SDKs and other output files that are ready to be used outside of the build system. By default, this directory resides within the Build Directory [http://www.yoctoproject.org/docs/1.7.2/dev-manual/dev-manual.html#build-directory] as ${TMPDIR}/deploy.

For more information on the structure of the Build Directory, see "The Build Directory - build/" section. For more detail on the contents of the deploy directory, see the "Images" and "Application Development SDK" sections.

DEPLOY_DIR_IMAGE

Points to the area that the OpenEmbedded build system uses to place images and other associated output files that are ready to be deployed onto the target machine. The directory is machine-specific as it contains the ${MACHINE} name. By default, this directory resides within the Build Directory [http://www.yoctoproject.org/docs/1.7.2/dev-manual/dev-manual.html#build-directory] as ${DEPLOY_DIR}/images/${MACHINE}/.

For more information on the structure of the Build Directory, see "The Build Directory - build/" section. For more detail on the contents of the deploy directory, see the "Images" and "Application Development SDK" sections.

DEPLOYDIR

When inheriting the deploy class, the DEPLOYDIR points to a temporary work area for deployed files that is set in the deploy class as follows:

```
DEPLOYDIR = "${WORKDIR}/deploy-${PN}"
```

Recipes inheriting the deploy class should copy files to be deployed into DEPLOYDIR, and the class will take care of copying them into DEPLOY_DIR_IMAGE afterwards.

DESCRIPTION

The package description used by package managers. If not set, DESCRIPTION takes the value of the SUMMARY variable.

DISK_SIGNATURE

A 32-bit MBR disk signature used by directdisk images.

By default, the signature is set to an automatically generated random value that allows the OpenEmbedded build system to create a boot loader. You can override the signature in the image recipe by setting DISK_SIGNATURE to an 8-digit hex string. You might want to override DISK_SIGNATURE if you want the disk signature to remain constant between image builds.

When using Linux 3.8 or later, you can use DISK_SIGNATURE to specify the root by UUID to allow the kernel to locate the root device even if the device name changes due to differences in hardware configuration. By default, SYSLINUX_ROOT is set as follows:

```
SYSLINUX_ROOT = "root=/dev/sda2"
```

However, you can change this to locate the root device using the disk signature instead:

```
SYSLINUX_ROOT = "root=PARTUUID=${DISK_SIGNATURE}-02"
```

As previously mentioned, it is possible to set the DISK_SIGNATURE variable in your local.conf file to a fixed value if you do not want syslinux.cfg changing for each build. You might find this useful when you want to upgrade the root filesystem on a device without having to recreate or modify the master boot record.

DISTRO

The short name of the distribution. This variable corresponds to a distribution configuration file whose root name is the same as the variable's argument and whose filename extension is .conf. For example, the distribution configuration file for the Poky distribution is named poky.conf and resides in the meta-yocto/conf/distro directory of the Source Directory [http://www.yoctoproject.org/docs/1.7.2/dev-manual/dev-manual.html#source-directory].

Within that poky.conf file, the DISTRO variable is set as follows:

```
DISTRO = "poky"
```

Distribution configuration files are located in a conf/distro directory within the Metadata [http://www.yoctoproject.org/docs/1.7.2/dev-manual/dev-manual.html#metadata] that contains the distribution configuration. The value for DISTRO must not contain spaces, and is typically all lower-case.

Note

If the DISTRO variable is blank, a set of default configurations are used, which are specified within meta/conf/distro/defaultsetup.conf also in the Source Directory.

DISTRO_EXTRA_RDEPENDS

Specifies a list of distro-specific packages to add to all images. This variable takes affect through packagegroup-base so the variable only really applies to the more full-featured images that include packagegroup-base. You can use this variable to keep distro policy out of generic images. As with all other distro variables, you set this variable in the distro .conf file.

DISTRO_EXTRA_RRECOMMENDS Specifies a list of distro-specific packages to add to all images if the packages exist. The packages might not exist or be empty (e.g. kernel modules). The list of packages are automatically installed but you can remove them.

DISTRO_FEATURES The software support you want in your distribution for various features. You define your distribution features in the distribution configuration file.

In most cases, the presence or absence of a feature in DISTRO_FEATURES is translated to the appropriate option supplied to the configure script during the do_configure task for recipes that optionally support the feature. For example, specifying "x11" in DISTRO_FEATURES, causes every piece of software built for the target that can optionally support X11 to have its X11 support enabled.

Two more examples are Bluetooth and NFS support. For a more complete list of features that ships with the Yocto Project and that you can provide with this variable, see the "Distro Features" section.

DISTRO_FEATURES_BACKFILL Features to be added to DISTRO_FEATURES if not also present in DISTRO_FEATURES_BACKFILL_CONSIDERED.

This variable is set in the meta/conf/bitbake.conf file. It is not intended to be user-configurable. It is best to just reference the variable to see which distro features are being backfilled for all distro configurations. See the Feature backfilling section for more information.

DISTRO_FEATURES_BACKFILL_CONSIDERED Features from DISTRO_FEATURES_BACKFILL that should not be backfilled (i.e. added to DISTRO_FEATURES) during the build. See the "Feature Backfilling" section for more information.

DISTRO_NAME The long name of the distribution.

DISTRO_PN_ALIAS Alias names used for the recipe in various Linux distributions.

See the "Handling a Package Name Alias [http://www.yoctoproject.org/docs/1.7.2/dev-manual/dev-manual.html#usingpoky-configuring-DISTRO_PN_ALIAS]" section in the Yocto Project Development Manual for more information.

DISTRO_VERSION The version of the distribution.

DISTROOVERRIDES This variable lists overrides specific to the current distribution. By default, the variable list includes the value of the DISTRO variable. You can extend the variable to apply any variable overrides you want as part of the distribution and are not already in OVERRIDES through some other means.

DL_DIR The central download directory used by the build process to store downloads. By default, DL_DIR gets files suitable for mirroring for everything except Git repositories. If you want tarballs of Git repositories, use the BB_GENERATE_MIRROR_TARBALLS variable.

You can set this directory by defining the DL_DIR variable in the conf/local.conf file. This directory is self-maintaining and you should not have to touch it. By default, the directory is downloads in the Build Directory [http://www.yoctoproject.org/docs/1.7.2/dev-manual/dev-manual.html#build-directory].

```
#DL_DIR ?= "${TOPDIR}/downloads"
```

To specify a different download directory, simply remove the comment from the line and provide your directory.

During a first build, the system downloads many different source code tarballs from various upstream projects. Downloading can take a while, particularly if your network connection is slow. Tarballs are all stored in the directory defined by DL_DIR and the build system looks there first to find source tarballs.

Note
When wiping and rebuilding, you can preserve this directory to speed up this part of subsequent builds.

You can safely share this directory between multiple builds on the same development machine. For additional information on how the build process gets source files when working behind a firewall or proxy server, see this specific question in the "FAQ [213]" chapter.

DOC_COMPRESS

When inheriting the compress_doc class, this variable sets the compression policy used when the OpenEmbedded build system compresses man pages and info pages. By default, the compression method used is gz (gzip). Other policies available are xz and bz2.

For information on policies and on how to use this variable, see the comments in the meta/classes/compress_doc.bbclass file.

E

EFI_PROVIDER

When building bootable images (i.e. where hddimg or vmdk is in IMAGE_FSTYPES), The EFI_PROVIDER variable specifies the EFI bootloader to use. The default is "grub-efi", but "gummiboot" can be used instead.

See the gummiboot class for more information.

ENABLE_BINARY_LOCALE_GENERATION

Variable that controls which locales for glibc are generated during the build (useful if the target device has 64Mbytes of RAM or less).

ERROR_QA

Specifies the quality assurance checks whose failures are reported as errors by the OpenEmbedded build system. You set this variable in your distribution configuration file. For a list of the checks you can control with this variable, see the "insane.bbclass" section.

ERR_REPORT_DIR

When used with the report-error class, specifies the path used for storing the debug files created by the error reporting tool [http://www.yoctoproject.org/docs/1.7.2/dev-manual/dev-manual.html#using-the-error-reporting-tool], which allows you to submit build errors you encounter to a central database. By default, the value of this variable is ${LOG_DIR}/error-report.

You can set ERR_REPORT_DIR to the path you want the error reporting tool to store the debug files as follows in your local.conf file:

```
ERR_REPORT_DIR = "path"
```

EXCLUDE_FROM_WORLD

Directs BitBake to exclude a recipe from world builds (i.e. bitbake world). During world builds, BitBake locates, parses and builds all recipes found in every layer exposed in the bblayers.conf configuration file.

To exclude a recipe from a world build using this variable, set the variable to "1" in the recipe.

Note
Recipes added to EXCLUDE_FROM_WORLD may still be built during a world build in order to satisfy dependencies of

other recipes. Adding a recipe to EXCLUDE_FROM_WORLD only ensures that the recipe is not explicitly added to the list of build targets in a world build.

EXTENDPE

Used with file and pathnames to create a prefix for a recipe's version based on the recipe's PE value. If PE is set and greater than zero for a recipe, EXTENDPE becomes that value (e.g if PE is equal to "1" then EXTENDPE becomes "1_"). If a recipe's PE is not set (the default) or is equal to zero, EXTENDPE becomes "".

See the STAMP variable for an example.

EXTENDPKGV

The full package version specification as it appears on the final packages produced by a recipe. The variable's value is normally used to fix a runtime dependency to the exact same version of another package in the same recipe:

```
RDEPENDS_${PN}-additional-module = "${PN} (= ${EXTENDPKGV})"
```

The dependency relationships are intended to force the package manager to upgrade these types of packages in lock-step.

EXTERNALSRC

When inheriting the externalsrc class, this variable points to the source tree, which is outside of the OpenEmbedded build system. When set, this variable sets the S variable, which is what the OpenEmbedded build system uses to locate unpacked recipe source code.

For more information on externalsrc.bbclass, see the "externalsrc.bbclass" section. You can also find information on how to use this variable in the "Building Software from an External Source [http://www.yoctoproject.org/docs/1.7.2/dev-manual/dev-manual.html#building-software-from-an-external-source]" section in the Yocto Project Development Manual.

EXTERNALSRC_BUILD

When inheriting the externalsrc class, this variable points to the directory in which the recipe's source code is built, which is outside of the OpenEmbedded build system. When set, this variable sets the B variable, which is what the OpenEmbedded build system uses to locate the Build Directory.

For more information on externalsrc.bbclass, see the "externalsrc.bbclass" section. You can also find information on how to use this variable in the "Building Software from an External Source [http://www.yoctoproject.org/docs/1.7.2/dev-manual/dev-manual.html#building-software-from-an-external-source]" section in the Yocto Project Development Manual.

EXTRA_IMAGE_FEATURES

The list of additional features to include in an image. Typically, you configure this variable in your local.conf file, which is found in the Build Directory [http://www.yoctoproject.org/docs/1.7.2/dev-manual/dev-manual.html#build-directory]. Although you can use this variable from within a recipe, best practices dictate that you do not.

Note
To enable primary features from within the image recipe, use the IMAGE_FEATURES variable.

Here are some examples of features you can add:

```
"dbg-pkgs" - Adds -dbg packages for all installed packages
             including symbol information for debugging and
```

```
                              profiling.

        "debug-tweaks" - Makes an image suitable for development.
                         For example, ssh root access has a blank
                         password.  You should remove this feature
                         before you produce a production image.

        "dev-pkgs" - Adds -dev packages for all installed packages.
                     This is useful if you want to develop against
                     the libraries in the image.

        "read-only-rootfs" - Creates an image whose root
                             filesystem is read-only. See the
                             "Creating a Read-Only Root Filesystem [http://ww
                             section in the Yocto Project
                             Development Manual for more
                             information

        "tools-debug" - Adds debugging tools such as gdb and
                        strace.

        "tools-profile" - Adds profiling tools such as oprofile,
                          exmap, lttng and valgrind (x86 only).

        "tools-sdk" - Adds development tools such as gcc, make,
                      pkgconfig and so forth.

        "tools-testapps" - Adds useful testing tools such as
                           ts_print, aplay, arecord and so
                           forth.
```

For a complete list of image features that ships with the Yocto Project, see the "Image Features" section.

For an example that shows how to customize your image by using this variable, see the "Customizing Images Using Custom IMAGE_FEATURES and EXTRA_IMAGE_FEATURES [http://www.yoctoproject.org/docs/1.7.2/ dev-manual/dev-manual.html#usingpoky-extend-customimage- imagefeatures]" section in the Yocto Project Development Manual.

EXTRA_IMAGECMD	Specifies additional options for the image creation command that has been specified in IMAGE_CMD. When setting this variable, you should use an override for the associated type. Here is an example:

```
        EXTRA_IMAGECMD_ext3 ?= "-i 4096"
```

EXTRA_IMAGEDEPENDS

A list of recipes to build that do not provide packages for installing into the root filesystem.

Sometimes a recipe is required to build the final image but is not needed in the root filesystem. You can use the EXTRA_IMAGEDEPENDS variable to list these recipes and thus specify the dependencies. A typical example is a required bootloader in a machine configuration.

Note
To add packages to the root filesystem, see the various *RDEPENDS and *RRECOMMENDS variables.

EXTRA_OECMAKE	Additional cmake options.
EXTRA_OECONF	Additional configure script options.

EXTRA_OEMAKE	Additional GNU make options.
EXTRA_OESCONS	When inheriting the scons class, this variable specifies additional configuration options you want to pass to the scons command line.
EXTRA_QMAKEVARS_POST	Configuration variables or options you want to pass to qmake. Use this variable when the arguments need to be after the .pro file list on the command line.
	This variable is used with recipes that inherit the qmake_base class or other classes that inherit qmake_base.
EXTRA_QMAKEVARS_PRE	Configuration variables or options you want to pass to qmake. Use this variable when the arguments need to be before the .pro file list on the command line.
	This variable is used with recipes that inherit the qmake_base class or other classes that inherit qmake_base.
EXTRA_USERS_PARAMS	When inheriting the extrausers class, this variable provides image level user and group operations. This is a more global method of providing user and group configuration as compared to using the useradd class, which ties user and group configurations to a specific recipe.

The set list of commands you can configure using the EXTRA_USERS_PARAMS is shown in the extrausers class. These commands map to the normal Unix commands of the same names:

```
# EXTRA_USERS_PARAMS = "\
# useradd -p '' tester; \
# groupadd developers; \
# userdel nobody; \
# groupdel -g video; \
# groupmod -g 1020 developers; \
# usermod -s /bin/sh tester; \
# "
```

F

FEATURE_PACKAGES	Defines one or more packages to include in an image when a specific item is included in IMAGE_FEATURES. When setting the value, FEATURE_PACKAGES should have the name of the feature item as an override. Here is an example:

```
FEATURE_PACKAGES_widget = "package1 package2"
```

In this example, if "widget" were added to IMAGE_FEATURES, package1 and package2 would be included in the image.

Note
Packages installed by features defined through FEATURE_PACKAGES are often package groups. While similarly named, you should not confuse the FEATURE_PACKAGES variable with package groups, which are discussed elsewhere in the documentation.

FEED_DEPLOYDIR_BASE_URI	Points to the base URL of the server and location within the document-root that provides the metadata and packages required by OPKG to support runtime package management of IPK packages. You set this variable in your local.conf file.

Consider the following example:

```
FEED_DEPLOYDIR_BASE_URI = "http://192.168.7.1/BOARD-dir"
```

This example assumes you are serving your packages over HTTP and your databases are located in a directory named BOARD-dir, which is underneath your HTTP server's document-root. In this case, the OpenEmbedded build system generates a set of configuration files for you in your target that work with the feed.

FILES

The list of directories or files that are placed in packages.

To use the FILES variable, provide a package name override that identifies the resulting package. Then, provide a space-separated list of files or paths that identify the files you want included as part of the resulting package. Here is an example:

```
FILES_${PN} += "${bindir}/mydir1/ ${bindir}/mydir2/myfile"
```

Note

When specifying paths as part of the FILES variable, it is good practice to use appropriate path variables. For example, use ${sysconfdir} rather than /etc, or ${bindir} rather than /usr/bin. You can find a list of these variables at the top of the meta/conf/bitbake.conf file in the Source Directory [http://www.yoctoproject.org/docs/1.7.2/dev-manual/dev-manual.html#source-directory].

If some of the files you provide with the FILES variable are editable and you know they should not be overwritten during the package update process by the Package Management System (PMS), you can identify these files so that the PMS will not overwrite them. See the CONFFILES variable for information on how to identify these files to the PMS.

FILESEXTRAPATHS

Extends the search path the OpenEmbedded build system uses when looking for files and patches as it processes recipes and append files. The default directories BitBake uses when it processes recipes are initially defined by the FILESPATH variable. You can extend FILESPATH variable by using FILESEXTRAPATHS.

Best practices dictate that you accomplish this by using FILESEXTRAPATHS from within a .bbappend file and that you prepend paths as follows:

```
FILESEXTRAPATHS_prepend := "${THISDIR}/${PN}:"
```

In the above example, the build system first looks for files in a directory that has the same name as the corresponding append file.

Note

When extending FILESEXTRAPATHS, be sure to use the immediate expansion (:=) operator. Immediate expansion makes sure that BitBake evaluates THISDIR at the time the directive is encountered rather than at some later time when expansion might result in a directory that does not contain the files you need.

Also, include the trailing separating colon character if you are prepending. The trailing colon character is necessary because you are directing BitBake to extend the path by prepending directories to the search path.
Here is another common use:

```
FILESEXTRAPATHS_prepend := "${THISDIR}/files:"
```

In this example, the build system extends the FILESPATH variable to include a directory named files that is in the same directory as the corresponding append file.

Here is a final example that specifically adds three paths:

```
FILESEXTRAPATHS_prepend := "path_1:path_2:path_3:"
```

By prepending paths in .bbappend files, you allow multiple append files that reside in different layers but are used for the same recipe to correctly extend the path.

FILESOVERRIDES

A subset of OVERRIDES used by the OpenEmbedded build system for creating FILESPATH. You can find more information on how overrides are handled in the BitBake Manual [http://www.yoctoproject.org/docs/1.7.2/bitbake-user-manual/bitbake-user-manual.html].

By default, the FILESOVERRIDES variable is defined as:

```
FILESOVERRIDES = "${TRANSLATED_TARGET_ARCH}:${MACHINEOVERRIDES}:$
```

Note
Do not hand-edit the FILESOVERRIDES variable. The values match up with expected overrides and are used in an expected manner by the build system.

FILESPATH

The default set of directories the OpenEmbedded build system uses when searching for patches and files. During the build process, BitBake searches each directory in FILESPATH in the specified order when looking for files and patches specified by each file:// URI in a recipe.

The default value for the FILESPATH variable is defined in the base.bbclass class found in meta/classes in the Source Directory [http://www.yoctoproject.org/docs/1.7.2/dev-manual/dev-manual.html#source-directory]:

```
FILESPATH = "${@base_set_filespath(["${FILE_DIRNAME}/${BP}", \
    "${FILE_DIRNAME}/${BPN}", "${FILE_DIRNAME}/files"], d)}"
```

Note
Do not hand-edit the FILESPATH variable. If you want the build system to look in directories other than the defaults, extend the FILESPATH variable by using the FILESEXTRAPATHS variable.
Be aware that the default FILESPATH directories do not map to directories in custom layers where append files (.bbappend) are used. If you want the build system to find patches or files that reside

with your append files, you need to extend the FILESPATH variable by using the FILESEXTRAPATHS variable.

FILESYSTEM_PERMS_TABLES   Allows you to define your own file permissions settings table as part of your configuration for the packaging process. For example, suppose you need a consistent set of custom permissions for a set of groups and users across an entire work project. It is best to do this in the packages themselves but this is not always possible.

By default, the OpenEmbedded build system uses the fs-perms.txt, which is located in the meta/files folder in the Source Directory [http://www.yoctoproject.org/docs/1.7.2/dev-manual/dev-manual.html#source-directory]. If you create your own file permissions setting table, you should place it in your layer or the distro's layer.

You define the FILESYSTEM_PERMS_TABLES variable in the conf/local.conf file, which is found in the Build Directory [http://www.yoctoproject.org/docs/1.7.2/dev-manual/dev-manual.html#build-directory], to point to your custom fs-perms.txt. You can specify more than a single file permissions setting table. The paths you specify to these files must be defined within the BBPATH variable.

For guidance on how to create your own file permissions settings table file, examine the existing fs-perms.txt.

FONT_PACKAGES   When inheriting the fontcache class, this variable identifies packages containing font files that need to be cached by Fontconfig. By default, the fontcache class assumes that fonts are in the recipe's main package (i.e. ${PN}). Use this variable if fonts you need are in a package other than that main package.

FULL_OPTIMIZATION   The options to pass in TARGET_CFLAGS and CFLAGS when compiling an optimized system. This variable defaults to "-O2 -pipe ${DEBUG_FLAGS}".

G

GLIBC_GENERATE_LOCALES   Specifies the list of GLIBC locales to generate should you not wish generate all LIBC locals, which can be time consuming.

Note

If you specifically remove the locale en_US.UTF-8, you must set IMAGE_LINGUAS appropriately.

You can set GLIBC_GENERATE_LOCALES in your local.conf file. By default, all locales are generated.

```
GLIBC_GENERATE_LOCALES = "en_GB.UTF-8 en_US.UTF-8"
```

GROUPADD_PARAM   When inheriting the useradd class, this variable specifies for a package what parameters should be passed to the groupadd command if you wish to add a group to the system when the package is installed.

Here is an example from the dbus recipe:

```
GROUPADD_PARAM_${PN} = "-r netdev"
```

For information on the standard Linux shell command groupadd, see http://linux.die.net/man/8/groupadd.

GROUPMEMS_PARAM   When inheriting the useradd class, this variable specifies for a package what parameters should be passed to the groupmems command if you wish to modify the members of a group when the package is installed.

For information on the standard Linux shell command groupmems, see http://linux.die.net/man/8/groupmems.

GRUB_GFXSERIAL   Configures the GNU GRand Unified Bootloader (GRUB) to have graphics and serial in the boot menu. Set this variable to "1" in your local.conf or distribution configuration file to enable graphics and serial in the menu.

See the grub-efi class for more information on how this variable is used.

GRUB_OPTS   Additional options to add to the GNU GRand Unified Bootloader (GRUB) configuration. Use a semi-colon character (;) to separate multiple options.

The GRUB_OPTS variable is optional. See the grub-efi class for more information on how this variable is used.

GRUB_TIMEOUT   Specifies the timeout before executing the default LABEL in the GNU GRand Unified Bootloader (GRUB).

The GRUB_TIMEOUT variable is optional. See the grub-efi class for more information on how this variable is used.

GTKIMMODULES_PACKAGES   When inheriting the gtk-immodules-cache class, this variable specifies the packages that contain the GTK+ input method modules being installed when the modules are in packages other than the main package.

GUMMIBOOT_CFG   When EFI_PROVIDER is set to "gummiboot", the GUMMIBOOT_CFG variable specifies the configuration file that should be used. By default, the gummiboot class sets the GUMMIBOOT_CFG as follows:

```
GUMMIBOOT_CFG ?= "${S}/loader.conf"
```

For information on Gummiboot, see the Gummiboot documentation [http://freedesktop.org/wiki/Software/gummiboot/].

GUMMIBOOT_ENTRIES   When EFI_PROVIDER is set to "gummiboot", the GUMMIBOOT_ENTRIES variable specifies a list of entry files (*.conf) to be installed containing one boot entry per file. By default, the gummiboot class sets the GUMMIBOOT_ENTRIES as follows:

```
GUMMIBOOT_ENTRIES ?= ""
```

For information on Gummiboot, see the Gummiboot documentation [http://freedesktop.org/wiki/Software/gummiboot/].

GUMMIBOOT_TIMEOUT   When EFI_PROVIDER is set to "gummiboot", the GUMMIBOOT_TIMEOUT variable specifies the boot menu timeout in seconds. By default, the gummiboot class sets the GUMMIBOOT_TIMEOUT as follows:

```
GUMMIBOOT_TIMEOUT ?= "10"
```

For information on Gummiboot, see the Gummiboot documentation [http://freedesktop.org/wiki/Software/gummiboot/].

H

HOMEPAGE — Website where more information about the software the recipe is building can be found.

HOST_CC_ARCH — Specifies architecture-specific compiler flags that are passed to the C compiler.

Default initialization for HOST_CC_ARCH varies depending on what is being built:

- TARGET_CC_ARCH when building for the target

- BUILD_CC_ARCH when building for the build host (i.e. native)

- BUILDSDK_CC_ARCH when building for an SDK (i.e. nativesdk)

HOST_SYS — Specifies the system, including the architecture and the operating system, for with the build is occurring in the context of the current recipe. The OpenEmbedded build system automatically sets this variable. You do not need to set the variable yourself.

Here are two examples:

- Given a native recipe on a 32-bit x86 machine running Linux, the value is "i686-linux".

- Given a recipe being built for a little-endian MIPS target running Linux, the value might be "mipsel-linux".

I

ICECC_DISABLED — Disables or enables the icecc (Icecream) function. For more information on this function and best practices for using this variable, see the "icecc.bbclass" section.

Setting this variable to "1" in your local.conf disables the function:

```
ICECC_DISABLED ??= "1"
```

To enable the function, set the variable as follows:

```
ICECC_DISABLED = ""
```

ICECC_ENV_EXEC — Points to the icecc-create-env script that you provide. This variable is used by the icecc class. You set this variable in your local.conf file.

If you do not point to a script that you provide, the OpenEmbedded build system uses the default script provided by the icecc-create-env.bb recipe, which is a modified version and not the one that comes with icecc.

ICECC_PARALLEL_MAKE — Extra options passed to the make command during the do_compile task that specify parallel compilation. This variable usually takes the form of -j 4, where the number represents the maximum number of parallel threads make can run.

Note

The options passed affect builds on all enabled machines on the network, which are machines running the `iceccd` daemon.

If your enabled machines support multiple cores, coming up with the maximum number of parallel threads that gives you the best performance could take some experimentation since machine speed, network lag, available memory, and existing machine loads can all affect build time. Consequently, unlike the PARALLEL_MAKE variable, there is no rule-of-thumb for setting ICECC_PARALLEL_MAKE to achieve optimal performance.

If you do not set ICECC_PARALLEL_MAKE, the build system does not use it (i.e. the system does not detect and assign the number of cores as is done with PARALLEL_MAKE).

ICECC_PATH | The location of the `icecc` binary. You can set this variable in your `local.conf` file. If your `local.conf` file does not define this variable, the `icecc` class attempts to define it by locating `icecc` using `which`.

ICECC_USER_CLASS_BL | Identifies user classes that you do not want the Icecream distributed compile support to consider. This variable is used by the `icecc` class. You set this variable in your `local.conf` file.

When you list classes using this variable, you are "blacklisting" them from distributed compilation across remote hosts. Any classes you list will be distributed and compiled locally.

ICECC_USER_PACKAGE_BL | Identifies user recipes that you do not want the Icecream distributed compile support to consider. This variable is used by the `icecc` class. You set this variable in your `local.conf` file.

When you list packages using this variable, you are "blacklisting" them from distributed compilation across remote hosts. Any packages you list will be distributed and compiled locally.

ICECC_USER_PACKAGE_WL | Identifies user recipes that use an empty PARALLEL_MAKE variable that you want to force remote distributed compilation on using the Icecream distributed compile support. This variable is used by the `icecc` class. You set this variable in your `local.conf` file.

IMAGE_BASENAME | The base name of image output files. This variable defaults to the recipe name (${PN}).

IMAGE_BOOT_FILES | A space-separated list of files installed into the boot partition when preparing an image. By default, the files are installed under the same name as the source files. To change the installed name, separate it from the original name with a semi-colon (;). Source files need to be located in DEPLOY_DIR_IMAGE. Here are two examples:

```
IMAGE_BOOT_FILES = "u-boot.img uImage;kernel"
IMAGE_BOOT_FILES = "u-boot.${UBOOT_SUFFIX} ${KERNEL_IMAGETYPE}"
```

IMAGE_CLASSES | A list of classes that all images should inherit. You typically use this variable to specify the list of classes that register the different types of images the OpenEmbedded build system creates.

The default value for IMAGE_CLASSES is `image_types`. You can set this variable in your `local.conf` or in a distribution configuration file.

For more information, see `meta/classes/image_types.bbclass` in the Source Directory [http://www.yoctoproject.org/docs/1.7.2/dev-manual/dev-manual.html#source-directory].

IMAGE_CMD   Specifies the command to create the image file for a specific image type, which corresponds to the value set set in IMAGE_FSTYPES, (e.g. ext3, btrfs, and so forth). When setting this variable, you should use an override for the associated type. Here is an example:

```
IMAGE_CMD_jffs2 = "mkfs.jffs2 --root=${IMAGE_ROOTFS} \
    --faketime --output=${DEPLOY_DIR_IMAGE}/${IMAGE_NAME}.rootfs.
    ${EXTRA_IMAGECMD}"
```

You typically do not need to set this variable unless you are adding support for a new image type. For more examples on how to set this variable, see the image_types class file, which is meta/classes/image_types.bbclass.

IMAGE_DEVICE_TABLES   Specifies one or more files that contain custom device tables that are passed to the makedevs command as part of creating an image. These files list basic device nodes that should be created under /dev within the image. If IMAGE_DEVICE_TABLES is not set, files/device_table-minimal.txt is used, which is located by BBPATH. For details on how you should write device table files, see meta/files/device_table-minimal.txt as an example.

IMAGE_FEATURES   The primary list of features to include in an image. Typically, you configure this variable in an image recipe. Although you can use this variable from your local.conf file, which is found in the Build Directory [http://www.yoctoproject.org/docs/1.7.2/dev-manual/dev-manual.html#build-directory], best practices dictate that you do not.

Note

To enable extra features from outside the image recipe, use the EXTRA_IMAGE_FEATURES variable.
For a list of image features that ships with the Yocto Project, see the "Image Features" section.

For an example that shows how to customize your image by using this variable, see the "Customizing Images Using Custom IMAGE_FEATURES and EXTRA_IMAGE_FEATURES [http://www.yoctoproject.org/docs/1.7.2/dev-manual/dev-manual.html#usingpoky-extend-customimage-imagefeatures]" section in the Yocto Project Development Manual.

IMAGE_FSTYPES   Specifies the formats the OpenEmbedded build system uses during the build when creating the root filesystem. For example, setting IMAGE_FSTYPES as follows causes the build system to create root filesystems using two formats: .ext3 and .tar.bz2:

```
IMAGE_FSTYPES = "ext3 tar.bz2"
```

For the complete list of supported image formats from which you can choose, see IMAGE_TYPES.

Note

If you add "live" to IMAGE_FSTYPES inside an image recipe, be sure that you do so prior to the "inherit image" line of the recipe or the live image will not build.

Note

Due to the way this variable is processed, it is not possible to update its contents using _append or _prepend. To add one or more additional options to this variable the += operator must be used.

IMAGE_INSTALL

Specifies the packages to install into an image. The IMAGE_INSTALL variable is a mechanism for an image recipe and you should use it with care to avoid ordering issues.

Note

When working with an core-image-minimal-initramfs [118] image, do not use the IMAGE_INSTALL variable to specify packages for installation. Instead, use the PACKAGE_INSTALL variable, which allows the initial RAM disk (initramfs) recipe to use a fixed set of packages and not be affected by IMAGE_INSTALL.

Image recipes set IMAGE_INSTALL to specify the packages to install into an image through image.bbclass. Additionally, "helper" classes exist, such as core-image.bbclass, that can take IMAGE_FEATURES lists and turn these into auto-generated entries in IMAGE_INSTALL in addition to its default contents.

Using IMAGE_INSTALL with the += operator from the /conf/local.conf file or from within an image recipe is not recommended as it can cause ordering issues. Since core-image.bbclass sets IMAGE_INSTALL to a default value using the ?= operator, using a += operation against IMAGE_INSTALL will result in unexpected behavior when used in conf/local.conf. Furthermore, the same operation from within an image recipe may or may not succeed depending on the specific situation. In both these cases, the behavior is contrary to how most users expect the += operator to work.

When you use this variable, it is best to use it as follows:

```
IMAGE_INSTALL_append = " package-name"
```

Be sure to include the space between the quotation character and the start of the package name or names.

IMAGE_LINGUAS

Specifies the list of locales to install into the image during the root filesystem construction process. The OpenEmbedded build system automatically splits locale files, which are used for localization, into separate packages. Setting the IMAGE_LINGUAS variable ensures that any locale packages that correspond to packages already selected for installation into the image are also installed. Here is an example:

```
IMAGE_LINGUAS = "pt-br de-de"
```

In this example, the build system ensures any Brazilian Portuguese and German locale files that correspond to packages in the image are installed (i.e. *-locale-pt-br and *-locale-de-de as well as *-locale-pt and *-locale-de, since some software packages only provide locale files by language and not by country-specific language).

See the GLIBC_GENERATE_LOCALES variable for information on generating GLIBC locales.

IMAGE_MANIFEST

The manifest file for the image. This file lists all the installed packages that make up the image. The file contains package information on a line-per-package basis as follows:

```
packagename packagearch version
```

The image class defines the manifest file as follows:

```
IMAGE_MANIFEST = "${DEPLOY_DIR_IMAGE}/${IMAGE_NAME}.rootfs.mani
```

The location is derived using the DEPLOY_DIR_IMAGE and IMAGE_NAME variables. You can find information on how the image is created in the "Image Generation" section.

IMAGE_NAME

The name of the output image files minus the extension. This variable is derived using the IMAGE_BASENAME, MACHINE, and DATETIME variables:

```
IMAGE_NAME = "${IMAGE_BASENAME}-${MACHINE}-${DATETIME}"
```

IMAGE_OVERHEAD_FACTOR

Defines a multiplier that the build system applies to the initial image size for cases when the multiplier times the returned disk usage value for the image is greater than the sum of IMAGE_ROOTFS_SIZE and IMAGE_ROOTFS_EXTRA_SPACE. The result of the multiplier applied to the initial image size creates free disk space in the image as overhead. By default, the build process uses a multiplier of 1.3 for this variable. This default value results in 30% free disk space added to the image when this method is used to determine the final generated image size. You should be aware that post install scripts and the package management system uses disk space inside this overhead area. Consequently, the multiplier does not produce an image with all the theoretical free disk space. See IMAGE_ROOTFS_SIZE for information on how the build system determines the overall image size.

The default 30% free disk space typically gives the image enough room to boot and allows for basic post installs while still leaving a small amount of free disk space. If 30% free space is inadequate, you can increase the default value. For example, the following setting gives you 50% free space added to the image:

```
IMAGE_OVERHEAD_FACTOR = "1.5"
```

Alternatively, you can ensure a specific amount of free disk space is added to the image by using the IMAGE_ROOTFS_EXTRA_SPACE variable.

IMAGE_PKGTYPE

Defines the package type (DEB, RPM, IPK, or TAR) used by the OpenEmbedded build system. The variable is defined appropriately by the package_deb, package_rpm, package_ipk, or package_tar class.

The package_sdk_base and image classes use the IMAGE_PKGTYPE for packaging up images and SDKs.

You should not set the IMAGE_PKGTYPE manually. Rather, the variable is set indirectly through the appropriate package_* class using the PACKAGE_CLASSES variable. The OpenEmbedded build system uses the first package type (e.g. DEB, RPM, or IPK) that appears with the variable

Note

Files using the `.tar` format are never used as a substitute packaging format for DEB, RPM, and IPK formatted files for your image or SDK.

IMAGE_POSTPROCESS_COMMAND Added by classes to run post processing commands once the OpenEmbedded build system has created the image. You can specify shell commands separated by semicolons:

```
IMAGE_POSTPROCESS_COMMAND += "shell_command; ... "
```

If you need to pass the path to the root filesystem within the command, you can use ${IMAGE_ROOTFS}, which points to the root filesystem image.

IMAGE_ROOTFS The location of the root filesystem while it is under construction (i.e. during the do_rootfs task). This variable is not configurable. Do not change it.

IMAGE_ROOTFS_ALIGNMENT Specifies the alignment for the output image file in Kbytes. If the size of the image is not a multiple of this value, then the size is rounded up to the nearest multiple of the value. The default value is "1". See IMAGE_ROOTFS_SIZE for additional information.

IMAGE_ROOTFS_EXTRA_SPACE Defines additional free disk space created in the image in Kbytes. By default, this variable is set to "0". This free disk space is added to the image after the build system determines the image size as described in IMAGE_ROOTFS_SIZE.

This variable is particularly useful when you want to ensure that a specific amount of free disk space is available on a device after an image is installed and running. For example, to be sure 5 Gbytes of free disk space is available, set the variable as follows:

```
IMAGE_ROOTFS_EXTRA_SPACE = "5242880"
```

For example, the Yocto Project Build Appliance specifically requests 40 Gbytes of extra space with the line:

```
IMAGE_ROOTFS_EXTRA_SPACE = "41943040"
```

IMAGE_ROOTFS_SIZE Defines the size in Kbytes for the generated image. The OpenEmbedded build system determines the final size for the generated image using an algorithm that takes into account the initial disk space used for the generated image, a requested size for the image, and requested additional free disk space to be added to the image. Programatically, the build system determines the final size of the generated image as follows:

```
if (image-du * overhead) < rootfs-size:
internal-rootfs-size = rootfs-size + xspace
    else:
internal-rootfs-size = (image-du * overhead) + xspace

    where:

    image-du = Returned value of the du command on
               the image.
```

```
overhead = IMAGE_OVERHEAD_FACTOR

rootfs-size = IMAGE_ROOTFS_SIZE

internal-rootfs-size = Initial root filesystem
                          size before any modifications.

xspace = IMAGE_ROOTFS_EXTRA_SPACE
```

See the IMAGE_OVERHEAD_FACTOR and IMAGE_ROOTFS_EXTRA_SPACE variables for related information.

IMAGE_TYPEDEP
Specifies a dependency from one image type on another. Here is an example from the image-live class:

```
IMAGE_TYPEDEP_live = "ext3"
```

In the previous example, the variable ensures that when "live" is listed with the IMAGE_FSTYPES variable, the OpenEmbedded build system produces an ext3 image first since one of the components of the live image is an ext3 formatted partition containing the root filesystem.

IMAGE_TYPES
Specifies the complete list of supported image types by default:

```
jffs2
jffs2.sum
cramfs
ext2
ext2.gz
ext2.bz2
ext3
ext3.gz
ext2.lzma
btrfs
live
squashfs
squashfs-xz
ubi
ubifs
tar
tar.gz
tar.bz2
tar.xz
cpio
cpio.gz
cpio.xz
cpio.lzma
vmdk
elf
```

For more information about these types of images, see meta/classes/image_types*.bbclass in the Source Directory [http://www.yoctoproject.org/docs/1.7.2/dev-manual/dev-manual.html#source-directory].

INC_PR
Helps define the recipe revision for recipes that share a common include file. You can think of this variable as part of the recipe revision as set from within an include file.

Suppose, for example, you have a set of recipes that are used across several projects. And, within each of those recipes the revision (its PR value) is set accordingly. In this case, when the revision of those recipes changes, the burden is on you to find all those recipes and be sure that they get changed to reflect the updated version of the recipe. In this scenario, it can get complicated when recipes that are used in many places and provide common functionality are upgraded to a new revision.

A more efficient way of dealing with this situation is to set the INC_PR variable inside the `include` files that the recipes share and then expand the INC_PR variable within the recipes to help define the recipe revision.

The following provides an example that shows how to use the INC_PR variable given a common `include` file that defines the variable. Once the variable is defined in the `include` file, you can use the variable to set the PR values in each recipe. You will notice that when you set a recipe's PR you can provide more granular revisioning by appending values to the INC_PR variable:

```
recipes-graphics/xorg-font/xorg-font-common.inc:INC_PR = "r2"
recipes-graphics/xorg-font/encodings_1.0.4.bb:PR = "${INC_PR}.1"
recipes-graphics/xorg-font/font-util_1.3.0.bb:PR = "${INC_PR}.0"
recipes-graphics/xorg-font/font-alias_1.0.3.bb:PR = "${INC_PR}.3"
```

The first line of the example establishes the baseline revision to be used for all recipes that use the `include` file. The remaining lines in the example are from individual recipes and show how the PR value is set.

INCOMPATIBLE_LICENSE
Specifies a space-separated list of license names (as they would appear in LICENSE) that should be excluded from the build. Recipes that provide no alternatives to listed incompatible licenses are not built. Packages that are individually licensed with the specified incompatible licenses will be deleted.

Note
This functionality is only regularly tested using the following setting:

```
INCOMPATIBLE_LICENSE = "GPL-3.0 LGPL-3.0 AGPL-3.0"
```

Although you can use other settings, you might be required to remove dependencies on or provide alternatives to components that are required to produce a functional system image.

INHIBIT_DEFAULT_DEPS
Prevents the default dependencies, namely the C compiler and standard C library (libc), from being added to DEPENDS. This variable is usually used within recipes that do not require any compilation using the C compiler.

Set the variable to "1" to prevent the default dependencies from being added.

INHIBIT_PACKAGE_DEBUG_SPLIT
Prevents the OpenEmbedded build system from splitting out debug information during packaging. By default, the build system splits out debugging information during the do_package task. For more information on how debug information is split out, see the PACKAGE_DEBUG_SPLIT_STYLE variable.

To prevent the build system from splitting out debug information during packaging, set the INHIBIT_PACKAGE_DEBUG_SPLIT variable as follows:

```
INHIBIT_PACKAGE_DEBUG_SPLIT = "1"
```

INHIBIT_PACKAGE_STRIP   If set to "1", causes the build to not strip binaries in resulting packages.

INHERIT   Causes the named class to be inherited at this point during parsing. The variable is only valid in configuration files.

INHERIT_DISTRO   Lists classes that will be inherited at the distribution level. It is unlikely that you want to edit this variable.

The default value of the variable is set as follows in the meta/conf/distro/defaultsetup.conf file:

```
INHERIT_DISTRO ?= "debian devshell sstate license"
```

INITRAMFS_FSTYPES   Defines the format for the output image of an initial RAM disk (initramfs), which is used during boot. Supported formats are the same as those supported by the IMAGE_FSTYPES variable.

INITRAMFS_IMAGE   Causes the OpenEmbedded build system to build an additional recipe as a dependency to your root filesystem recipe (e.g. core-image-sato). The additional recipe is used to create an initial RAM disk (initramfs) that might be needed during the initial boot of the target system to accomplish such things as loading kernel modules prior to mounting the root file system.

When you set the variable, specify the name of the initramfs you want created. The following example, which is set in the local.conf configuration file, causes a separate recipe to be created that results in an initramfs image named core-image-sato-initramfs.bb to be created:

```
INITRAMFS_IMAGE = "core-image-minimal-initramfs"
```

By default, the kernel class sets this variable to a null string as follows:

```
INITRAMFS_IMAGE = ""
```

See the local.conf.sample.extended [http://git.yoctoproject.org/cgit/cgit.cgi/poky/tree/meta-yocto/conf/local.conf.sample.extended] file for additional information. You can also reference the kernel.bbclass [http://git.yoctoproject.org/cgit/cgit.cgi/poky/tree/meta/classes/kernel.bbclass] file to see how the variable is used.

INITRAMFS_IMAGE_BUNDLE   Controls whether or not the image recipe specified by INITRAMFS_IMAGE is run through an extra pass during kernel compilation in order to build a single binary that contains both the kernel image and the initial RAM disk (initramfs). Using an extra compilation pass ensures that when a kernel attempts to use an initramfs, it does not encounter circular dependencies should the initramfs include kernel modules.

The combined binary is deposited into the tmp/deploy directory, which is part of the Build Directory [http://www.yoctoproject.org/docs/1.7.2/dev-manual/dev-manual.html#build-directory].

Setting the variable to "1" in a configuration file causes the OpenEmbedded build system to make the extra pass during kernel compilation:

```
INITRAMFS_IMAGE_BUNDLE = "1"
```

By default, the kernel class sets this variable to a null string as follows:

```
INITRAMFS_IMAGE_BUNDLE = ""
```

Note

You must set the INITRAMFS_IMAGE_BUNDLE variable in a configuration file. You cannot set the variable in a recipe file. See the local.conf.sample.extended [http://git.yoctoproject.org/cgit/cgit.cgi/poky/tree/meta-yocto/conf/local.conf.sample.extended] file for additional information.

INITRD	Indicates list of filesystem images to concatenate and use as an initial RAM disk (initrd). The INITRD variable is an optional variable used with the bootimg class.
INITRD_IMAGE	When building a "live" bootable image (i.e. when IMAGE_FSTYPES contains "live"), INITRD_IMAGE specifies the image recipe that should be built to provide the initial RAM disk image. The default value is "core-image-minimal-initramfs". See the image-live class for more information.
INITSCRIPT_NAME	The filename of the initialization script as installed to ${sysconfdir}/init.d. This variable is used in recipes when using update-rc.d.bbclass. The variable is mandatory.
INITSCRIPT_PACKAGES	A list of the packages that contain initscripts. If multiple packages are specified, you need to append the package name to the other INITSCRIPT_* as an override. This variable is used in recipes when using update-rc.d.bbclass. The variable is optional and defaults to the PN variable.
INITSCRIPT_PARAMS	Specifies the options to pass to update-rc.d. Here is an example: `INITSCRIPT_PARAMS = "start 99 5 2 . stop 20 0 1 6 ."` In this example, the script has a runlevel of 99, starts the script in initlevels 2 and 5, and stops the script in levels 0, 1 and 6. The variable's default value is "defaults", which is set in the update-rc.d class. The value in INITSCRIPT_PARAMS is passed through to the update-rc.d command. For more information on valid parameters,

please see the update-rc.d manual page at http://www.tin.org/bin/man.cgi?section=8&topic=update-rc.d.

INSANE_SKIP

Specifies the QA checks to skip for a specific package within a recipe. For example, to skip the check for symbolic link .so files in the main package of a recipe, add the following to the recipe. The package name override must be used, which in this example is ${PN}:

```
INSANE_SKIP_${PN} += "dev-so"
```

See the "insane.bbclass" section for a list of the valid QA checks you can specify using this variable.

IPK_FEED_URIS

When the IPK backend is in use and package management is enabled on the target, you can use this variable to set up opkg in the target image to point to package feeds on a nominated server. Once the feed is established, you can perform installations or upgrades using the package manager at runtime.

K

KARCH

Defines the kernel architecture used when assembling the configuration. Architectures supported for this release are:

```
powerpc
i386
x86_64
arm
qemu
mips
```

You define the KARCH variable in the BSP Descriptions [http://www.yoctoproject.org/docs/1.7.2/kernel-dev/kernel-dev.html#bsp-descriptions].

KBRANCH

A regular expression used by the build process to explicitly identify the kernel branch that is validated, patched and configured during a build. The KBRANCH variable is optional. You can use it to trigger checks to ensure the exact kernel branch you want is being used by the build process.

Values for this variable are set in the kernel's recipe file and the kernel's append file. For example, if you are using the Yocto Project kernel that is based on the Linux 3.10 kernel, the kernel recipe file is the meta/recipes-kernel/linux/linux-yocto_3.10.bb file. Following is the default value for KBRANCH and the default override for the architectures the Yocto Project supports:

```
KBRANCH_DEFAULT = "standard/base"
KBRANCH = "${KBRANCH_DEFAULT}"
```

This branch exists in the linux-yocto-3.10 kernel Git repository http://git.yoctoproject.org/cgit.cgi/linux-yocto-3.10/refs/heads.

This variable is also used from the kernel's append file to identify the kernel branch specific to a particular machine or target hardware. The kernel's append file is located in the BSP layer for a given machine. For example, the kernel append file for the Crown Bay BSP is in the meta-intel Git repository and is named meta-crownbay/recipes-kernel/linux/linux-yocto_3.10.bbappend. Here are the related statements from the append file:

```
COMPATIBLE_MACHINE_crownbay = "crownbay"
KMACHINE_crownbay = "crownbay"
KBRANCH_crownbay = "standard/crownbay"
KERNEL_FEATURES_append_crownbay = " features/drm-emgd/drm-emgd-1.

COMPATIBLE_MACHINE_crownbay-noemgd = "crownbay-noemgd"
KMACHINE_crownbay-noemgd = "crownbay"
KBRANCH_crownbay-noemgd = "standard/crownbay"
KERNEL_FEATURES_append_crownbay-noemgd = " cfg/vesafb"
```

The KBRANCH_* statements identify the kernel branch to use when building for the Crown Bay BSP. In this case there are two identical statements: one for each type of Crown Bay machine.

KBRANCH_DEFAULT	Defines the Linux kernel source repository's default branch used to build the Linux kernel. The KBRANCH_DEFAULT value is the default value for KBRANCH. Unless you specify otherwise, KBRANCH_DEFAULT initializes to "master".
KERNEL_EXTRA_ARGS	Specifies additional make command-line arguments the OpenEmbedded build system passes on when compiling the kernel.
KERNEL_FEATURES	Includes additional metadata from the Yocto Project kernel Git repository. In the OpenEmbedded build system, the default Board Support Packages (BSPs) Metadata [http://www.yoctoproject.org/docs/1.7.2/dev-manual/dev-manual.html#metadata] is provided through the KMACHINE and KBRANCH variables. You can use the KERNEL_FEATURES variable to further add metadata for all BSPs.

The metadata you add through this variable includes config fragments and features descriptions, which usually includes patches as well as config fragments. You typically override the KERNEL_FEATURES variable for a specific machine. In this way, you can provide validated, but optional, sets of kernel configurations and features.

For example, the following adds netfilter to all the Yocto Project kernels and adds sound support to the qemux86 machine:

```
# Add netfilter to all linux-yocto kernels
KERNEL_FEATURES="features/netfilter"

# Add sound support to the qemux86 machine
KERNEL_FEATURES_append_qemux86=" cfg/sound"
```

KERNEL_IMAGE_BASE_NAME	The base name of the kernel image. This variable is set in the kernel class as follows:

```
KERNEL_IMAGE_BASE_NAME ?= "${KERNEL_IMAGETYPE}-${PKGE}-${PKGV}-${
```

See the KERNEL_IMAGETYPE, PKGE, PKGV, PKGR, MACHINE, and DATETIME variables for additional information.

KERNEL_IMAGETYPE	The type of kernel to build for a device, usually set by the machine configuration files and defaults to "zImage". This variable is used when building the kernel and is passed to make as the target to build.
KERNEL_MODULE_AUTOLOAD	Lists kernel modules that need to be auto-loaded during boot.

Note

This variable replaces the deprecated `module_autoload` variable.

You can use the KERNEL_MODULE_AUTOLOAD variable anywhere that it can be recognized by the kernel recipe or by an out-of-tree kernel module recipe (e.g. a machine configuration file, a distribution configuration file, an append file for the recipe, or the recipe itself).

Specify it as follows:

```
KERNEL_MODULE_AUTOLOAD += "module_name1 module_name2 module_nam
```

Including KERNEL_MODULE_AUTOLOAD causes the OpenEmbedded build system to populate the `/etc/modules-load.d/modname.conf` file with the list of modules to be auto-loaded on boot. The modules appear one-per-line in the file. Here is an example of the most common use case:

```
KERNEL_MODULE_AUTOLOAD += "module_name"
```

For information on how to populate the `modname.conf` file with `modprobe.d` syntax lines, see the KERNEL_MODULE_PROBECONF variable.

KERNEL_MODULE_PROBECONF Provides a list of modules for which the OpenEmbedded build system expects to find `module_conf_modname` values that specify configuration for each of the modules. For information on how to provide those module configurations, see the `module_conf_*` variable.

KERNEL_PATH The location of the kernel sources. This variable is set to the value of the STAGING_KERNEL_DIR within the module class. For information on how this variable is used, see the "Incorporating Out-of-Tree Modules [http://www.yoctoproject.org/docs/1.7.2/kernel-dev/kernel-dev.html#incorporating-out-of-tree-modules]" section.

To help maximize compatibility with out-of-tree drivers used to build modules, the OpenEmbedded build system also recognizes and uses the KERNEL_SRC variable, which is identical to the KERNEL_PATH variable. Both variables are common variables used by external Makefiles to point to the kernel source directory.

KERNEL_SRC The location of the kernel sources. This variable is set to the value of the STAGING_KERNEL_DIR within the module class. For information on how this variable is used, see the "Incorporating Out-of-Tree Modules [http://www.yoctoproject.org/docs/1.7.2/kernel-dev/kernel-dev.html#incorporating-out-of-tree-modules]" section.

To help maximize compatibility with out-of-tree drivers used to build modules, the OpenEmbedded build system also recognizes and uses the KERNEL_PATH variable, which is identical to the KERNEL_SRC variable. Both variables are common variables used by external Makefiles to point to the kernel source directory.

KFEATURE_DESCRIPTION Provides a short description of a configuration fragment. You use this variable in the `.scc` file that describes a configuration fragment file. Here is the variable used in a file named `smp.scc` to describe SMP being enabled:

```
define KFEATURE_DESCRIPTION "Enable SMP"
```

KMACHINE
The machine as known by the kernel. Sometimes the machine name used by the kernel does not match the machine name used by the OpenEmbedded build system. For example, the machine name that the OpenEmbedded build system understands as qemuarm goes by a different name in the Linux Yocto kernel. The kernel understands that machine as arm_versatile926ejs. For cases like these, the KMACHINE variable maps the kernel machine name to the OpenEmbedded build system machine name.

Kernel machine names are initially defined in the Yocto Linux Kernel's meta branch. From the meta branch, look in the meta/cfg/kernel-cache/bsp/<bsp_name>/<bsp-name>-<kernel-type>.scc file. For example, from the meta branch in the linux-yocto-3.0 kernel, the meta/cfg/kernel-cache/bsp/cedartrail/cedartrail-standard.scc file has the following:

```
define KMACHINE cedartrail
define KTYPE standard
define KARCH i386

include ktypes/standard
branch cedartrail

include cedartrail.scc
```

You can see that the kernel understands the machine name for the Cedar Trail Board Support Package (BSP) as cedartrail.

If you look in the Cedar Trail BSP layer in the meta-intel Source Repositories [http://www.yoctoproject.org/docs/1.7.2/dev-manual/dev-manual.html#source-repositories] at meta-cedartrail/recipes-kernel/linux/linux-yocto_3.0.bbappend, you will find the following statements among others:

```
COMPATIBLE_MACHINE_cedartrail = "cedartrail"
KMACHINE_cedartrail  = "cedartrail"
KBRANCH_cedartrail  = "yocto/standard/cedartrail"
KERNEL_FEATURES_append_cedartrail += "bsp/cedartrail/cedartrail-p
KERNEL_FEATURES_append_cedartrail += "cfg/efi-ext.scc"

COMPATIBLE_MACHINE_cedartrail-nopvr = "cedartrail"
KMACHINE_cedartrail-nopvr  = "cedartrail"
KBRANCH_cedartrail-nopvr  = "yocto/standard/cedartrail"
KERNEL_FEATURES_append_cedartrail-nopvr += " cfg/smp.scc"
```

The KMACHINE statements in the kernel's append file make sure that the OpenEmbedded build system and the Yocto Linux kernel understand the same machine names.

This append file uses two KMACHINE statements. The first is not really necessary but does ensure that the machine known to the OpenEmbedded build system as cedartrail maps to the machine in the kernel also known as cedartrail:

```
KMACHINE_cedartrail  = "cedartrail"
```

The second statement is a good example of why the KMACHINE variable is needed. In this example, the OpenEmbedded build system uses the cedartrail-nopvr machine name to refer to the Cedar Trail BSP that does not support the proprietary PowerVR driver. The kernel, however, uses the machine name cedartrail. Thus, the append file must map the cedartrail-nopvr machine name to the kernel's cedartrail name:

```
KMACHINE_cedartrail-nopvr  = "cedartrail"
```

BSPs that ship with the Yocto Project release provide all mappings between the Yocto Project kernel machine names and the OpenEmbedded machine names. Be sure to use the KMACHINE if you create a BSP and the machine name you use is different than that used in the kernel.

KTYPE

Defines the kernel type to be used in assembling the configuration. The linux-yocto recipes define "standard", "tiny", and "preempt-rt" kernel types. See the "Kernel Types [http://www.yoctoproject.org/docs/1.7.2/kernel-dev/kernel-dev.html#kernel-types]" section in the Yocto Project Linux Kernel Development Manual for more information on kernel types.

You define the KTYPE variable in the BSP Descriptions [http://www.yoctoproject.org/docs/1.7.2/kernel-dev/kernel-dev.html#bsp-descriptions]. The value you use must match the value used for the LINUX_KERNEL_TYPE value used by the kernel recipe.

L

LABELS

Provides a list of targets for automatic configuration.

See the grub-efi class for more information on how this variable is used.

LAYERDEPENDS

Lists the layers that this recipe depends upon, separated by spaces. Optionally, you can specify a specific layer version for a dependency by adding it to the end of the layer name with a colon, (e.g. "anotherlayer:3" to be compared against LAYERVERSION_anotherlayer in this case). An error will be produced if any dependency is missing or the version numbers do not match exactly (if specified). This variable is used in the conf/layer.conf file and must be suffixed with the name of the specific layer (e.g. LAYERDEPENDS_mylayer).

LAYERDIR

When used inside the layer.conf configuration file, this variable provides the path of the current layer. This variable is not available outside of layer.conf and references are expanded immediately when parsing of the file completes.

LAYERVERSION

Optionally specifies the version of a layer as a single number. You can use this within LAYERDEPENDS for another layer in order to depend on a specific version of the layer. This variable is used in the conf/layer.conf file and must be suffixed with the name of the specific layer (e.g. LAYERVERSION_mylayer).

LDFLAGS

Specifies the flags to pass to the linker. This variable is exported to an environment variable and thus made visible to the software being built during the compilation step.

Default initialization for LDFLAGS varies depending on what is being built:

• TARGET_LDFLAGS when building for the target

- BUILD_LDFLAGS when building for the build host (i.e. -native)

- BUILDSDK_LDFLAGS when building for an SDK (i.e. nativesdk-)

LEAD_SONAME
Specifies the lead (or primary) compiled library file (.so) that the debian class applies its naming policy to given a recipe that packages multiple libraries.

This variable works in conjunction with the debian class.

LIC_FILES_CHKSUM
Checksums of the license text in the recipe source code.

This variable tracks changes in license text of the source code files. If the license text is changed, it will trigger a build failure, which gives the developer an opportunity to review any license change.

This variable must be defined for all recipes (unless LICENSE is set to "CLOSED").

For more information, see the " Tracking License Changes" section.

LICENSE
The list of source licenses for the recipe. Follow these rules:

- Do not use spaces within individual license names.

- Separate license names using | (pipe) when there is a choice between licenses.

- Separate license names using & (ampersand) when multiple licenses exist that cover different parts of the source.

- You can use spaces between license names.

- For standard licenses, use the names of the files in meta/files/ common-licenses/ or the SPDXLICENSEMAP flag names defined in meta/conf/licenses.conf.

Here are some examples:

```
LICENSE = "LGPLv2.1 | GPLv3"
LICENSE = "MPL-1 & LGPLv2.1"
LICENSE = "GPLv2+"
```

The first example is from the recipes for Qt, which the user may choose to distribute under either the LGPL version 2.1 or GPL version 3. The second example is from Cairo where two licenses cover different parts of the source code. The final example is from sysstat, which presents a single license.

You can also specify licenses on a per-package basis to handle situations where components of the output have different licenses. For example, a piece of software whose code is licensed under GPLv2 but has accompanying documentation licensed under the GNU Free Documentation License 1.2 could be specified as follows:

```
LICENSE = "GFDL-1.2 & GPLv2"
LICENSE_${PN} = "GPLv2"
LICENSE_${PN}-doc = "GFDL-1.2"
```

LICENSE_FLAGS
Specifies additional flags for a recipe you must whitelist through LICENSE_FLAGS_WHITELIST in order to allow the recipe to be built. When providing multiple flags, separate them with spaces.

This value is independent of LICENSE and is typically used to mark recipes that might require additional licenses in order to be used in a commercial product. For more information, see the "Enabling Commercially Licensed Recipes" section.

LICENSE_FLAGS_WHITELIST   Lists license flags that when specified in LICENSE_FLAGS within a recipe should not prevent that recipe from being built. This practice is otherwise known as "whitelisting" license flags. For more information, see the Enabling Commercially Licensed Recipes" section.

LICENSE_PATH   Path to additional licenses used during the build. By default, the OpenEmbedded build system uses COMMON_LICENSE_DIR to define the directory that holds common license text used during the build. The LICENSE_PATH variable allows you to extend that location to other areas that have additional licenses:

LICENSE_PATH += "path-to-additional-common-licenses"

LINUX_KERNEL_TYPE   Defines the kernel type to be used in assembling the configuration. The linux-yocto recipes define "standard", "tiny", and "preempt-rt" kernel types. See the "Kernel Types [http://www.yoctoproject.org/docs/1.7.2/kernel-dev/kernel-dev.html#kernel-types]" section in the Yocto Project Linux Kernel Development Manual for more Information on kernel types.

If you do not specify a LINUX_KERNEL_TYPE, it defaults to "standard". Together with KMACHINE, the LINUX_KERNEL_TYPE variable defines the search arguments used by the kernel tools to find the appropriate description within the kernel Metadata [http://www.yoctoproject.org/docs/1.7.2/dev-manual/dev-manual.html#metadata] with which to build out the sources and configuration.

LINUX_VERSION   The Linux version from kernel.org on which the Linux kernel image being built using the OpenEmbedded build system is based. You define this variable in the kernel recipe. For example, the linux-yocto-3.4.bb kernel recipe found in meta/recipes-kernel/linux defines the variables as follows:

LINUX_VERSION ?= "3.4.24"

The LINUX_VERSION variable is used to define PV for the recipe:

PV = "${LINUX_VERSION}+git${SRCPV}"

LINUX_VERSION_EXTENSION   A string extension compiled into the version string of the Linux kernel built with the OpenEmbedded build system. You define this variable in the kernel recipe. For example, the linux-yocto kernel recipes all define the variable as follows:

LINUX_VERSION_EXTENSION ?= "-yocto-${LINUX_KERNEL_TYPE}"

Defining this variable essentially sets the Linux kernel configuration item CONFIG_LOCALVERSION, which is visible through the uname command. Here is an example that shows the extension assuming it was set as previously shown:

$ uname -r

3.7.0-rc8-custom

LOG_DIR — Specifies the directory to which the OpenEmbedded build system writes overall log files. The default directory is ${TMPDIR}/log.

For the directory containing logs specific to each task, see the T variable.

M

MACHINE — Specifies the target device for which the image is built. You define MACHINE in the local.conf file found in the Build Directory [http://www.yoctoproject.org/docs/1.7.2/dev-manual/dev-manual.html#build-directory]. By default, MACHINE is set to "qemux86", which is an x86-based architecture machine to be emulated using QEMU:

```
MACHINE ?= "qemux86"
```

The variable corresponds to a machine configuration file of the same name, through which machine-specific configurations are set. Thus, when MACHINE is set to "qemux86" there exists the corresponding qemux86.conf machine configuration file, which can be found in the Source Directory [http://www.yoctoproject.org/docs/1.7.2/dev-manual/dev-manual.html#source-directory] in meta/conf/machine.

The list of machines supported by the Yocto Project as shipped include the following:

```
MACHINE ?= "qemuarm"
MACHINE ?= "qemumips"
MACHINE ?= "qemuppc"
MACHINE ?= "qemux86"
MACHINE ?= "qemux86-64"
MACHINE ?= "genericx86"
MACHINE ?= "genericx86-64"
MACHINE ?= "beaglebone"
MACHINE ?= "mpc8315e-rdb"
MACHINE ?= "edgerouter"
```

The last five are Yocto Project reference hardware boards, which are provided in the meta-yocto-bsp layer.

Note
Adding additional Board Support Package (BSP) layers to your configuration adds new possible settings for MACHINE.

MACHINE_ARCH — Specifies the name of the machine-specific architecture. This variable is set automatically from MACHINE or TUNE_PKGARCH. You should not hand-edit the MACHINE_ARCH variable.

MACHINE_ESSENTIAL_EXTRA_RDEPENDS — Specifies required machine-specific packages to install as part of the image being built. The build process depends on these packages being present. Furthermore, because this is a "machine essential" variable, the list of packages are essential for the machine to boot. The impact of this variable affects images based on packagegroup-core-boot, including the core-image-minimal image.

This variable is similar to the MACHINE_ESSENTIAL_EXTRA_RRECOMMENDS variable with the exception that the image being built has a build dependency on the variable's list of packages. In other words, the image will not build if a file in this list is not found.

As an example, suppose the machine for which you are building requires example-init to be run during boot to initialize the hardware. In this case, you would use the following in the machine's .conf configuration file:

MACHINE_ESSENTIAL_EXTRA_RDEPENDS += "example-init"

MACHINE_ESSENTIAL_EXTRA_RRECOMMENDS A list of recommended machine-specific packages to install as part of the image being built. The build process does not depend on these packages being present. However, because this is a "machine essential" variable, the list of packages are essential for the machine to boot. The impact of this variable affects images based on packagegroup-core-boot, including the core-image-minimal image.

This variable is similar to the MACHINE_ESSENTIAL_EXTRA_RDEPENDS variable with the exception that the image being built does not have a build dependency on the variable's list of packages. In other words, the image will still build if a package in this list is not found. Typically, this variable is used to handle essential kernel modules, whose functionality may be selected to be built into the kernel rather than as a module, in which case a package will not be produced.

Consider an example where you have a custom kernel where a specific touchscreen driver is required for the machine to be usable. However, the driver can be built as a module or into the kernel depending on the kernel configuration. If the driver is built as a module, you want it to be installed. But, when the driver is built into the kernel, you still want the build to succeed. This variable sets up a "recommends" relationship so that in the latter case, the build will not fail due to the missing package. To accomplish this, assuming the package for the module was called kernel-module-ab123, you would use the following in the machine's .conf configuration file:

MACHINE_ESSENTIAL_EXTRA_RRECOMMENDS += "kernel-module-ab123"

Some examples of these machine essentials are flash, screen, keyboard, mouse, or touchscreen drivers (depending on the machine).

MACHINE_EXTRA_RDEPENDS A list of machine-specific packages to install as part of the image being built that are not essential for the machine to boot. However, the build process for more fully-featured images depends on the packages being present.

This variable affects all images based on packagegroup-base, which does not include the core-image-minimal or core-image-full-cmdline images.

The variable is similar to the MACHINE_EXTRA_RRECOMMENDS variable with the exception that the image being built has a build dependency on the variable's list of packages. In other words, the image will not build if a file in this list is not found.

An example is a machine that has WiFi capability but is not essential for the machine to boot the image. However, if you are building a more fully-featured image, you want to enable the WiFi. The package containing the firmware for the WiFi hardware is always expected to exist, so it is acceptable for the build process to depend upon finding the package. In this case, assuming the package for the firmware was called wifidriver-firmware, you would use the following in the .conf file for the machine:

```
MACHINE_EXTRA_RDEPENDS += "wifidriver-firmware"
```

MACHINE_EXTRA_RRECOMMENDS A list of machine-specific packages to install as part of the image being built that are not essential for booting the machine. The image being built has no build dependency on this list of packages.

This variable affects only images based on packagegroup-base, which does not include the core-image-minimal or core-image-full-cmdline images.

This variable is similar to the MACHINE_EXTRA_RDEPENDS variable with the exception that the image being built does not have a build dependency on the variable's list of packages. In other words, the image will build if a file in this list is not found.

An example is a machine that has WiFi capability but is not essential For the machine to boot the image. However, if you are building a more fully-featured image, you want to enable WiFi. In this case, the package containing the WiFi kernel module will not be produced if the WiFi driver is built into the kernel, in which case you still want the build to succeed instead of failing as a result of the package not being found. To accomplish this, assuming the package for the module was called kernel-module-examplewifi, you would use the following in the .conf file for the machine:

```
MACHINE_EXTRA_RRECOMMENDS += "kernel-module-examplewifi"
```

MACHINE_FEATURES Specifies the list of hardware features the MACHINE is capable of supporting. For related information on enabling features, see the DISTRO_FEATURES, COMBINED_FEATURES, and IMAGE_FEATURES variables.

For a list of hardware features supported by the Yocto Project as shipped, see the "Machine Features" section.

MACHINE_FEATURES_BACKFILL Features to be added to MACHINE_FEATURES if not also present in MACHINE_FEATURES_BACKFILL_CONSIDERED.

This variable is set in the meta/conf/bitbake.conf file. It is not intended to be user-configurable. It is best to just reference the variable to see which machine features are being backfilled for all machine configurations. See the "Feature backfilling" section for more information.

MACHINE_FEATURES_BACKFILL_CONSIDERED Features from MACHINE_FEATURES_BACKFILL that should not be backfilled (i.e. added to MACHINE_FEATURES) during the build. See the "Feature backfilling" section for more information.

MACHINEOVERRIDES Lists overrides specific to the current machine. By default, this list includes the value of MACHINE. You can extend the list to apply variable overrides for classes of machines. For example, all QEMU emulated machines (e.g. qemuarm, qemux86, and so forth) include a common file named meta/conf/machine/include/qemu.inc that prepends MACHINEOVERRIDES with the following variable override:

```
MACHINEOVERRIDES =. "qemuall:"
```

Applying an override like qemuall affects all QEMU emulated machines elsewhere. Here is an example from the connman-conf recipe:

```
SRC_URI_append_qemuall = "file://wired.config \
                          file://wired-setup \
                          "
```

MAINTAINER

The email address of the distribution maintainer.

MIRRORS

Specifies additional paths from which the OpenEmbedded build system gets source code. When the build system searches for source code, it first tries the local download directory. If that location fails, the build system tries locations defined by PREMIRRORS, the upstream source, and then locations specified by MIRRORS in that order.

Assuming your distribution (DISTRO) is "poky", the default value for MIRRORS is defined in the conf/distro/poky.conf file in the meta-yocto Git repository.

MLPREFIX

Specifies a prefix has been added to PN to create a special version of a recipe or package, such as a Multilib version. The variable is used in places where the prefix needs to be added to or removed from a the name (e.g. the BPN variable). MLPREFIX gets set when a prefix has been added to PN.

module_autoload

This variable has been replaced by the KERNEL_MODULE_AUTOLOAD variable. You should replace all occurrences of module_autoload with additions to KERNEL_MODULE_AUTOLOAD, for example:

```
module_autoload_rfcomm = "rfcomm"
```

should now be replaced with:

```
KERNEL_MODULE_AUTOLOAD += "rfcomm"
```

See the KERNEL_MODULE_AUTOLOAD variable for more information.

module_conf

Specifies modprobe.d [http://linux.die.net/man/5/modprobe.d] syntax lines for inclusion in the /etc/modprobe.d/modname.conf file.

You can use this variable anywhere that it can be recognized by the kernel recipe or out-of-tree kernel module recipe (e.g. a machine configuration file, a distribution configuration file, an append file for the recipe, or the recipe itself). If you use this variable, you must also be sure to list the module name in the KERNEL_MODULE_AUTOLOAD variable.

Here is the general syntax:

```
module_conf_module_name = "modprobe.d-syntax"
```

You must use the kernel module name override.

Run man modprobe.d in the shell to find out more information on the exact syntax you want to provide with module_conf.

Including `module_conf` causes the OpenEmbedded build system to populate the `/etc/modprobe.d/modname.conf` file with `modprobe.d` syntax lines. Here is an example that adds the options `arg1` and `arg2` to a module named mymodule:

```
module_conf_mymodule = "options mymodule arg1=val1 arg2=val2"
```

For information on how to specify kernel modules to auto-load on boot, see the `KERNEL_MODULE_AUTOLOAD` variable.

MODULE_IMAGE_BASE_NAME The base name of the kernel modules tarball. This variable is set in the kernel class as follows:

```
MODULE_IMAGE_BASE_NAME ?= "modules-${PKGE}-${PKGV}-${PKGR}-${MACH
```

See the `PKGE`, `PKGV`, `PKGR`, `MACHINE`, and `DATETIME` variables for additional information.

MODULE_TARBALL_DEPLOY Controls creation of the `modules-*.tgz` file. Set this variable to "0" to disable creation of this file, which contains all of the kernel modules resulting from a kernel build.

MULTIMACH_TARGET_SYS Separates files for different machines such that you can build for multiple target machines using the same output directories. See the `STAMP` variable for an example.

N

NATIVELSBSTRING A string identifying the host distribution. Strings consist of the host distributor ID followed by the release, as reported by the `lsb_release` tool or as read from `/etc/lsb-release`. For example, when running a build on Ubuntu 12.10, the value is "Ubuntu-12.10". If this information is unable to be determined, the value resolves to "Unknown".

This variable is used by default to isolate native shared state packages for different distributions (e.g. to avoid problems with `glibc` version incompatibilities). Additionally, the variable is checked against `SANITY_TESTED_DISTROS` if that variable is set.

NO_RECOMMENDATIONS Prevents installation of all "recommended-only" packages. Recommended-only packages are packages installed only through the `RRECOMMENDS` variable). Setting the `NO_RECOMMENDATIONS` variable to "1" turns this feature on:

```
NO_RECOMMENDATIONS = "1"
```

You can set this variable globally in your `local.conf` file or you can attach it to a specific image recipe by using the recipe name override:

```
NO_RECOMMENDATIONS_pn-target_image = "package_name"
```

It is important to realize that if you choose to not install packages using this variable and some other packages are dependent on them (i.e. listed in a recipe's `RDEPENDS` variable), the OpenEmbedded build system ignores your request and will install the packages to avoid dependency errors.

Note

Some recommended packages might be required for certain system functionality, such as kernel modules. It is up to you to add packages with the IMAGE_INSTALL variable.

Support for this variable exists only when using the IPK and RPM packaging backend. Support does not exist for DEB.

See the BAD_RECOMMENDATIONS and the PACKAGE_EXCLUDE variables for related information.

NOHDD
: Causes the OpenEmbedded build system to skip building the .hddimg image. The NOHDD variable is used with the bootimg class. Set the variable to "1" to prevent the .hddimg image from being built.

NOISO
: Causes the OpenEmbedded build system to skip building the ISO image. The NOISO variable is used with the bootimg class. Set the variable to "1" to prevent the ISO image from being built. To enable building an ISO image, set the variable to "0".

O

OE_BINCONFIG_EXTRA_MANGLE
: When inheriting the binconfig class, this variable specifies additional arguments passed to the "sed" command. The sed command alters any paths in configuration scripts that have been set up during compilation. Inheriting this class results in all paths in these scripts being changed to point into the sysroots/ directory so that all builds that use the script will use the correct directories for the cross compiling layout.

See the meta/classes/binconfig.bbclass in the Source Directory [http://www.yoctoproject.org/docs/1.7.2/dev-manual/dev-manual.html#source-directory] for details on how this class applies these additional sed command arguments. For general information on the binconfig.bbclass class, see the "Binary Configuration Scripts - binconfig.bbclass" section.

OE_IMPORTS
: An internal variable used to tell the OpenEmbedded build system what Python modules to import for every Python function run by the system.

Note

Do not set this variable. It is for internal use only.

OE_TERMINAL
: Controls how the OpenEmbedded build system spawns interactive terminals on the host development system (e.g. using the BitBake command with the -c devshell command-line option). For more information, see the "Using a Development Shell [http://www.yoctoproject.org/docs/1.7.2/dev-manual/dev-manual.html#platdev-appdev-devshell]" section in the Yocto Project Development Manual.

You can use the following values for the OE_TERMINAL variable:

```
auto
gnome
xfce
rxvt
screen
konsole
none
```

Note

Konsole support only works for KDE 3.x. Also, "auto" is the default behavior for OE_TERMINAL

OEROOT

The directory from which the top-level build environment setup script is sourced. The Yocto Project makes two top-level build environment setup scripts available: oe-init-build-env and oe-init-build-env-memres. When you run one of these scripts, the OEROOT variable resolves to the directory that contains the script.

For additional information on how this variable is used, see the initialization scripts.

OLDEST_KERNEL

Declares the oldest version of the Linux kernel that the produced binaries must support. This variable is passed into the build of the Embedded GNU C Library (glibc).

The default for this variable comes from the meta/conf/bitbake.conf configuration file. You can override this default by setting the variable in a custom distribution configuration file.

OVERRIDES

BitBake uses OVERRIDES to control what variables are overridden after BitBake parses recipes and configuration files. You can find more information on how overrides are handled in the "Conditional Syntax (Overrides) [http://www.yoctoproject.org/docs/1.7.2/bitbake-user-manual/bitbake-user-manual.html#conditional-syntax-overrides]" section of the BitBake User Manual.

P

P

The recipe name and version. P is comprised of the following:

```
${PN}-${PV}
```

PACKAGE_ARCH

The architecture of the resulting package or packages.

By default, the value of this variable is set to TUNE_PKGARCH when building for the target, BUILD_ARCH when building for the build host and "${SDK_ARCH}-${SDKPKGSUFFIX}" when building for the SDK. However, if your recipe's output packages are built specific to the target machine rather than general for the architecture of the machine, you should set PACKAGE_ARCH to the value of MACHINE_ARCH in the recipe as follows:

```
PACKAGE_ARCH = "${MACHINE_ARCH}"
```

PACKAGE_ARCHS

Specifies a list of architectures compatible with the target machine. This variable is set automatically and should not normally be hand-edited. Entries are separated using spaces and listed in order of priority. The default value for PACKAGE_ARCHS is "all any noarch ${PACKAGE_EXTRA_ARCHS} ${MACHINE_ARCH}".

PACKAGE_BEFORE_PN

Enables easily adding packages to PACKAGES before ${PN} so that those added packages can pick up files that would normally be included in the default package.

PACKAGE_CLASSES

This variable, which is set in the local.conf configuration file found in the conf folder of the Build Directory [http://www.yoctoproject.org/docs/1.7.2/dev-manual/dev-manual.html#build-directory], specifies the package manager the OpenEmbedded build system uses when packaging data.

You can provide one or more of the following arguments for the variable:

```
PACKAGE_CLASSES ?= "package_rpm package_deb package_ipk package
```

The build system uses only the first argument in the list as the package manager when creating your image or SDK. However, packages will be created using any additional packaging classes you specify. For example, if you use the following in your local.conf file:

```
PACKAGE_CLASSES ?= "package_ipk package_tar"
```

The OpenEmbedded build system uses the IPK package manager to create your image or SDK as well as generating TAR packages.

You cannot specify the package_tar class first in the list. Files using the .tar format cannot be used as a substitute packaging format for DEB, RPM, and IPK formatted files for your image or SDK.

For information on packaging and build performance effects as a result of the package manager in use, see the "package.bbclass" section.

PACKAGE_DEBUG_SPLIT_STYLE   Determines how to split up the binary and debug information when creating *-dbg packages to be used with the GNU Project Debugger (GDB).

With the PACKAGE_DEBUG_SPLIT_STYLE variable, you can control where debug information, which can include or exclude source files, is stored:

- ".debug": Debug symbol files are placed next to the binary in a .debug directory on the target. For example, if a binary is installed into /bin, the corresponding debug symbol files are installed in /bin/.debug. Source files are placed in /usr/src/debug. This is the default behavior.

- "debug-file-directory": Debug symbol files are placed under /usr/lib/debug on the target, and separated by the path from where the binary is installed. For example, if a binary is installed in /bin, the corresponding debug symbols are installed in /usr/lib/debug/bin. Source files are placed in /usr/src/debug.

- "debug-without-src": The same behavior as ".debug" previously described with the exception that no source files are installed.

You can find out more about debugging using GDB by reading the "Debugging With the GNU Project Debugger (GDB) Remotely [http://www.yoctoproject.org/docs/1.7.2/dev-manual/dev-manual.html#platdev-gdb-remotedebug]" section in the Yocto Project Development Manual.

PACKAGE_EXCLUDE   Lists packages that should not be installed into an image. For example:

```
PACKAGE_EXCLUDE = "package_name package_name package_name ..."
```

You can set this variable globally in your local.conf file or you can attach it to a specific image recipe by using the recipe name override:

```
PACKAGE_EXCLUDE_pn-target_image = "package_name"
```

If you choose to not install a package using this variable and some other package is dependent on it (i.e. listed in a recipe's RDEPENDS variable), the OpenEmbedded build system generates a fatal installation error. Because the build system halts the process with a fatal error, you can use the variable with an iterative development process to remove specific components from a system.

Support for this variable exists only when using the IPK and RPM packaging backend. Support does not exist for DEB.

See the NO_RECOMMENDATIONS and the BAD_RECOMMENDATIONS variables for related information.

PACKAGE_EXTRA_ARCHS   Specifies the list of architectures compatible with the device CPU. This variable is useful when you build for several different devices that use miscellaneous processors such as XScale and ARM926-EJS).

PACKAGE_GROUP   The PACKAGE_GROUP variable has been renamed to FEATURE_PACKAGES. See the variable description for FEATURE_PACKAGES for information.

If if you use the PACKAGE_GROUP variable, the OpenEmbedded build system issues a warning message.

PACKAGE_INSTALL   The final list of packages passed to the package manager for installation into the image.

Because the package manager controls actual installation of all packages, the list of packages passed using PACKAGE_INSTALL is not the final list of packages that are actually installed. This variable is internal to the image construction code. Consequently, in general, you should use the IMAGE_INSTALL variable to specify packages for installation. The exception to this is when working with the core-image-minimal-initramfs [118] image. When working with an initial RAM disk (initramfs) image, use the PACKAGE_INSTALL variable.

PACKAGE_PREPROCESS_FUNCS   Specifies a list of functions run to pre-process the PKGD directory prior to splitting the files out to individual packages.

PACKAGECONFIG   This variable provides a means of enabling or disabling features of a recipe on a per-recipe basis. PACKAGECONFIG blocks are defined in recipes when you specify features and then arguments that define feature behaviors. Here is the basic block structure:

```
PACKAGECONFIG ??= "f1 f2 f3 ..."
PACKAGECONFIG[f1] = "--with-f1,--without-f1,build-deps-f1,rt-deps
PACKAGECONFIG[f2] = "--with-f2,--without-f2,build-deps-f2,rt-deps
PACKAGECONFIG[f3] = "--with-f3,--without-f3,build-deps-f3,rt-deps
```

The PACKAGECONFIG variable itself specifies a space-separated list of the features to enable. Following the features, you can determine the behavior of each feature by providing up to four order-dependent arguments, which are separated by commas. You can omit any argument you like but must retain the separating commas. The order is important and specifies the following:

1. Extra arguments that should be added to the configure script argument list (EXTRA_OECONF) if the feature is enabled.

2. Extra arguments that should be added to EXTRA_OECONF if the feature is disabled.

3. Additional build dependencies (DEPENDS) that should be added if the feature is enabled.

4. Additional runtime dependencies (RDEPENDS) that should be added if the feature is enabled.

Consider the following PACKAGECONFIG block taken from the librsvg recipe. In this example the feature is croco, which has three arguments that determine the feature's behavior.

```
PACKAGECONFIG ??= "croco"
PACKAGECONFIG[croco] = "--with-croco,--without-croco,libcroco"
```

The --with-croco and libcroco arguments apply only if the feature is enabled. In this case, --with-croco is added to the configure script argument list and libcroco is added to DEPENDS. On the other hand, if the feature is disabled say through a .bbappend file in another layer, then the second argument --without-croco is added to the configure script rather than --with-croco.

The basic PACKAGECONFIG structure previously described holds true regardless of whether you are creating a block or changing a block. When creating a block, use the structure inside your recipe.

If you want to change an existing PACKAGECONFIG block, you can do so one of two ways:

• Append file: Create an append file named recipename.bbappend in your layer and override the value of PACKAGECONFIG. You can either completely override the variable:

```
PACKAGECONFIG="f4 f5"
```

Or, you can just append the variable:

```
PACKAGECONFIG_append = " f4"
```

• Configuration file: This method is identical to changing the block through an append file except you edit your local.conf or mydistro.conf file. As with append files previously described, you can either completely override the variable:

```
PACKAGECONFIG_pn-recipename="f4 f5"
```

Or, you can just amend the variable:

```
PACKAGECONFIG_append_pn-recipename = " f4"
```

PACKAGES

The list of packages to be created from the recipe. The default value is the following:

```
${PN}-dbg ${PN}-staticdev ${PN}-dev ${PN}-doc ${PN}-locale ${PAC
```

PACKAGESPLITFUNCS	Specifies a list of functions run to perform additional splitting of files into individual packages. Recipes can either prepend to this variable or prepend to the populate_packages function in order to perform additional package splitting. In either case, the function should set PACKAGES, FILES, RDEPENDS and other packaging variables appropriately in order to perform the desired splitting.
PACKAGES_DYNAMIC	A promise that your recipe satisfies runtime dependencies for optional modules that are found in other recipes. PACKAGES_DYNAMIC does not actually satisfy the dependencies, it only states that they should be satisfied. For example, if a hard, runtime dependency (RDEPENDS) of another package is satisfied at build time through the PACKAGES_DYNAMIC variable, but a package with the module name is never actually produced, then the other package will be broken. Thus, if you attempt to include that package in an image, you will get a dependency failure from the packaging system during the do_rootfs task.
	Typically, if there is a chance that such a situation can occur and the package that is not created is valid without the dependency being satisfied, then you should use RRECOMMENDS (a soft runtime dependency) instead of RDEPENDS.
	For an example of how to use the PACKAGES_DYNAMIC variable when you are splitting packages, see the "Handling Optional Module Packaging [http://www.yoctoproject.org/docs/1.7.2/dev-manual/dev-manual.html#handling-optional-module-packaging]" section in the Yocto Project Development Manual.
PARALLEL_MAKE	Extra options passed to the make command during the do_compile task in order to specify parallel compilation on the local build host. This variable is usually in the form "-j <x>", where x represents the maximum number of parallel threads make can run.
	If your development host supports multiple cores, a good rule of thumb is to set this variable to twice the number of cores on the host. If you do not set PARALLEL_MAKE, it defaults to the number of cores your build system has.

Note
Individual recipes might clear out this variable if the software being built has problems running its make process in parallel.

PARALLEL_MAKEINST	Extra options passed to the make install command during the do_install task in order to specify parallel installation. This variable defaults to the value of PARALLEL_MAKE.

Note
Individual recipes might clear out this variable if the software being built has problems running its make install process in parallel.

PATCHRESOLVE	Determines the action to take when a patch fails. You can set this variable to one of two values: "noop" and "user".
	The default value of "noop" causes the build to simply fail when the OpenEmbedded build system cannot successfully apply a patch. Setting the value to "user" causes the build system to launch a shell and places you in the right location so that you can manually resolve the conflicts.
	Set this variable in your local.conf file.

PATCHTOOL

Specifies the utility used to apply patches for a recipe during the do_patch task. You can specify one of three utilities: "patch", "quilt", or "git". The default utility used is "quilt" except for the quilt-native recipe itself. Because the quilt tool is not available at the time quilt-native is being patched, it uses "patch".

If you wish to use an alternative patching tool, set the variable in the recipe using one of the following:

```
PATCHTOOL = "patch"
PATCHTOOL = "quilt"
PATCHTOOL = "git"
```

PE

The epoch of the recipe. By default, this variable is unset. The variable is used to make upgrades possible when the versioning scheme changes in some backwards incompatible way.

PF

Specifies the recipe or package name and includes all version and revision numbers (i.e. glibc-2.13-r20+svnr15508/ and bash-4.2-r1/). This variable is comprised of the following:

```
${PN}-${EXTENDPE}${PV}-${PR}
```

PIXBUF_PACKAGES

When inheriting the pixbufcache class, this variable identifies packages that contain the pixbuf loaders used with gdk-pixbuf. By default, the pixbufcache class assumes that the loaders are in the recipe's main package (i.e. ${PN}). Use this variable if the loaders you need are in a package other than that main package.

PKG

The name of the resulting package created by the OpenEmbedded build system.

Note
When using the PKG variable, you must use a package name override.
For example, when the debian class renames the output package, it does so by setting PKG_packagename.

PKGD

Points to the destination directory for files to be packaged before they are split into individual packages. This directory defaults to the following:

```
${WORKDIR}/package
```

Do not change this default.

PKGDATA_DIR

Points to a shared, global-state directory that holds data generated during the packaging process. During the packaging process, the do_packagedata task packages data for each recipe and installs it into this temporary, shared area. This directory defaults to the following:

```
${STAGING_DIR_HOST}/pkgdata
```

Do not change this default.

PKGDEST

Points to the parent directory for files to be packaged after they have been split into individual packages. This directory defaults to the following:

```
${WORKDIR}/packages-split
```

Under this directory, the build system creates directories for each package specified in PACKAGES. Do not change this default.

PKGDESTWORK   Points to a temporary work area used by the do_package task to write output from the do_packagedata task. The PKGDESTWORK location defaults to the following:

```
${WORKDIR}/pkgdata
```

The do_packagedata task then packages the data in the temporary work area and installs it into a shared directory pointed to by PKGDATA_DIR.

Do not change this default.

PKGE   The epoch of the output package built by the OpenEmbedded build system. By default, PKGE is set to PE.

PKGR   The revision of the output package built by the OpenEmbedded build system. By default, PKGR is set to PR.

PKGV   The version of the output package built by the OpenEmbedded build system. By default, PKGV is set to PV.

PN   This variable can have two separate functions depending on the context: a recipe name or a resulting package name.

PN refers to a recipe name in the context of a file used by the OpenEmbedded build system as input to create a package. The name is normally extracted from the recipe file name. For example, if the recipe is named expat_2.0.1.bb, then the default value of PN will be "expat".

The variable refers to a package name in the context of a file created or produced by the OpenEmbedded build system.

If applicable, the PN variable also contains any special suffix or prefix. For example, using bash to build packages for the native machine, PN is bash-native. Using bash to build packages for the target and for Multilib, PN would be bash and lib64-bash, respectively.

PNBLACKLIST   Lists recipes you do not want the OpenEmbedded build system to build. This variable works in conjunction with the blacklist class, which the recipe must inherit globally.

To prevent a recipe from being built, inherit the class globally and use the variable in your local.conf file. Here is an example that prevents myrecipe from being built:

```
INHERIT += "blacklist"
PNBLACKLIST[myrecipe] = "Not supported by our organization."
```

PR   The revision of the recipe. The default value for this variable is "r0".

PREFERRED_PROVIDER   If multiple recipes provide an item, this variable determines which recipe should be given preference. You should always suffix the variable with the name of the provided item, and you should set it to the PN of the recipe to which you want to give precedence. Some examples:

```
PREFERRED_PROVIDER_virtual/kernel ?= "linux-yocto"
PREFERRED_PROVIDER_virtual/xserver = "xserver-xf86"
PREFERRED_PROVIDER_virtual/libgl ?= "mesa"
```

PREFERRED_VERSION

If there are multiple versions of recipes available, this variable determines which recipe should be given preference. You must always suffix the variable with the PN you want to select, and you should set the PV accordingly for precedence. You can use the "%" character as a wildcard to match any number of characters, which can be useful when specifying versions that contain long revision numbers that could potentially change. Here are two examples:

```
PREFERRED_VERSION_python = "2.7.3"
PREFERRED_VERSION_linux-yocto = "3.10%"
```

PREMIRRORS

Specifies additional paths from which the OpenEmbedded build system gets source code. When the build system searches for source code, it first tries the local download directory. If that location fails, the build system tries locations defined by PREMIRRORS, the upstream source, and then locations specified by MIRRORS in that order.

Assuming your distribution (DISTRO) is "poky", the default value for PREMIRRORS is defined in the conf/distro/poky.conf file in the meta-yocto Git repository.

Typically, you could add a specific server for the build system to attempt before any others by adding something like the following to the local.conf configuration file in the Build Directory [http://www.yoctoproject.org/docs/1.7.2/dev-manual/dev-manual.html#build-directory]:

```
PREMIRRORS_prepend = "\
git://.*/.* http://www.yoctoproject.org/sources/ \n \
ftp://.*/.* http://www.yoctoproject.org/sources/ \n \
http://.*/.* http://www.yoctoproject.org/sources/ \n \
https://.*/.* http://www.yoctoproject.org/sources/ \n"
```

These changes cause the build system to intercept Git, FTP, HTTP, and HTTPS requests and direct them to the http:// sources mirror. You can use file:// URLs to point to local directories or network shares as well.

PRINC

The PRINC variable has been deprecated and triggers a warning if detected during a build. For PR increments on changes, use the PR service instead. You can find out more about this service in the "Working With a PR Service [http://www.yoctoproject.org/docs/1.7.2/dev-manual/dev-manual.html#working-with-a-pr-service]" section in the Yocto Project Development Manual.

PRIVATE_LIBS

Specifies libraries installed within a recipe that should be ignored by the OpenEmbedded build system's shared library resolver. This variable is typically used when software being built by a recipe has its own private versions of a library normally provided by another recipe. In this case, you would not want the package containing the private libraries to be set as a dependency on other unrelated packages that should instead depend on the package providing the standard version of the library.

Libraries specified in this variable should be specified by their file name. For example, from the Firefox recipe in meta-browser:

```
PRIVATE_LIBS = "libmozjs.so \
                libxpcom.so \
                libnspr4.so \
                libxul.so \
                libmozalloc.so \
                libplc4.so \
                libplds4.so"
```

PROVIDES

A list of aliases by which a particular recipe can be known. By default, a recipe's own PN is implicitly already in its PROVIDES list. If a recipe uses PROVIDES, the additional aliases are synonyms for the recipe and can be useful satisfying dependencies of other recipes during the build as specified by DEPENDS.

Consider the following example PROVIDES statement from a recipe file libav_0.8.11.bb:

```
PROVIDES += "libpostproc"
```

The PROVIDES statement results in the "libav" recipe also being known as "libpostproc".

PRSERV_HOST

The network based PR service host and port.

The conf/local.conf.sample.extended configuration file in the Source Directory [http://www.yoctoproject.org/docs/1.7.2/dev-manual/dev-manual.html#source-directory] shows how the PRSERV_HOST variable is set:

```
PRSERV_HOST = "localhost:0"
```

You must set the variable if you want to automatically start a local PR service [http://www.yoctoproject.org/docs/1.7.2/dev-manual/dev-manual.html#working-with-a-pr-service]. You can set PRSERV_HOST to other values to use a remote PR service.

PTEST_ENABLED

Specifies whether or not Package Test [http://www.yoctoproject.org/docs/1.7.2/dev-manual/dev-manual.html#testing-packages-with-ptest] (ptest) functionality is enabled when building a recipe. You should not set this variable directly. Enabling and disabling building Package Tests at build time should be done by adding "ptest" to (or removing it from) DISTRO_FEATURES.

PV

The version of the recipe. The version is normally extracted from the recipe filename. For example, if the recipe is named expat_2.0.1.bb, then the default value of PV will be "2.0.1". PV is generally not overridden within a recipe unless it is building an unstable (i.e. development) version from a source code repository (e.g. Git or Subversion).

PYTHON_ABI

When used by recipes that inherit the distutils3, setuptools3, distutils, or setuptools classes, denotes the Application Binary Interface (ABI) currently in use for Python. By default, the ABI is "m". You do not have to set this variable as the OpenEmbedded build system sets it for you.

The OpenEmbedded build system uses the ABI to construct directory names used when installing the Python headers and libraries in sysroot (e.g. .../python3.3m/...).

Recipes that inherit the distutils class during cross-builds also use this variable to locate the headers and libraries of the appropriate Python that the extension is targeting.

PYTHON_PN

When used by recipes that inherit the distutils3, setuptools3, distutils, or setuptools classes, specifies the major Python version being built. For Python 2.x, PYTHON_PN would be "python2". For Python 3.x, the variable would be "python3". You do not have to set this variable as the OpenEmbedded build system automatically sets it for you.

The variable allows recipes to use common infrastructure such as the following:

```
DEPENDS += "${PYTHON_PN}-native"
```

In the previous example, the version of the dependency is PYTHON_PN.

Q

QMAKE_PROFILES

Specifies your own subset of .pro files to be built for use with qmake. If you do not set this variable, all .pro files in the directory pointed to by S will be built by default.

This variable is used with recipes that inherit the qmake_base class or other classes that inherit qmake_base.

R

RCONFLICTS

The list of packages that conflict with packages. Note that packages will not be installed if conflicting packages are not first removed.

Like all package-controlling variables, you must always use them in conjunction with a package name override. Here is an example:

```
RCONFLICTS_${PN} = "another-conflicting-package-name"
```

BitBake, which the OpenEmbedded build system uses, supports specifying versioned dependencies. Although the syntax varies depending on the packaging format, BitBake hides these differences from you. Here is the general syntax to specify versions with the RCONFLICTS variable:

```
RCONFLICTS_${PN} = "package (operator version)"
```

For operator, you can specify the following:

```
=
<
>
<=
>=
```

For example, the following sets up a dependency on version 1.2 or greater of the package foo:

```
RCONFLICTS_${PN} = "foo (>= 1.2)"
```

RDEPENDS

Lists a package's runtime dependencies (i.e. other packages) that must be installed in order for the built package to run correctly. If a package in this list cannot be found during the build, you will get a build error.

When you use the RDEPENDS variable in a recipe, you are essentially stating that the recipe's do_build task depends on the existence of a specific package. Consider this simple example for two recipes named "a" and "b" that produce similarly named IPK packages. In this example, the RDEPENDS statement appears in the "a" recipe:

```
RDEPENDS_${PN} = "b"
```

Here, the dependency is such that the do_build task for recipe "a" depends on the do_package_write_ipk task of recipe "b". This means the package file for "b" must be available when the output for recipe "a" has been completely built. More importantly, package "a" will be marked as depending on package "b" in a manner that is understood by the package manager.

The names of the packages you list within RDEPENDS must be the names of other packages - they cannot be recipe names. Although package names and recipe names usually match, the important point here is that you are providing package names within the RDEPENDS variable. For an example of the default list of packages created from a recipe, see the PACKAGES variable.

Because the RDEPENDS variable applies to packages being built, you should always use the variable in a form with an attached package name. For example, suppose you are building a development package that depends on the perl package. In this case, you would use the following RDEPENDS statement:

```
RDEPENDS_${PN}-dev += "perl"
```

In the example, the development package depends on the perl package. Thus, the RDEPENDS variable has the ${PN}-dev package name as part of the variable.

The package name you attach to the RDEPENDS variable must appear as it would in the PACKAGES namespace before any renaming of the output package by classes like debian.

In many cases you do not need to explicitly add runtime dependencies using RDEPENDS since some automatic handling occurs:

- shlibdeps: If a runtime package contains a shared library (.so), the build processes the library in order to determine other libraries to which it is dynamically linked. The build process adds these libraries to RDEPENDS when creating the runtime package.

- pcdeps: If the package ships a pkg-config information file, the build process uses this file to add items to the RDEPENDS variable to create the runtime packages.

BitBake, which the OpenEmbedded build system uses, supports specifying versioned dependencies. Although the syntax varies depending on the packaging format, BitBake hides these differences from you. Here is the general syntax to specify versions with the RDEPENDS variable:

```
RDEPENDS_${PN} = "package (operator version)"
```

For operator, you can specify the following:

```
=
<
>
<=
>=
```

For example, the following sets up a dependency on version 1.2 or greater of the package foo:

```
RDEPENDS_${PN} = "foo (>= 1.2)"
```

For information on build-time dependencies, see the DEPENDS variable.

REQUIRED_DISTRO_FEATURES When inheriting the distro_features_check class, this variable identifies distribution features that must exist in the current configuration in order for the OpenEmbedded build system to build the recipe. In other words, if the REQUIRED_DISTRO_FEATURES variable lists a feature that does not appear in DISTRO_FEATURES within the current configuration, an error occurs and the build stops.

RM_OLD_IMAGE Reclaims disk space by removing previously built versions of the same image from the images directory pointed to by the DEPLOY_DIR variable.

Set this variable to "1" in your local.conf file to remove these images.

RM_WORK_EXCLUDE With rm_work enabled, this variable specifies a list of recipes whose work directories should not be removed. See the "rm_work.bbclass" section for more details.

ROOT_HOME Defines the root home directory. By default, this directory is set as follows in the BitBake configuration file:

```
ROOT_HOME ??= "/home/root"
```

Note
This default value is likely used because some embedded solutions prefer to have a read-only root filesystem and prefer to keep writeable data in one place.

You can override the default by setting the variable in any layer or in the local.conf file. Because the default is set using a "weak" assignment (i.e. "??="), you can use either of the following forms to define your override:

```
ROOT_HOME = "/root"
ROOT_HOME ?= "/root"
```

These override examples use /root, which is probably the most commonly used override.

ROOTFS

Indicates a filesystem image to include as the root filesystem.

The ROOTFS variable is an optional variable used with the bootimg class.

ROOTFS_POSTPROCESS_COMMAND Added by classes to run post processing commands once the OpenEmbedded build system has created the root filesystem. You can specify shell commands separated by semicolons:

```
ROOTFS_POSTPROCESS_COMMAND += "shell_command; ... "
```

If you need to pass the path to the root filesystem within the command, you can use ${IMAGE_ROOTFS}, which points to the root filesystem image. See the IMAGE_ROOTFS variable for more information.

RPROVIDES

A list of package name aliases that a package also provides. These aliases are useful for satisfying runtime dependencies of other packages both during the build and on the target (as specified by RDEPENDS).

Note

A package's own name is implicitly already in its RPROVIDES list.

As with all package-controlling variables, you must always use the variable in conjunction with a package name override. Here is an example:

```
RPROVIDES_${PN} = "widget-abi-2"
```

RRECOMMENDS

A list of packages that extends the usability of a package being built. The package being built does not depend on this list of packages in order to successfully build, but rather uses them for extended usability. To specify runtime dependencies for packages, see the RDEPENDS variable.

The package manager will automatically install the RRECOMMENDS list of packages when installing the built package. However, you can prevent listed packages from being installed by using the BAD_RECOMMENDATIONS, NO_RECOMMENDATIONS, and PACKAGE_EXCLUDE variables.

Packages specified in RRECOMMENDS need not actually be produced. However, a recipe must exist that provides each package, either through the PACKAGES or PACKAGES_DYNAMIC variables or the RPROVIDES variable, or an error will occur during the build. If such a recipe does exist and the package is not produced, the build continues without error.

Because the RRECOMMENDS variable applies to packages being built, you should always attach an override to the variable to specify the particular package whose usability is being extended. For example, suppose you are building a development package that is extended to support wireless functionality. In this case, you would use the following:

```
RRECOMMENDS_${PN}-dev += "wireless_package_name"
```

In the example, the package name (${PN}-dev) must appear as it would in the PACKAGES namespace before any renaming of the output package by classes such as debian.bbclass.

BitBake, which the OpenEmbedded build system uses, supports specifying versioned recommends. Although the syntax varies depending on the packaging format, BitBake hides these differences from you. Here is the general syntax to specify versions with the RRECOMMENDS variable:

```
RRECOMMENDS_${PN} = "package (operator version)"
```

For operator, you can specify the following:

```
=
<
>
<=
>=
```

For example, the following sets up a recommend on version 1.2 or greater of the package foo:

```
RRECOMMENDS_${PN} = "foo (>= 1.2)"
```

RREPLACES

A list of packages replaced by a package. The package manager uses this variable to determine which package should be installed to replace other package(s) during an upgrade. In order to also have the other package(s) removed at the same time, you must add the name of the other package to the RCONFLICTS variable.

As with all package-controlling variables, you must use this variable in conjunction with a package name override. Here is an example:

```
RREPLACES_${PN} = "other-package-being-replaced"
```

BitBake, which the OpenEmbedded build system uses, supports specifying versioned replacements. Although the syntax varies depending on the packaging format, BitBake hides these differences from you. Here is the general syntax to specify versions with the RREPLACES variable:

```
RREPLACES_${PN} = "package (operator version)"
```

For operator, you can specify the following:

```
=
<
>
<=
>=
```

For example, the following sets up a replacement using version 1.2 or greater of the package foo:

```
RREPLACES_${PN} = "foo (>= 1.2)"
```

RSUGGESTS

A list of additional packages that you can suggest for installation by the package manager at the time a package is installed. Not all package managers support this functionality.

As with all package-controlling variables, you must always use this variable in conjunction with a package name override. Here is an example:

```
RSUGGESTS_${PN} = "useful-package another-package"
```

S

S

The location in the Build Directory [http://www.yoctoproject.org/docs/1.7.2/dev-manual/dev-manual.html#build-directory] where unpacked recipe source code resides. This location is within the work directory (WORKDIR), which is not static. The unpacked source location depends on the recipe name (PN) and recipe version (PV) as follows:

```
${WORKDIR}/${PN}-${PV}
```

As an example, assume a Source Directory [http://www.yoctoproject.org/docs/1.7.2/dev-manual/dev-manual.html#source-directory] top-level folder named poky and a default Build Directory at poky/build. In this case, the work directory the build system uses to keep the unpacked recipe for db is the following:

```
poky/build/tmp/work/qemux86-poky-linux/db/5.1.19-r3/db-5.1.19
```

SANITY_REQUIRED_UTILITIES

Specifies a list of command-line utilities that should be checked for during the initial sanity checking process when running BitBake. If any of the utilities are not installed on the build host, then BitBake immediately exits with an error.

SANITY_TESTED_DISTROS

A list of the host distribution identifiers that the build system has been tested against. Identifiers consist of the host distributor ID followed by the release, as reported by the lsb_release tool or as read from /etc/lsb-release. Separate the list items with explicit newline characters (\n). If SANITY_TESTED_DISTROS is not empty and the current value of NATIVELSBSTRING does not appear in the list, then the build system reports a warning that indicates the current host distribution has not been tested as a build host.

SDK_ARCH

The target architecture for the SDK. Typically, you do not directly set this variable. Instead, use SDKMACHINE.

SDK_DEPLOY

The directory set up and used by the populate_sdk_base to which the SDK is deployed. The populate_sdk_base class defines SDK_DEPLOY as follows:

```
SDK_DEPLOY = "${TMPDIR}/deploy/sdk"
```

SDK_DIR   The parent directory used by the OpenEmbedded build system when creating SDK output. The `populate_sdk_base` class defines the variable as follows:

```
SDK_DIR = "${WORKDIR}/sdk"
```

Note
The `SDK_DIR` directory is a temporary directory as it is part of WORKDIR. The final output directory is SDK_DEPLOY.

SDK_NAME   The base name for SDK output files. The name is derived from the DISTRO, TCLIBC, SDK_ARCH, IMAGE_BASENAME, and TUNE_PKGARCH variables:

```
SDK_NAME = "${DISTRO}-${TCLIBC}-${SDK_ARCH}-${IMAGE_BASENAME}-${
```

SDK_OUTPUT   The location used by the OpenEmbedded build system when creating SDK output. The `populate_sdk_base` class defines the variable as follows:

```
SDK_OUTPUT = "${SDK_DIR}/image"
```

Note
The `SDK_OUTPUT` directory is a temporary directory as it is part of WORKDIR by way of SDK_DIR. The final output directory is SDK_DEPLOY.

SDK_PACKAGE_ARCHS   Specifies a list of architectures compatible with the SDK machine. This variable is set automatically and should not normally be hand-edited. Entries are separated using spaces and listed in order of priority. The default value for SDK_PACKAGE_ARCHS is "all any noarch ${SDK_ARCH}-${SDKPKGSUFFIX}".

SDKIMAGE_FEATURES   Equivalent to IMAGE_FEATURES. However, this variable applies to the SDK generated from an image using the following command:

```
$ bitbake -c populate_sdk imagename
```

SDKMACHINE   The machine for which the Application Development Toolkit (ADT) or SDK is built. In other words, the SDK or ADT is built such that it runs on the target you specify with the SDKMACHINE value. The value points to a corresponding .conf file under conf/machine-sdk/.

You can use "i686" and "x86_64" as possible values for this variable. The variable defaults to "i686" and is set in the local.conf file in the Build Directory.

```
SDKMACHINE ?= "i686"
```

Note
You cannot set the SDKMACHINE variable in your distribution configuration file. If you do, the configuration will not take affect.

SDKPATH	Defines the path offered to the user for installation of the SDK that is generated by the OpenEmbedded build system. The path appears as the default location for installing the SDK when you run the SDK's installation script. You can override the offered path when you run the script.
SECTION	The section in which packages should be categorized. Package management utilities can make use of this variable.
SELECTED_OPTIMIZATION	Specifies the optimization flags passed to the C compiler when building for the target. The flags are passed through the default value of the TARGET_CFLAGS variable.

The SELECTED_OPTIMIZATION variable takes the value of FULL_OPTIMIZATION unless DEBUG_BUILD = "1". If that is the case, the value of DEBUG_OPTIMIZATION is used.

SERIAL_CONSOLE — Defines a serial console (TTY) to enable using getty. Provide a value that specifies the baud rate followed by the TTY device name separated by a space. You cannot specify more than one TTY device:

```
SERIAL_CONSOLE = "115200 ttyS0"
```

Note
The SERIAL_CONSOLE variable is deprecated. Please use the SERIAL_CONSOLES variable.

SERIAL_CONSOLES — Defines the serial consoles (TTYs) to enable using getty. Provide a value that specifies the baud rate followed by the TTY device name separated by a semicolon. Use spaces to separate multiple devices:

```
SERIAL_CONSOLES = "115200;ttyS0 115200;ttyS1"
```

SERIAL_CONSOLES_CHECK — Similar to SERIAL_CONSOLES except the device is checked for existence before attempting to enable it. This variable is currently only supported with SysVinit (i.e. not with systemd).

SIGGEN_EXCLUDE_SAFE_RECIPE_DEPS — A list of recipe dependencies that should not be used to determine signatures of tasks from one recipe when they depend on tasks from another recipe. For example:

```
SIGGEN_EXCLUDE_SAFE_RECIPE_DEPS += "intone->mplayer2"
```

In this example, intone depends on mplayer2.

Use of this variable is one mechanism to remove dependencies that affect task signatures and thus force rebuilds when a recipe changes.

Caution
If you add an inappropriate dependency for a recipe relationship, the software might break during runtime if the interface of the second recipe was changed after the first recipe had been built.

SIGGEN_EXCLUDERECIPES_ABISAFE — A list of recipes that are completely stable and will never change. The ABI for the recipes in the list are presented by output from the tasks run to build the recipe. Use of this variable is one way to remove dependencies from one recipe on another that affect task signatures and thus force rebuilds when the recipe changes.

Caution

If you add an inappropriate variable to this list, the software might break at runtime if the interface of the recipe was changed after the other had been built.

SITEINFO_BITS Specifies the number of bits for the target system CPU. The value should be either "32" or "64".

SITEINFO_ENDIANNESS Specifies the endian byte order of the target system. The value should be either "le" for little-endian or "be" for big-endian.

SOC_FAMILY Groups together machines based upon the same family of SOC (System On Chip). You typically set this variable in a common .inc file that you include in the configuration files of all the machines.

Note

You must include conf/machine/include/soc-family.inc for this variable to appear in MACHINEOVERRIDES.

SOLIBS Defines the suffix for shared libraries used on the target platform. By default, this suffix is ".so.*" for all Linux-based systems and is defined in the meta/conf/bitbake.conf configuration file.

You will see this variable referenced in the default values of FILES_${PN}.

SOLIBSDEV Defines the suffix for the development symbolic link (symlink) for shared libraries on the target platform. By default, this suffix is ".so" for Linux-based systems and is defined in the meta/conf/bitbake.conf configuration file.

You will see this variable referenced in the default values of FILES_${PN}-dev.

SOURCE_MIRROR_URL Defines your own PREMIRRORS from which to first fetch source before attempting to fetch from the upstream specified in SRC_URI.

To use this variable, you must globally inherit the own-mirrors class and then provide the URL to your mirrors. Here is an example:

```
INHERIT += "own-mirrors"
SOURCE_MIRROR_URL = "http://example.com/my-source-mirror"
```

Note

You can specify only a single URL in SOURCE_MIRROR_URL.

SPDXLICENSEMAP Maps commonly used license names to their SPDX counterparts found in meta/files/common-licenses/. For the default SPDXLICENSEMAP mappings, see the meta/conf/licenses.conf file.

For additional information, see the LICENSE variable.

SPECIAL_PKGSUFFIX A list of prefixes for PN used by the OpenEmbedded build system to create variants of recipes or packages. The list specifies the prefixes to strip off during certain circumstances such as the generation of the BPN variable.

SRC_URI The list of source files - local or remote. This variable tells the OpenEmbedded build system which bits to pull in for the build and how to pull them in. For example, if the recipe or append file only needs to fetch a tarball from the Internet, the recipe or append file uses a single SRC_URI entry. On the other hand, if the recipe or append file needs to fetch a tarball, apply two patches, and include a custom file, the recipe or append file would include four instances of the variable.

The following list explains the available URI protocols:

- `file://` - Fetches files, which are usually files shipped with the Metadata [http://www.yoctoproject.org/docs/1.7.2/dev-manual/dev-manual.html#metadata], from the local machine. The path is relative to the FILESPATH variable. Thus, the build system searches, in order, from the following directories, which are assumed to be a subdirectories of the directory in which the recipe file (`.bb`) or append file (`.bbappend`) resides:

  - `${BPN}` - The base recipe name without any special suffix or version numbers.

  - `${BP}` - `${BPN}-${PV}`. The base recipe name and version but without any special package name suffix.

  - files - Files within a directory, which is named `files` and is also alongside the recipe or append file.

    ## Note
    If you want the build system to pick up files specified through a SRC_URI statement from your append file, you need to be sure to extend the FILESPATH variable by also using the FILESEXTRAPATHS variable from within your append file.

- `bzr://` - Fetches files from a Bazaar revision control repository.

- `git://` - Fetches files from a Git revision control repository.

- `osc://` - Fetches files from an OSC (OpenSUSE Build service) revision control repository.

- `repo://` - Fetches files from a repo (Git) repository.

- `ccrc://` - Fetches files from a ClearCase repository.

- `http://` - Fetches files from the Internet using `http`.

- `https://` - Fetches files from the Internet using `https`.

- `ftp://` - Fetches files from the Internet using `ftp`.

- `cvs://` - Fetches files from a CVS revision control repository.

- `hg://` - Fetches files from a Mercurial (hg) revision control repository.

- `p4://` - Fetches files from a Perforce (p4) revision control repository.

- `ssh://` - Fetches files from a secure shell.

- `svn://` - Fetches files from a Subversion (`svn`) revision control repository.

Standard and recipe-specific options for SRC_URI exist. Here are standard options:

- `apply` - Whether to apply the patch or not. The default action is to apply the patch.

- `striplevel` - Which striplevel to use when applying the patch. The default level is 1.

- patchdir - Specifies the directory in which the patch should be applied. The default is ${S}.

Here are options specific to recipes building code from a revision control system:

- mindate - Apply the patch only if SRCDATE is equal to or greater than mindate.

- maxdate - Apply the patch only if SRCDATE is not later than mindate.

- minrev - Apply the patch only if SRCREV is equal to or greater than minrev.

- maxrev - Apply the patch only if SRCREV is not later than maxrev.

- rev - Apply the patch only if SRCREV is equal to rev.

- notrev - Apply the patch only if SRCREV is not equal to rev.

Here are some additional options worth mentioning:

- unpack - Controls whether or not to unpack the file if it is an archive. The default action is to unpack the file.

- subdir - Places the file (or extracts its contents) into the specified subdirectory of WORKDIR. This option is useful for unusual tarballs or other archives that do not have their files already in a subdirectory within the archive.

- name - Specifies a name to be used for association with SRC_URI checksums when you have more than one file specified in SRC_URI.

- downloadfilename - Specifies the filename used when storing the downloaded file.

SRC_URI_OVERRIDES_PACKAGE_ARCH	By default, the OpenEmbedded build system automatically detects whether SRC_URI contains files that are machine-specific. If so, the build system automatically changes PACKAGE_ARCH. Setting this variable to "0" disables this behavior.
SRCDATE	The date of the source code used to build the package. This variable applies only if the source was fetched from a Source Code Manager (SCM).
SRCPV	Returns the version string of the current package. This string is used to help define the value of PV.

The SRCPV variable is defined in the meta/ conf/bitbake.conf configuration file in the Source Directory [http://www.yoctoproject.org/docs/1.7.2/dev-manual/dev-manual.html#source-directory] as follows:

```
SRCPV = "${@bb.fetch2.get_srcrev(d)}"
```

Recipes that need to define PV do so with the help of the SRCPV. For example, the ofono recipe (ofono_git.bb) located in meta/ recipes-connectivity in the Source Directory defines PV as follows:

```
PV = "0.12-git${SRCPV}"
```

SRCREV	The revision of the source code used to build the package. This variable applies to Subversion, Git, Mercurial and Bazaar only. Note

that if you wish to build a fixed revision and you wish to avoid performing a query on the remote repository every time BitBake parses your recipe, you should specify a SRCREV that is a full revision identifier and not just a tag.

SSTATE_DIR   The directory for the shared state cache.

SSTATE_MIRROR_ALLOW_NETWORK When set to "1", allows fetches from mirrors that are specified in SSTATE_MIRRORS to work even when fetching from the network has been disabled by setting BB_NO_NETWORK to "1". Using the SSTATE_MIRROR_ALLOW_NETWORK variable is useful if you have set SSTATE_MIRRORS to point to an internal server for your shared state cache, but you want to disable any other fetching from the network.

SSTATE_MIRRORS   Configures the OpenEmbedded build system to search other mirror locations for prebuilt cache data objects before building out the data. This variable works like fetcher MIRRORS and PREMIRRORS and points to the cache locations to check for the shared objects.

You can specify a filesystem directory or a remote URL such as HTTP or FTP. The locations you specify need to contain the shared state cache (sstate-cache) results from previous builds. The sstate-cache you point to can also be from builds on other machines.

If a mirror uses the same structure as SSTATE_DIR, you need to add "PATH" at the end as shown in the examples below. The build system substitutes the correct path within the directory structure.

```
SSTATE_MIRRORS ?= "\
file://.* http://someserver.tld/share/sstate/PATH \n \
file://.* file:///some-local-dir/sstate/PATH"
```

STAGING_BASE_LIBDIR_NATIVE Specifies the path to the /lib subdirectory of the sysroot directory for the build host.

STAGING_BASELIBDIR   Specifies the path to the /lib subdirectory of the sysroot directory for the target for which the current recipe is being built (STAGING_DIR_HOST).

STAGING_BINDIR   Specifies the path to the /usr/bin subdirectory of the sysroot directory for the target for which the current recipe is being built (STAGING_DIR_HOST).

STAGING_BINDIR_CROSS   Specifies the path to the directory containing binary configuration scripts. These scripts provide configuration information for other software that wants to make use of libraries or include files provided by the software associated with the script.

Note
This style of build configuration has been largely replaced by pkg-config. Consequently, if pkg-config is supported by the library to which you are linking, it is recommended you use pkg-config instead of a provided configuration script.

STAGING_BINDIR_NATIVE   Specifies the path to the /usr/bin subdirectory of the sysroot directory for the build host.

STAGING_DATADIR   Specifies the path to the /usr/share subdirectory of the sysroot directory for the target for which the current recipe is being built (STAGING_DIR_HOST).

STAGING_DIR   Specifies the path to the top-level sysroots directory (i.e. ${TMPDIR}/ sysroots).

Note

Recipes should never write files directly under this directory because the OpenEmbedded build system manages the directory automatically. Instead, files should be installed to ${D} within your recipe's do_install task and then the OpenEmbedded build system will stage a subset of those files into the sysroot.

STAGING_DIR_HOST	Specifies the path to the primary sysroot directory for which the target is being built. Depending on the type of recipe and the build target, the recipe's value is as follows: • For recipes building for the target machine, the value is "${STAGING_DIR}/${MACHINE}". • For native recipes building for the build host, the value is empty given the assumption that when building for the build host, the build host's own directories should be used. • For nativesdk recipes that Build for the SDK, the value is "${STAGING_DIR}/${MULTIMACH_HOST_SYS}".
STAGING_DATADIR_NATIVE	Specifies the path to the /usr/share subdirectory of the sysroot directory for the build host.
STAGING_DIR_NATIVE	Specifies the path to the sysroot directory for the build host.
STAGING_DIR_TARGET	Specifies the path to the sysroot directory for the target for which the current recipe is being built. In most cases, this path is the STAGING_DIR_HOST. Some recipes build binaries that can run on the target system but those binaries in turn generate code for another different system (e.g. cross-canadian recipes). Using terminology from GNU, the primary system is referred to as the "HOST" and the secondary, or different, system is referred to as the "TARGET". Thus, the binaries run on the "HOST" system and and generate binaries for the "TARGET" system. STAGING_DIR_TARGET points to the sysroot used for the "TARGET" system.
STAGING_ETCDIR_NATIVE	Specifies the path to the /etc subdirectory of the sysroot directory for the build host.
STAGING_EXECPREFIXDIR	Specifies the path to the /usr subdirectory of the sysroot directory for the target for which the current recipe is being built (STAGING_DIR_HOST).
STAGING_INCDIR	Specifies the path to the /usr/include subdirectory of the sysroot directory for the target for which the current recipe being built (STAGING_DIR_HOST).
STAGING_INCDIR_NATIVE	Specifies the path to the /usr/include subdirectory of the sysroot directory for the build host.
STAGING_LIBDIR	Specifies the path to the /usr/lib subdirectory of the sysroot directory for the target for which the current recipe is being built (STAGING_DIR_HOST).
STAGING_LIBDIR_NATIVE	Specifies the path to the /usr/lib subdirectory of the sysroot directory for the build host.
STAGING_KERNEL_DIR	The directory with kernel headers that are required to build out-of-tree modules.
STAMP	Specifies the base path used to create recipe stamp files. The path to an actual stamp file is constructed by evaluating this string and then

appending additional information. Currently, the default assignment for STAMP as set in the meta/conf/bitbake.conf file is:

```
STAMP = "${STAMPS_DIR}/${MULTIMACH_TARGET_SYS}/${PN}/${EXTENDPE}$
```

See STAMPS_DIR, MULTIMACH_TARGET_SYS, PN, EXTENDPE, PV, and PR for related variable information.

STAMPS_DIR	Specifies the base directory in which the OpenEmbedded build system places stamps. The default directory is ${TMPDIR}/stamps.
SUMMARY	The short (72 characters or less) summary of the binary package for packaging systems such as opkg, rpm or dpkg. By default, SUMMARY is used to define the DESCRIPTION variable if DESCRIPTION is not set in the recipe.
SYSLINUX_DEFAULT_CONSOLE	Specifies the kernel boot default console. If you want to use a console other than the default, set this variable in your recipe as follows where "X" is the console number you want to use:

```
SYSLINUX_DEFAULT_CONSOLE = "console=ttyX"
```

The syslinux class initially sets this variable to null but then checks for a value later.

SYSLINUX_OPTS	Lists additional options to add to the syslinux file. You need to set this variable in your recipe. If you want to list multiple options, separate the options with a semicolon character (;).

The syslinux class uses this variable to create a set of options.

SYSLINUX_SERIAL	Specifies the alternate serial port or turns it off. To turn off serial, set this variable to an empty string in your recipe. The variable's default value is set in the syslinux as follows:

```
SYSLINUX_SERIAL ?= "0 115200"
```

The class checks for and uses the variable as needed.

SYSLINUX_SPLASH	An .LSS file used as the background for the VGA boot menu when you are using the boot menu. You need to set this variable in your recipe.

The syslinux class checks for this variable and if found, the OpenEmbedded build system installs the splash screen.

SYSLINUX_SERIAL_TTY	Specifies the alternate console=tty... kernel boot argument. The variable's default value is set in the syslinux as follows:

```
SYSLINUX_SERIAL_TTY ?= "console=ttyS0,115200"
```

The class checks for and uses the variable as needed.

SYSROOT_PREPROCESS_FUNCS	A list of functions to execute after files are staged into the sysroot. These functions are usually used to apply additional processing on the staged files, or to stage additional files.
SYSTEMD_AUTO_ENABLE	When inheriting the systemd class, this variable specifies whether the service you have specified in SYSTEMD_SERVICE should be started automatically or not. By default, the service is enabled to

automatically start at boot time. The default setting is in the systemd class as follows:

SYSTEMD_AUTO_ENABLE ??= "enable"

You can disable the service by setting the variable to "disable".

SYSTEMD_PACKAGES

When inheriting the systemd class, this variable locates the systemd unit files when they are not found in the main recipe's package. By default, the SYSTEMD_PACKAGES variable is set such that the systemd unit files are assumed to reside in the recipes main package:

SYSTEMD_PACKAGES ?= "${PN}"

If these unit files are not in this recipe's main package, you need to use SYSTEMD_PACKAGES to list the package or packages in which the build system can find the systemd unit files.

SYSTEMD_SERVICE

When inheriting the systemd class, this variable specifies the systemd service name for a package.

When you specify this file in your recipe, use a package name override to indicate the package to which the value applies. Here is an example from the connman recipe:

SYSTEMD_SERVICE_${PN} = "connman.service"

SYSVINIT_ENABLED_GETTYS

When using SysVinit [http://www.yoctoproject.org/docs/1.7.2/dev-manual/dev-manual.html#new-recipe-enabling-system-services], specifies a space-separated list of the virtual terminals that should be running a getty [http://en.wikipedia.org/wiki/Getty_%28Unix%29] (allowing login), assuming USE_VT is not set to "0".

The default value for SYSVINIT_ENABLED_GETTYS is "1" (i.e. only run a getty on the first virtual terminal).

T

T

This variable points to a directory were BitBake places temporary files, which consist mostly of task logs and scripts, when building a particular recipe. The variable is typically set as follows:

T = "${WORKDIR}/temp"

The WORKDIR is the directory into which BitBake unpacks and builds the recipe. The default bitbake.conf file sets this variable.

The T variable is not to be confused with the TMPDIR variable, which points to the root of the directory tree where BitBake places the output of an entire build.

TARGET_ARCH

The target machine's architecture. The OpenEmbedded build system supports many architectures. Here is an example list of architectures supported. This list is by no means complete as the architecture is configurable:

arm

```
i586
x86_64
powerpc
powerpc64
mips
mipsel
```

For additional information on machine architectures, see the TUNE_ARCH variable.

TARGET_AS_ARCH	Specifies architecture-specific assembler flags for the target system. TARGET_AS_ARCH is initialized from TUNE_ASARGS by default in the BitBake configuration file (meta/conf/bitbake.conf):

```
TARGET_AS_ARCH = "${TUNE_ASARGS}"
```

TARGET_CC_ARCH

Specifies architecture-specific C compiler flags for the target system. TARGET_CC_ARCH is initialized from TUNE_CCARGS by default.

Note
It is a common workaround to append LDFLAGS to TARGET_CC_ARCH in recipes that build software for the target that would not otherwise respect the exported LDFLAGS variable.

TARGET_CC_KERNEL_ARCH

This is a specific kernel compiler flag for a CPU or Application Binary Interface (ABI) tune. The flag is used rarely and only for cases where a userspace TUNE_CCARGS is not compatible with the kernel compilation. The TARGET_CC_KERNEL_ARCH variable allows the kernel (and associated modules) to use a different configuration. See the meta/conf/machine/include/arm/feature-arm-thumb.inc file in the Source Directory [http://www.yoctoproject.org/docs/1.7.2/dev-manual/dev-manual.html#source-directory] for an example.

TARGET_CFLAGS

Specifies the flags to pass to the C compiler when building for the target. When building in the target context, CFLAGS is set to the value of this variable by default.

Additionally, the SDK's environment setup script sets the CFLAGS variable in the environment to the TARGET_CFLAGS value so that executables built using the SDK also have the flags applied.

TARGET_CPPFLAGS

Specifies the flags to pass to the C pre-processor (i.e. to both the C and the C++ compilers) when building for the target. When building in the target context, CPPFLAGS is set to the value of this variable by default.

Additionally, the SDK's environment setup script sets the CPPFLAGS variable in the environment to the TARGET_CPPFLAGS value so that executables built using the SDK also have the flags applied.

TARGET_CXXFLAGS

Specifies the flags to pass to the C++ compiler when building for the target. When building in the target context, CXXFLAGS is set to the value of this variable by default.

Additionally, the SDK's environment setup script sets the CXXFLAGS variable in the environment to the TARGET_CXXFLAGS value so that executables built using the SDK also have the flags applied.

TARGET_FPU

Specifies the method for handling FPU code. For FPU-less targets, which include most ARM CPUs, the variable must be set to "soft". If not, the kernel emulation gets used, which results in a performance penalty.

TARGET_LD_ARCH	Specifies architecture-specific linker flags for the target system. TARGET_LD_ARCH is initialized from TUNE_LDARGS by default in the BitBake configuration file (meta/conf/bitbake.conf):

```
TARGET_LD_ARCH = "${TUNE_LDARGS}"
```

TARGET_LDFLAGS	Specifies the flags to pass to the linker when building for the target. When building in the target context, LDFLAGS is set to the value of this variable by default.
	Additionally, the SDK's environment setup script sets the LDFLAGS variable in the environment to the TARGET_LDFLAGS value so that executables built using the SDK also have the flags applied.
TARGET_OS	Specifies the target's operating system. The variable can be set to "linux" for glibc-based systems and to "linux-uclibc" for uclibc. For ARM/EABI targets, there are also "linux-gnueabi" and "linux-uclibc-gnueabi" values possible.
TCLIBC	Specifies the GNU standard C library (libc) variant to use during the build process. This variable replaces POKYLIBC, which is no longer supported.
	You can select "glibc" or "uclibc".
TCMODE	Specifies the toolchain selector. TCMODE controls the characteristics of the generated packages and images by telling the OpenEmbedded build system which toolchain profile to use. By default, the OpenEmbedded build system builds its own internal toolchain. The variable's default value is "default", which uses that internal toolchain.

Note

If TCMODE is set to a value other than "default", then it is your responsibility to ensure that the toolchain is compatible with the default toolchain. Using older or newer versions of these components might cause build problems. See the Release Notes [http://www.yoctoproject.org/downloads/core/dizzy172] for the specific components with which the toolchain must be compatible.

With additional layers, it is possible to use a pre-compiled external toolchain. One example is the Sourcery G++ Toolchain. The support for this toolchain resides in the separate meta-sourcery layer at http://github.com/MentorEmbedded/meta-sourcery/. You can use meta-sourcery as a template for adding support for other external toolchains.

The TCMODE variable points the build system to a file in conf/distro/include/tcmode-${TCMODE}.inc. Thus, for meta-sourcery, which has conf/distro/include/tcmode-external-sourcery.inc, you would set the variable as follows:

```
TCMODE ?= "external-sourcery"
```

The variable is similar to TCLIBC, which controls the variant of the GNU standard C library (libc) used during the build process: glibc or uclibc.

TEST_EXPORT_DIR	The location the OpenEmbedded build system uses to export tests when the TEST_EXPORT_ONLY variable is set to "1".

The TEST_EXPORT_DIR variable defaults to "${TMPDIR}/testimage/${PN}".

TEST_EXPORT_ONLY

Specifies to export the tests only. Set this variable to "1" if you do not want to run the tests but you want them to be exported in a manner that you to run them outside of the build system.

TEST_IMAGE

Automatically runs the series of automated tests for images when an image is successfully built.

These tests are written in Python making use of the unittest module, and the majority of them run commands on the target system over ssh. You can set this variable to "1" in your local.conf file in the Build Directory [http://www.yoctoproject.org/docs/1.7.2/dev-manual/dev-manual.html#build-directory] to have the OpenEmbedded build system automatically run these tests after an image successfully builds:

```
TEST_IMAGE = "1"
```

For more information on enabling, running, and writing these tests, see the "Performing Automated Runtime Testing [http://www.yoctoproject.org/docs/1.7.2/dev-manual/dev-manual.html#performing-automated-runtime-testing]" section in the Yocto Project Development Manual and the "testimage.bbclass" section.

TEST_LOG_DIR

Holds the SSH log and the boot log for QEMU machines. The TEST_LOG_DIR variable defaults to "${WORKDIR}/testimage".

Note
Actual test results reside in the task log (log.do_testimage), which is in the ${WORKDIR}/temp/ directory.

TEST_POWERCONTROL_CMD

For automated hardware testing, specifies the command to use to control the power of the target machine under test. Typically, this command would point to a script that performs the appropriate action (e.g. interacting with a web-enabled power strip). The specified command should expect to receive as the last argument "off", "on" or "cycle" specifying to power off, on, or cycle (power off and then power on) the device, respectively.

TEST_POWERCONTROL_EXTRA_ARGS

For automated hardware testing, specifies additional arguments to pass through to the command specified in TEST_POWERCONTROL_CMD. Setting TEST_POWERCONTROL_EXTRA_ARGS is optional. You can use it if you wish, for example, to separate the machine-specific and non-machine-specific parts of the arguments.

TEST_QEMUBOOT_TIMEOUT

The time in seconds allowed for an image to boot before automated runtime tests begin to run against an image. The default timeout period to allow the boot process to reach the login prompt is 500 seconds. You can specify a different value in the local.conf file.

For more information on testing images, see the "Performing Automated Runtime Testing [http://www.yoctoproject.org/docs/1.7.2/dev-manual/dev-manual.html#performing-automated-runtime-testing]" section in the Yocto Project Development Manual.

TEST_SERIALCONTROL_CMD

For automated hardware testing, specifies the command to use to connect to the serial console of the target machine under test. This command simply needs to connect to the serial console and forward that connection to standard input and output as any normal terminal program does.

For example, to use the Picocom terminal program on serial device /dev/ttyUSB0 at 115200bps, you would set the variable as follows:

```
TEST_SERIALCONTROL_CMD = "picocom /dev/ttyUSB0 -b 115200"
```

TEST_SERIALCONTROL_EXTRA_ARGS   For automated hardware testing, specifies additional arguments to pass through to the command specified in TEST_SERIALCONTROL_CMD. Setting TEST_SERIALCONTROL_EXTRA_ARGS is optional. You can use it if you wish, for example, to separate the machine-specific and non-machine-specific parts of the command.

TEST_SERVER_IP   The IP address of the build machine (host machine). This IP address is usually automatically detected. However, if detection fails, this variable needs to be set to the IP address of the build machine (i.e. where the build is taking place).

Note

The TEST_SERVER_IP variable is only used for a small number of tests such as the "smart" test suite, which needs to download packages from DEPLOY_DIR/rpm.

TEST_TARGET   Specifies the target controller to use when running tests against a test image. The default controller to use is "qemu":

```
TEST_TARGET = "qemu"
```

A target controller is a class that defines how an image gets deployed on a target and how a target is started. A layer can extend the controllers by adding a module in the layer's /lib/oeqa/controllers directory and by inheriting the BaseTarget class, which is an abstract class that cannot be used as a value of TEST_TARGET.

You can provide the following arguments with TEST_TARGET:

- "qemu" and "QemuTarget": Boots a QEMU image and runs the tests. See the "Enabling Runtime Tests on QEMU [http://www.yoctoproject.org/docs/1.7.2/dev-manual/dev-manual.html#qemu-image-enabling-tests]" section in the Yocto Project Development Manual for more information.

- "simpleremote" and "SimpleRemoteTarget": Runs the tests on target hardware that is already up and running. The hardware can be on the network or it can be a device running an image on QEMU. You must also set TEST_TARGET_IP when you use "simpleremote" or "SimpleRemoteTarget".

Note

This argument is defined in meta/lib/oeqa/targetcontrol.py. The small caps names are kept for compatibility reasons.

- "GummibootTarget": Automatically deploys and runs tests on an EFI-enabled machine that has a master image installed.

Note

This argument is defined in meta/lib/oeqa/controllers/masterimage.py.

For information on running tests on hardware, see the "Enabling Runtime Tests on Hardware [http://www.yoctoproject.org/docs/1.7.2/dev-manual/dev-manual.html#hardware-image-enabling-tests]" section in the Yocto Project Development Manual.

TEST_TARGET_IP   The IP address of your hardware under test. The TEST_TARGET_IP variable has no effect when TEST_TARGET is set to "qemu".

When you specify the IP address, you can also include a port. Here is an example:

```
TEST_TARGET_IP = "192.168.1.4:2201"
```

Specifying a port is useful when SSH is started on a non-standard port or in cases when your hardware under test is behind a firewall or network that is not directly accessible from your host and you need to do port address translation.

TEST_SUITES   An ordered list of tests (modules) to run against an image when performing automated runtime testing.

The OpenEmbedded build system provides a core set of tests that can be used against images.

Note
Currently, there is only support for running these tests under QEMU.

Tests include ping, ssh, df among others. You can add your own tests to the list of tests by appending TEST_SUITES as follows:

```
TEST_SUITES_append = " mytest"
```

Alternatively, you can provide the "auto" option to have all applicable tests run against the image.

```
TEST_SUITES_append = " auto"
```

Using this option causes the build system to automatically run tests that are applicable to the image. Tests that are not applicable are skipped.

The order in which tests are run is important. Tests that depend on another test must appear later in the list than the test on which they depend. For example, if you append the list of tests with two tests (test_A and test_B) where test_B is dependent on test_A, then you must order the tests as follows:

```
TEST_SUITES = " test_A test_B"
```

For more information on testing images, see the "Performing Automated Runtime Testing [http://www.yoctoproject.org/docs/1.7.2/dev-manual/dev-manual.html#performing-automated-runtime-testing]" section in the Yocto Project Development Manual.

THISDIR   The directory in which the file BitBake is currently parsing is located. Do not manually set this variable.

TMPDIR

This variable is the base directory the OpenEmbedded build system uses for all build output and intermediate files (other than the shared state cache). By default, the TMPDIR variable points to tmp within the Build Directory [http://www.yoctoproject.org/docs/1.7.2/dev-manual/dev-manual.html#build-directory].

If you want to establish this directory in a location other than the default, you can uncomment and edit the following statement in the conf/local.conf file in the Source Directory [http://www.yoctoproject.org/docs/1.7.2/dev-manual/dev-manual.html#source-directory]:

```
#TMPDIR = "${TOPDIR}/tmp"
```

An example use for this scenario is to set TMPDIR to a local disk, which does not use NFS, while having the Build Directory use NFS.

The filesystem used by TMPDIR must have standard filesystem semantics (i.e. mixed-case files are unique, POSIX file locking, and persistent inodes). Due to various issues with NFS and bugs in some implementations, NFS does not meet this minimum requirement. Consequently, TMPDIR cannot be on NFS.

TOOLCHAIN_HOST_TASK

This variable lists packages the OpenEmbedded build system uses when building an SDK, which contains a cross-development environment. The packages specified by this variable are part of the toolchain set that runs on the SDKMACHINE, and each package should usually have the prefix "nativesdk-". When building an SDK using bitbake -c populate_sdk <imagename>, a default list of packages is set in this variable, but you can add additional packages to the list.

For background information on cross-development toolchains in the Yocto Project development environment, see the "Cross-Development Toolchain Generation" section. For information on setting up a cross-development environment, see the "Installing the ADT and Toolchains [http://www.yoctoproject.org/docs/1.7.2/adt-manual/adt-manual.html#installing-the-adt]" section in the Yocto Project Application Developer's Guide.

TOOLCHAIN_TARGET_TASK

This variable lists packages the OpenEmbedded build system uses when it creates the target part of an SDK (i.e. the part built for the target hardware), which includes libraries and headers.

For background information on cross-development toolchains in the Yocto Project development environment, see the "Cross-Development Toolchain Generation" section. For information on setting up a cross-development environment, see the "Installing the ADT and Toolchains [http://www.yoctoproject.org/docs/1.7.2/adt-manual/adt-manual.html#installing-the-adt]" section in the Yocto Project Application Developer's Guide.

TOPDIR

The top-level Build Directory [http://www.yoctoproject.org/docs/1.7.2/dev-manual/dev-manual.html#build-directory]. BitBake automatically sets this variable when you initialize your build environment using either oe-init-build-env or oe-init-build-env-memres.

TRANSLATED_TARGET_ARCH

A sanitized version of TARGET_ARCH. This variable is used where the architecture is needed in a value where underscores are not allowed, for example within package filenames. In this case, dash characters replace any underscore characters used in TARGET_ARCH.

Do not edit this variable.

TUNE_ARCH

The GNU canonical architecture for a specific architecture (i.e. arm, armeb, mips, mips64, and so forth). BitBake uses this value to setup configuration.

TUNE_ARCH definitions are specific to a given architecture. The definitions can be a single static definition, or can be dynamically adjusted. You can see details for a given CPU family by looking at the architecture's README file. For example, the meta/conf/machine/include/mips/README file in the Source Directory [http://www.yoctoproject.org/docs/1.7.2/dev-manual/dev-manual.html#source-directory] provides information for TUNE_ARCH specific to the mips architecture.

TUNE_ARCH is tied closely to TARGET_ARCH, which defines the target machine's architecture. The BitBake configuration file (meta/conf/bitbake.conf) sets TARGET_ARCH as follows:

```
TARGET_ARCH = "${TUNE_ARCH}"
```

The following list, which is by no means complete since architectures are configurable, shows supported machine architectures:

```
arm
i586
x86_64
powerpc
powerpc64
mips
mipsel
```

TUNE_ASARGS

Specifies architecture-specific assembler flags for the target system. The set of flags is based on the selected tune features. TUNE_ASARGS is set using the tune include files, which are typically under meta/conf/machine/include/ and are influenced through TUNE_FEATURES. For example, the meta/conf/machine/include/x86/arch-x86.inc file defines the flags for the x86 architecture as follows:

```
TUNE_ASARGS += "${@bb.utils.contains("TUNE_FEATURES", "mx32", "-x
```

Note
Board Support Packages (BSPs) can supply their own set of flags.

TUNE_CCARGS

Specifies architecture-specific C compiler flags for the target system. The set of flags is based on the selected tune features. TUNE_CCARGS is set using the tune include files, which are typically under meta/conf/machine/include/ and are influenced through TUNE_FEATURES.

Note
Board Support Packages (BSPs) can supply their own set of flags.

TUNE_LDARGS

Specifies architecture-specific linker flags for the target system. The set of flags is based on the selected tune features. TUNE_LDARGS is set using the tune include files, which are typically under meta/conf/machine/include/ and are influenced through TUNE_FEATURES. For example, the meta/conf/machine/include/x86/arch-x86.inc file defines the flags for the x86 architecture as follows:

```
TUNE_LDARGS += "${@bb.utils.contains("TUNE_FEATURES", "mx32", "-
```

Note

Board Support Packages (BSPs) can supply their own set of flags.

TUNE_FEATURES

Features used to "tune" a compiler for optimal use given a specific processor. The features are defined within the tune files and allow arguments (i.e. TUNE_*ARGS) to be dynamically generated based on the features.

The OpenEmbedded build system verifies the features to be sure they are not conflicting and that they are supported.

The BitBake configuration file (meta/conf/bitbake.conf) defines TUNE_FEATURES as follows:

```
TUNE_FEATURES ??= "${TUNE_FEATURES_tune-${DEFAULTTUNE}}"
```

See the DEFAULTTUNE variable for more information.

TUNE_PKGARCH

The package architecture understood by the packaging system to define the architecture, ABI, and tuning of output packages.

TUNE_PKGARCH_tune

The CPU or Application Binary Interface (ABI) specific tuning of the TUNE_PKGARCH.

These tune-specific package architectures are defined in the machine include files. Here is an example of the "core2-32" tuning as used in the meta/conf/machine/include/tune-core2.inc file:

```
TUNE_PKGARCH_tune-core2-32 = "core2-32"
```

TUNEABI

An underlying Application Binary Interface (ABI) used by a particular tuning in a given toolchain layer. Providers that use prebuilt libraries can use the TUNEABI, TUNEABI_OVERRIDE, and TUNEABI_WHITELIST variables to check compatibility of tunings against their selection of libraries.

If TUNEABI is undefined, then every tuning is allowed. See the sanity class to see how the variable is used.

TUNEABI_OVERRIDE

If set, the OpenEmbedded system ignores the TUNEABI_WHITELIST variable. Providers that use prebuilt libraries can use the TUNEABI_OVERRIDE, TUNEABI_WHITELIST, and TUNEABI variables to check compatibility of a tuning against their selection of libraries.

See the sanity class to see how the variable is used.

TUNEABI_WHITELIST

A whitelist of permissible TUNEABI values. If TUNEABI_WHITELIST is not set, all tunes are allowed. Providers that use prebuilt libraries can use the TUNEABI_WHITELIST, TUNEABI_OVERRIDE, and TUNEABI variables to check compatibility of a tuning against their selection of libraries.

See the sanity class to see how the variable is used.

TUNECONFLICT[feature]

Specifies CPU or Application Binary Interface (ABI) tuning features that conflict with feature.

Known tuning conflicts are specified in the machine include files in the Source Directory [http://www.yoctoproject.org/docs/1.7.2/dev-manual/dev-manual.html#source-directory]. Here is an example from the meta/conf/machine/include/mips/arch-mips.inc include file that lists the "o32" and "n64" features as conflicting with the "n32" feature:

```
TUNECONFLICTS[n32] = "o32 n64"
```

TUNEVALID[feature]

Specifies a valid CPU or Application Binary Interface (ABI) tuning feature. The specified feature is stored as a flag. Valid features are specified in the machine include files (e.g. meta/conf/machine/include/arm/arch-arm.inc). Here is an example from that file:

```
TUNEVALID[bigendian] = "Enable big-endian mode."
```

See the machine include files in the Source Directory [http://www.yoctoproject.org/docs/1.7.2/dev-manual/dev-manual.html#source-directory] for these features.

U

UBOOT_CONFIG

Configures the UBOOT_MACHINE and can also define IMAGE_FSTYPES for individual cases.

Following is an example from the meta-fsl-arm layer.

```
UBOOT_CONFIG ??= "sd"
UBOOT_CONFIG[sd] = "mx6qsabreauto_config,sdcard"
UBOOT_CONFIG[eimnor] = "mx6qsabreauto_eimnor_config"
UBOOT_CONFIG[nand] = "mx6qsabreauto_nand_config,ubifs"
UBOOT_CONFIG[spinor] = "mx6qsabreauto_spinor_config"
```

In this example, "sd" is selected as the configuration of the possible four for the UBOOT_MACHINE. The "sd" configuration defines "mx6qsabreauto_config" as the value for UBOOT_MACHINE, while the "sdcard" specifies the IMAGE_FSTYPES to use for the U-boot image.

For more information on how the UBOOT_CONFIG is handled, see the uboot-config [http://git.yoctoproject.org/cgit/cgit.cgi/poky/tree/meta/classes/uboot-config.bbclass] class.

UBOOT_ENTRYPOINT

Specifies the entry point for the U-Boot image. During U-Boot image creation, the UBOOT_ENTRYPOINT variable is passed as a command-line parameter to the uboot-mkimage utility.

UBOOT_LOADADDRESS

Specifies the load address for the U-Boot image. During U-Boot image creation, the UBOOT_LOADADDRESS variable is passed as a command-line parameter to the uboot-mkimage utility.

UBOOT_LOCALVERSION

Appends a string to the name of the local version of the U-Boot image. For example, assuming the version of the U-Boot image built was "2013.10, the full version string reported by U-Boot would be "2013.10-yocto" given the following statement:

```
UBOOT_LOCALVERSION = "-yocto"
```

UBOOT_MACHINE	Specifies the value passed on the make command line when building a U-Boot image. The value indicates the target platform configuration. You typically set this variable from the machine configuration file (i.e. conf/machine/machine_name.conf). Please see the "Selection of Processor Architecture and Board Type" section in the U-Boot README for valid values for this variable.
UBOOT_MAKE_TARGET	Specifies the target called in the Makefile. The default target is "all".
UBOOT_SUFFIX	Points to the generated U-Boot extension. For example, u-boot.sb has a .sb extension. The default U-Boot extension is .bin
UBOOT_TARGET	Specifies the target used for building U-Boot. The target is passed directly as part of the "make" command (e.g. SPL and AIS). If you do not specifically set this variable, the OpenEmbedded build process passes and uses "all" for the target during the U-Boot building process.
USE_VT	When using SysVinit [http://www.yoctoproject.org/docs/1.7.2/dev-manual/dev-manual.html#new-recipe-enabling-system-services], determines whether or not to run a getty [http://en.wikipedia.org/wiki/Getty_%28Unix%29] on any virtual terminals in order to enable logging in through those terminals. The default value used for USE_VT is "1" when no default value is specifically set. Typically, you would set USE_VT to "0" in the machine configuration file for machines that do not have a graphical display attached and therefore do not need virtual terminal functionality.
USER_CLASSES	A list of classes to globally inherit. These classes are used by the OpenEmbedded build system to enable extra features (e.g. buildstats, image-mklibs, and so forth). The default list is set in your local.conf file: USER_CLASSES ?= "buildstats image-mklibs image-prelink" For more information, see meta-yocto/conf/local.conf.sample in the Source Directory [http://www.yoctoproject.org/docs/1.7.2/dev-manual/dev-manual.html#source-directory].
USERADD_ERROR_DYNAMIC	Forces the OpenEmbedded build system to produce an error if the user identification (uid) and group identification (gid) values are not defined in files/passwd and files/group files. The default behavior for the build system is to dynamically apply uid and gid values. Consequently, the USERADD_ERROR_DYNAMIC variable is by default not set. If you plan on using statically assigned gid and uid values, you should set the USERADD_ERROR_DYNAMIC variable in your local.conf file as follows: USERADD_ERROR_DYNAMIC = "1" Overriding the default behavior implies you are going to also take steps to set static uid and gid values through use of the USERADDEXTENSION, USERADD_UID_TABLES, and USERADD_GID_TABLES variables.
USERADD_GID_TABLES	Specifies a password file to use for obtaining static group identification (gid) values when the OpenEmbedded build system adds a group to the system during package installation.

When applying static group identification (gid) values, the OpenEmbedded build system looks in BBPATH for a `files/group` file and then applies those uid values. Set the variable as follows in your `local.conf` file:

```
USERADD_GID_TABLES = "files/group"
```

Note
Setting the `USERADDEXTENSION` variable to "useradd-staticids" causes the build system to use static gid values.

USERADD_UID_TABLES

Specifies a password file to use for obtaining static user identification (uid) values when the OpenEmbedded build system adds a user to the system during package installation.

When applying static user identification (uid) values, the OpenEmbedded build system looks in BBPATH for a `files/passwd` file and then applies those uid values. Set the variable as follows in your `local.conf` file:

```
USERADD_UID_TABLES = "files/passwd"
```

Note
Setting the `USERADDEXTENSION` variable to "useradd-staticids" causes the build system to use static uid values.

USERADD_PACKAGES

When inheriting the `useradd` class, this variable specifies the individual packages within the recipe that require users and/or groups to be added.

You must set this variable if the recipe inherits the class. For example, the following enables adding a user for the main package in a recipe:

```
USERADD_PACKAGES = "${PN}"
```

Note
If follows that if you are going to use the USERADD_PACKAGES variable, you need to set one or more of the USERADD_PARAM, GROUPADD_PARAM, or GROUPMEMS_PARAM variables.

USERADD_PARAM

When inheriting the `useradd` class, this variable specifies for a package what parameters should be passed to the `useradd` command if you wish to add a user to the system when the package is installed.

Here is an example from the dbus recipe:

```
USERADD_PARAM_${PN} = "--system --home ${localstatedir}/lib/dbus
                       --no-create-home --shell /bin/false \
                       --user-group messagebus"
```

For information on the standard Linux shell command `useradd`, see http://linux.die.net/man/8/useradd.

USERADDEXTENSION

When set to "useradd-staticids", causes the OpenEmbedded build system to base all user and group additions on a static passwd and group files found in BBPATH.

To use static user identification (uid) and group identification (gid) values, set the variable as follows in your local.conf file:

```
USERADDEXTENSION = "useradd-staticids"
```

Note
Setting this variable to use static uid and gid values causes the OpenEmbedded build system to employ the useradd-staticids class.

If you use static uid and gid information, you must also specify the files/passwd and files/group files by setting the USERADD_UID_TABLES and USERADD_GID_TABLES variables. Additionally, you should also set the USERADD_ERROR_DYNAMIC variable.

W

WARN_QA

Specifies the quality assurance checks whose failures are reported as warnings by the OpenEmbedded build system. You set this variable in your distribution configuration file. For a list of the checks you can control with this variable, see the "insane.bbclass" section.

WORKDIR

The pathname of the work directory in which the OpenEmbedded build system builds a recipe. This directory is located within the TMPDIR directory structure and is specific to the recipe being built and the system for which it is being built.

The WORKDIR directory is defined as follows:

```
${TMPDIR}/work/${MULTIMACH_TARGET_SYS}/${PN}/${EXTENDPE}${PV}-${
```

The actual directory depends on several things:

- TMPDIR: The top-level build output directory

- MULTIMACH_TARGET_SYS: The target system identifier

- PN: The recipe name

- EXTENDPE: The epoch - (if PE is not specified, which is usually the case for most recipes, then EXTENDPE is blank)

- PV: The recipe version

- PR: The recipe revision

As an example, assume a Source Directory top-level folder name poky, a default Build Directory at poky/build, and a qemux86-poky-linux machine target system. Furthermore, suppose your recipe is named foo_1.3.0-r0.bb. In this case, the work directory the build system uses to build the package would be as follows:

```
poky/build/tmp/work/qemux86-poky-linux/foo/1.3.0-r0
```

Chapter 13. Variable Context

While you can use most variables in almost any context such as .conf, .bbclass, .inc, and .bb files, some variables are often associated with a particular locality or context. This chapter describes some common associations.

13.1. Configuration

The following subsections provide lists of variables whose context is configuration: distribution, machine, and local.

13.1.1. Distribution (Distro)

This section lists variables whose configuration context is the distribution, or distro.

- DISTRO
- DISTRO_NAME
- DISTRO_VERSION
- MAINTAINER
- PACKAGE_CLASSES
- TARGET_OS
- TARGET_FPU
- TCMODE
- TCLIBC

13.1.2. Machine

This section lists variables whose configuration context is the machine.

- TARGET_ARCH
- SERIAL_CONSOLES
- PACKAGE_EXTRA_ARCHS
- IMAGE_FSTYPES
- MACHINE_FEATURES
- MACHINE_EXTRA_RDEPENDS
- MACHINE_EXTRA_RRECOMMENDS
- MACHINE_ESSENTIAL_EXTRA_RDEPENDS
- MACHINE_ESSENTIAL_EXTRA_RRECOMMENDS

13.1.3. Local

This section lists variables whose configuration context is the local configuration through the local.conf file.

- DISTRO
- MACHINE
- DL_DIR

- BBFILES

- EXTRA_IMAGE_FEATURES

- PACKAGE_CLASSES

- BB_NUMBER_THREADS

- BBINCLUDELOGS

- ENABLE_BINARY_LOCALE_GENERATION

13.2. Recipes

The following subsections provide lists of variables whose context is recipes: required, dependencies, path, and extra build information.

13.2.1. Required

This section lists variables that are required for recipes.

- LICENSE

- LIC_FILES_CHKSUM

- SRC_URI - used in recipes that fetch local or remote files.

13.2.2. Dependencies

This section lists variables that define recipe dependencies.

- DEPENDS

- RDEPENDS

- RRECOMMENDS

- RCONFLICTS

- RREPLACES

13.2.3. Paths

This section lists variables that define recipe paths.

- WORKDIR

- S

- FILES

13.2.4. Extra Build Information

This section lists variables that define extra build information for recipes.

- EXTRA_OECMAKE

- EXTRA_OECONF

- EXTRA_OEMAKE

- PACKAGES

- DEFAULT_PREFERENCE

Chapter 14. FAQ

14.1. How does Poky differ from OpenEmbedded [http://www.openembedded.org]?

The term "Poky [http://www.yoctoproject.org/docs/1.7.2/dev-manual/dev-manual.html#poky]" refers to the specific reference build system that the Yocto Project provides. Poky is based on OE-Core [http://www.yoctoproject.org/docs/1.7.2/dev-manual/dev-manual.html#oe-core] and BitBake [http://www.yoctoproject.org/docs/1.7.2/dev-manual/dev-manual.html#bitbake-term]. Thus, the generic term used here for the build system is the "OpenEmbedded build system." Development in the Yocto Project using Poky is closely tied to OpenEmbedded, with changes always being merged to OE-Core or BitBake first before being pulled back into Poky. This practice benefits both projects immediately.

14.2. My development system does not meet the required Git, tar, and Python versions. In particular, I do not have Python 2.7.3 or greater, or I do have Python 3.x, which is specifically not supported by the Yocto Project. Can I still use the Yocto Project?

You can get the required tools on your host development system a couple different ways (i.e. building a tarball or downloading a tarball). See the "Required Git, tar, and Python Versions" section for steps on how to update your build tools.

14.3. How can you claim Poky / OpenEmbedded-Core is stable?

There are three areas that help with stability;

- The Yocto Project team keeps OE-Core [http://www.yoctoproject.org/docs/1.7.2/dev-manual/dev-manual.html#oe-core] small and focused, containing around 830 recipes as opposed to the thousands available in other OpenEmbedded community layers. Keeping it small makes it easy to test and maintain.

- The Yocto Project team runs manual and automated tests using a small, fixed set of reference hardware as well as emulated targets.

- The Yocto Project uses an autobuilder, which provides continuous build and integration tests.

14.4. How do I get support for my board added to the Yocto Project?

Support for an additional board is added by creating a Board Support Package (BSP) layer for it. For more information on how to create a BSP layer, see the "Understanding and Creating Layers [http://www.yoctoproject.org/docs/1.7.2/dev-manual/dev-manual.html#understanding-and-creating-layers]" section in the Yocto Project Development Manual and the Yocto Project Board Support Package (BSP) Developer's Guide [http://www.yoctoproject.org/docs/1.7.2/bsp-guide/bsp-guide.html].

Usually, if the board is not completely exotic, adding support in the Yocto Project is fairly straightforward.

14.5. Are there any products built using the OpenEmbedded build system?

The software running on the Vernier LabQuest [http://vernier.com/labquest/] is built using the OpenEmbedded build system. See the Vernier LabQuest [http://www.vernier.com/products/interfaces/labq/] website for more information. There are a number of pre-production devices using the OpenEmbedded build system and the Yocto Project team announces them as soon as they are released.

14.6. What does the OpenEmbedded build system produce as output?

Because you can use the same set of recipes to create output of various formats, the output of an OpenEmbedded build depends on how you start it. Usually, the output is a flashable image ready for the target device.

14.7. How do I add my package to the Yocto Project?

To add a package, you need to create a BitBake recipe. For information on how to create a BitBake recipe, see the "Writing a New Recipe [http://www.yoctoproject.org/docs/1.7.2/dev-manual/dev-manual.html#new-recipe-writing-a-new-recipe]" in the Yocto Project Development Manual.

14.8. Do I have to reflash my entire board with a new Yocto Project image when recompiling a package?

The OpenEmbedded build system can build packages in various formats such as IPK for OPKG, Debian package (.deb), or RPM. You can then upgrade the packages using the package tools on the device, much like on a desktop distribution such as Ubuntu or Fedora. However, package management on the target is entirely optional.

14.9. What is GNOME Mobile and what is the difference between GNOME Mobile and GNOME?

GNOME Mobile is a subset of the GNOME [http://www.gnome.org] platform targeted at mobile and embedded devices. The main difference between GNOME Mobile and standard GNOME is that desktop-orientated libraries have been removed, along with deprecated libraries, creating a much smaller footprint.

14.10.I see the error 'chmod: XXXXX new permissions are r-xrwxrwx, not r-xr-xr-x'. What is wrong?

You are probably running the build on an NTFS filesystem. Use ext2, ext3, or ext4 instead.

14.11.I see lots of 404 responses for files on http://www.yoctoproject.org/sources/*. Is something wrong?

Nothing is wrong. The OpenEmbedded build system checks any configured source mirrors before downloading from the upstream sources. The build system does this searching for both source archives and pre-checked out versions of SCM-managed software. These checks help in large installations because it can reduce load on the SCM servers themselves. The address above is one of the default mirrors configured into the build system. Consequently, if an upstream source disappears, the team can place sources there so builds continue to work.

14.12.I have machine-specific data in a package for one machine only but the package is being marked as machine-specific in all cases, how do I prevent this?

Set SRC_URI_OVERRIDES_PACKAGE_ARCH = "0" in the .bb file but make sure the package is manually marked as machine-specific for the case that needs it. The code that handles SRC_URI_OVERRIDES_PACKAGE_ARCH is in the meta/classes/base.bbclass file.

14.13.I'm behind a firewall and need to use a proxy server. How do I do that?

Most source fetching by the OpenEmbedded build system is done by wget and you therefore need to specify the proxy settings in a .wgetrc file in your home directory. Here are some example settings:

```
http_proxy = http://proxy.yoyodyne.com:18023/
ftp_proxy = http://proxy.yoyodyne.com:18023/
```

The Yocto Project also includes a site.conf.sample file that shows how to configure CVS and Git proxy servers if needed.

14.14.What's the difference between target and target-native?

The *-native targets are designed to run on the system being used for the build. These are usually tools that are needed to assist the build in some way such as quilt-native, which is used to apply patches. The non-native version is the one that runs on the target device.

14.15.I'm seeing random build failures. Help?!

If the same build is failing in totally different and random ways, the most likely explanation is:

• The hardware you are running the build on has some problem.

• You are running the build under virtualization, in which case the virtualization probably has bugs.

The OpenEmbedded build system processes a massive amount of data that causes lots of network, disk and CPU activity and is sensitive to even single-bit failures in any of these areas. True random failures have always been traced back to hardware or virtualization issues.

14.16. What do we need to ship for license compliance?

This is a difficult question and you need to consult your lawyer for the answer for your specific case. It is worth bearing in mind that for GPL compliance, there needs to be enough information shipped to allow someone else to rebuild and produce the same end result you are shipping. This means sharing the source code, any patches applied to it, and also any configuration information about how that package was configured and built.

You can find more information on licensing in the "Licensing [http://www.yoctoproject.org/docs/1.7.2/dev-manual/dev-manual.html#licensing]" and "Maintaining Open Source License Compliance During Your Product's Lifecycle [http://www.yoctoproject.org/docs/1.7.2/dev-manual/dev-manual.html#maintaining-open-source-license-compliance-during-your-products-lifecycle]" sections, both of which are in the Yocto Project Development Manual.

14.17. How do I disable the cursor on my touchscreen device?

You need to create a form factor file as described in the "Miscellaneous BSP-Specific Recipe Files [http://www.yoctoproject.org/docs/1.7.2/bsp-guide/bsp-guide.html#bsp-filelayout-misc-recipes]" section in the Yocto Project Board Support Packages (BSP) Developer's Guide. Set the HAVE_TOUCHSCREEN variable equal to one as follows:

```
HAVE_TOUCHSCREEN=1
```

14.18. How do I make sure connected network interfaces are brought up by default?

The default interfaces file provided by the netbase recipe does not automatically bring up network interfaces. Therefore, you will need to add a BSP-specific netbase that includes an interfaces file. See the "Miscellaneous BSP-Specific Recipe Files [http://www.yoctoproject.org/docs/1.7.2/bsp-guide/bsp-guide.html#bsp-filelayout-misc-recipes]" section in the Yocto Project Board Support Packages (BSP) Developer's Guide for information on creating these types of miscellaneous recipe files.

For example, add the following files to your layer:

```
meta-MACHINE/recipes-bsp/netbase/netbase/MACHINE/interfaces
meta-MACHINE/recipes-bsp/netbase/netbase_5.0.bbappend
```

14.19. How do I create images with more free space?

By default, the OpenEmbedded build system creates images that are 1.3 times the size of the populated root filesystem. To affect the image size, you need to set various configurations:

- Image Size: The OpenEmbedded build system uses the IMAGE_ROOTFS_SIZE variable to define the size of the image in Kbytes. The build system determines the size by taking into account the initial root filesystem size before any modifications such as requested size for the image and any requested additional free disk space to be added to the image.

- Overhead: Use the IMAGE_OVERHEAD_FACTOR variable to define the multiplier that the build system applies to the initial image size, which is 1.3 by default.

- Additional Free Space: Use the IMAGE_ROOTFS_EXTRA_SPACE variable to add additional free space to the image. The build system adds this space to the image after it determines its IMAGE_ROOTFS_SIZE.

14.20. Why don't you support directories with spaces in the pathnames?

The Yocto Project team has tried to do this before but too many of the tools the OpenEmbedded build system depends on, such as autoconf, break when they find spaces in pathnames. Until that situation changes, the team will not support spaces in pathnames.

14.21 How do I use an external toolchain?

The toolchain configuration is very flexible and customizable. It is primarily controlled with the TCMODE variable. This variable controls which tcmode-*.inc file to include from the meta/conf/distro/include directory within the Source Directory [http://www.yoctoproject.org/docs/1.7.2/dev-manual/dev-manual.html#source-directory].

The default value of TCMODE is "default", which tells the OpenEmbedded build system to use its internally built toolchain (i.e. tcmode-default.inc). However, other patterns are accepted. In particular, "external-*" refers to external toolchains. One example is the Sourcery G++ Toolchain. The support for this toolchain resides in the separate meta-sourcery layer at http://github.com/MentorEmbedded/meta-sourcery/.

In addition to the toolchain configuration, you also need a corresponding toolchain recipe file. This recipe file needs to package up any pre-built objects in the toolchain such as libgcc, libstdcc++, any locales, and libc.

14.22 How does the OpenEmbedded build system obtain source code and will it work behind my firewall or proxy server?

The way the build system obtains source code is highly configurable. You can setup the build system to get source code in most environments if HTTP transport is available.

When the build system searches for source code, it first tries the local download directory. If that location fails, Poky tries PREMIRRORS, the upstream source, and then MIRRORS in that order.

Assuming your distribution is "poky", the OpenEmbedded build system uses the Yocto Project source PREMIRRORS by default for SCM-based sources, upstreams for normal tarballs, and then falls back to a number of other mirrors including the Yocto Project source mirror if those fail.

As an example, you could add a specific server for the build system to attempt before any others by adding something like the following to the local.conf configuration file:

```
PREMIRRORS_prepend = "\
git://.*/.* http://www.yoctoproject.org/sources/ \n \
ftp://.*/.* http://www.yoctoproject.org/sources/ \n \
http://.*/.* http://www.yoctoproject.org/sources/ \n \
https://.*/.* http://www.yoctoproject.org/sources/ \n"
```

These changes cause the build system to intercept Git, FTP, HTTP, and HTTPS requests and direct them to the http:// sources mirror. You can use file:// URLs to point to local directories or network shares as well.

Aside from the previous technique, these options also exist:

```
BB_NO_NETWORK = "1"
```

This statement tells BitBake to issue an error instead of trying to access the Internet. This technique is useful if you want to ensure code builds only from local sources.

Here is another technique:

```
BB_FETCH_PREMIRRORONLY = "1"
```

This statement limits the build system to pulling source from the PREMIRRORS only. Again, this technique is useful for reproducing builds.

Here is another technique:

```
BB_GENERATE_MIRROR_TARBALLS = "1"
```

This statement tells the build system to generate mirror tarballs. This technique is useful if you want to create a mirror server. If not, however, the technique can simply waste time during the build.

Finally, consider an example where you are behind an HTTP-only firewall. You could make the following changes to the local.conf configuration file as long as the PREMIRRORS server is current:

```
PREMIRRORS_prepend = "\
ftp://.*/.* http://www.yoctoproject.org/sources/ \n \
http://.*/.* http://www.yoctoproject.org/sources/ \n \
https://.*/.* http://www.yoctoproject.org/sources/ \n"
BB_FETCH_PREMIRRORONLY = "1"
```

These changes would cause the build system to successfully fetch source over HTTP and any network accesses to anything other than the PREMIRRORS would fail.

The build system also honors the standard shell environment variables http_proxy, ftp_proxy, https_proxy, and all_proxy to redirect requests through proxy servers.

Note

You can find more information on the "Working Behind a Network Proxy [https://wiki.yoctoproject.org/wiki/Working_Behind_a_Network_Proxy]" Wiki page.

14.23.Can I get rid of build output so I can start over?

Yes - you can easily do this. When you use BitBake to build an image, all the build output goes into the directory created when you run the build environment setup script (i.e. oe-init-build-env or oe-init-build-env-memres). By default, this Build Directory [http://www.yoctoproject.org/docs/1.7.2/dev-manual/dev-manual.html#build-directory] is named build but can be named anything you want.

Within the Build Directory, is the tmp directory. To remove all the build output yet preserve any source code or downloaded files from previous builds, simply remove the tmp directory.

14.24.Why do ${bindir} and ${libdir} have strange values for -native recipes?

Executables and libraries might need to be used from a directory other than the directory into which they were initially installed. Complicating this situation is the fact that sometimes these executables and libraries are compiled with the expectation of being run from that initial installation target directory. If this is the case, moving them causes problems.

This scenario is a fundamental problem for package maintainers of mainstream Linux distributions as well as for the OpenEmbedded build system. As such, a well-established solution exists. Makefiles, Autotools configuration scripts, and other build systems are expected to respect environment variables such as bindir, libdir, and sysconfdir that indicate where executables, libraries, and data reside when a program is actually run. They are also expected to respect a DESTDIR environment variable, which is prepended to all the other variables when the build system actually installs the files. It is understood that the program does not actually run from within DESTDIR.

When the OpenEmbedded build system uses a recipe to build a target-architecture program (i.e. one that is intended for inclusion on the image being built), that program eventually runs from the root file system of that image. Thus, the build system provides a value of "/usr/bin" for bindir, a value of "/usr/lib" for libdir, and so forth.

Meanwhile, DESTDIR is a path within the Build Directory [http://www.yoctoproject.org/docs/1.7.2/dev-manual/dev-manual.html#build-directory]. However, when the recipe builds a native program (i.e. one that is intended to run on the build machine), that program is never installed directly to the build machine's root file system. Consequently, the build system uses paths within the Build Directory for DESTDIR, bindir and related variables. To better understand this, consider the following two paths where the first is relatively normal and the second is not:

Note

Due to these lengthy examples, the paths are artificially broken across lines for readability.

```
/home/maxtothemax/poky-bootchart2/build/tmp/work/i586-poky-linux/zlib/
    1.2.8-r0/sysroot-destdir/usr/bin
```

```
/home/maxtothemax/poky-bootchart2/build/tmp/work/x86_64-linux/
    zlib-native/1.2.8-r0/sysroot-destdir/home/maxtothemax/poky-bootchart2/
    build/tmp/sysroots/x86_64-linux/usr/bin
```

Even if the paths look unusual, they both are correct - the first for a target and the second for a native recipe. These paths are a consequence of the DESTDIR mechanism and while they appear strange, they are correct and in practice very effective.

14.25.The files provided by my -native recipe do not appear to be available to other recipes. Files are missing from the native sysroot, my recipe is installing to the wrong place, or I am getting permissions errors during the do_install task in my recipe! What is wrong?

This situation results when a build system does not recognize the environment variables supplied to it by BitBake [http://www.yoctoproject.org/docs/1.7.2/dev-manual/dev-manual.html#bitbake-term]. The incident that prompted this FAQ entry involved a Makefile that used an environment variable named BINDIR instead of the more standard variable bindir. The makefile's hardcoded default value of "/usr/bin" worked most of the time, but not for the recipe's -native variant. For another example, permissions errors might be caused by a Makefile that ignores DESTDIR or uses a different name for that environment variable. Check the the build system to see if these kinds of issues exist.

Chapter 15. Contributing to the Yocto Project

15.1. Introduction

The Yocto Project team is happy for people to experiment with the Yocto Project. A number of places exist to find help if you run into difficulties or find bugs. To find out how to download source code, see the "Yocto Project Release [http://www.yoctoproject.org/docs/1.7.2/dev-manual/dev-manual.html#local-yp-release]" section in the Yocto Project Development Manual.

15.2. Tracking Bugs

If you find problems with the Yocto Project, you should report them using the Bugzilla application at http://bugzilla.yoctoproject.org.

15.3. Mailing lists

A number of mailing lists maintained by the Yocto Project exist as well as related OpenEmbedded mailing lists for discussion, patch submission and announcements. To subscribe to one of the following mailing lists, click on the appropriate URL in the following list and follow the instructions:

- http://lists.yoctoproject.org/listinfo/yocto - General Yocto Project discussion mailing list.

- http://lists.openembedded.org/mailman/listinfo/openembedded-core - Discussion mailing list about OpenEmbedded-Core (the core metadata).

- http://lists.openembedded.org/mailman/listinfo/openembedded-devel - Discussion mailing list about OpenEmbedded.

- http://lists.openembedded.org/mailman/listinfo/bitbake-devel - Discussion mailing list about the BitBake [http://www.yoctoproject.org/docs/1.7.2/dev-manual/dev-manual.html#bitbake-term] build tool.

- http://lists.yoctoproject.org/listinfo/poky - Discussion mailing list about Poky [http://www.yoctoproject.org/docs/1.7.2/dev-manual/dev-manual.html#poky].

- http://lists.yoctoproject.org/listinfo/yocto-announce - Mailing list to receive official Yocto Project release and milestone announcements.

For more Yocto Project-related mailing lists, see the Yocto Project community mailing lists page here [http://www.yoctoproject.org/tools-resources/community/mailing-lists].

15.4. Internet Relay Chat (IRC)

Two IRC channels on freenode are available for the Yocto Project and Poky discussions:

- #yocto

- #poky

15.5. Links

Here is a list of resources you will find helpful:

- The Yocto Project website [http://www.yoctoproject.org]: The home site for the Yocto Project.

- Intel Corporation [http://www.intel.com/]: The company that acquired OpenedHand in 2008 and began development on the Yocto Project.

- OpenEmbedded [http://www.openembedded.org]: The upstream, generic, embedded distribution used as the basis for the build system in the Yocto Project. Poky derives from and contributes back to the OpenEmbedded project.

- BitBake [http://www.openembedded.org/wiki/BitBake]: The tool used to process metadata.

- BitBake User Manual [http://www.yoctoproject.org/docs/1.7.2/bitbake-user-manual/bitbake-user-manual.html]: A comprehensive guide to the BitBake tool. In the Source Directory [http://www.yoctoproject.org/docs/1.7.2/dev-manual/dev-manual.html#source-directory], you can find the BitBake User Manual in the `bitbake/doc/bitbake-user-manual` directory.

- QEMU [http://wiki.qemu.org/Index.html]: An open source machine emulator and virtualizer.

15.6. Contributions

The Yocto Project gladly accepts contributions. You can submit changes to the project either by creating and sending pull requests, or by submitting patches through email. For information on how to do both as well as information on how to identify the maintainer for each area of code, see the "How to Submit a Change [http://www.yoctoproject.org/docs/1.7.2/dev-manual/dev-manual.html#how-to-submit-a-change]" section in the Yocto Project Development Manual.

www.ingramcontent.com/pod-product-compliance
Lightning Source LLC
LaVergne TN
LVHW060139070326
832902LV00018B/2857

* 9 7 8 9 8 8 8 3 8 1 9 8 2 *